Harbrace
ESSENTIALS

THIRD EDITION

Cheryl Glenn
The Pennsylvania State University

Loretta Gray
Central Washington University

D0144175

CENGAGE

Australia • Brazil • Mexico • Singapore • United Kingdom • United States

CENGAGE

***Harbrace Essentials*,**
Third Edition
Cheryl Glenn, Loretta Gray

Product Manager: Laura Ross

Senior Content Developer:
Kathy Sands-Boehmer

Product Assistant: Shelby
Nathanson

Senior Marketing Manager:
Kina Lara

Content Project Manager:
Rebecca Donahue

Manufacturing Planner: Fola
Orekoya

IP Analyst: Ann Hoffman

IP Project Manager: Betsy
Hathaway

Production Service/Compositor:
SPi Global

Senior Art Director: Marissa
Falco

Text Designer: Alisha Webber,
Cenveo Publisher Services

Cover Designer: Marissa Falco

Cover Image: Michael Wertz

For product information and technology
assistance, contact us at **Cengage Learning
Customer & Sales Support, 1-800-354-9706**

For permission to use material from this text or
product, submit all requests online at
www.cengage.com/permissions.

Further permissions questions can be emailed to
permissionrequest@cengage.com.

Library of Congress Control Number:

Student Edition:
ISBN: 978-1-337-55688-0

Cengage Learning
20 Channel Center Street
Boston, MA 02210
USA

Cengage Learning is a leading provider of customize
learning solutions with employees residing in nearly
40 different countries and sales in more than 125
countries around the world. Find your local represen
tative at **www.cengage.com**.

Cengage Learning products are represented in
Canada by Nelson Education, Ltd.

To learn more about Cengage Learning Solutions,
visit **www.cengage.com**.

To register or access your online learning solution or
purchase materials for your course, visit
www.cengagebrain.com.

Printed in China
Print Number: 01   Print Year: 2017

Preface

Whether you are writing for school or on the job, *Harbrace Essentials* provides the practical advice, helpful strategies, and examples of effective writing that will help you make your writer's voice heard.

Finding What You Need

Harbrace Essentials puts all the information you need at your fingertips.

- **Brief Contents.** Use the brief table of contents on the inside front cover to find the chapter you need. For quick reference, the brief table of contents also provides a guide to the color-coded parts of the book—you'll find the color for each part on related page tabs.
- **Contents.** When you need to locate more specific information, consult the detailed table of contents on the inside back cover. You can then flip to the sections you need, such as 4a or 15c, using the section locators at the top of each page.
- **User-Friendly Index.** You can find the specific pages on which any topic is mentioned by consulting the index (p. 463). The index includes entries that reflect the terminology of the book (for example, *conjunction*) as well as entries in everyday language for when you're not certain what topic to check (such as *and* if you don't know that this word is a conjunction). It provides not only page numbers but also chapter and section references for each topic.

- **Advice on MLA, APA, CMS, and CSE.** For quick access to documentation styles, open to the tab that says MLA and then scan the next page for the style you are using. A directory of Citation Maps can be found at the end of the book (p. 485). These Citation Maps explain the process of citing common sources in each style (MLA, APA, CMS, and CSE). The chapters on MLA and APA documentation are preceded by tabbed dividers for quick access.

- **Knowledge Transfer.** We have included additional assignments for writing in other courses, writing in the workplace, and writing in the public sphere so you can quickly see that what you are learning in your writing classes are transferrable skills and content.

- **Glossaries.** If you need help with words that are commonly confused or misused (such as *accept* and *except*), consult the Glossary of Usage on page 525. The Glossary of Terms (p. 449) defines grammatical and rhetorical terms, including those that appear in boldface throughout the book.

- **Revision Symbols.** If your instructor gives you feedback that includes revision symbols, use this list to lead you to sections of the book that offer strategies and detailed help for revision. The list appears on p. 486, one page in from the inside back cover.

- **Resources for Multilingual Writers.** Refer to the checklists and tips throughout the book for key advice on special topics. For quick access to grammar help designed especially for multilingual writers, the directory at the end of the book (p. 485) points you to help with specific topics throughout the book.

- **Answers to Exercises.** *Harbrace Essentials* offers answers to even-numbered exercise items so that you can work through material and test your own understanding.

Although we believe *Harbrace Essentials* will help you answer any question you may have about writing, if you have suggestions for improving the next edition or if we can assist you in any way, don't hesitate to write to us c/o Cengage Learning, English Editorial, 20 Channel Center Street, Boston, MA 02210.

Cheryl Glenn
Loretta Gray

Teaching and Learning Resources

Instructor Manual with Answer Key

An Instructor Manual with an Answer Key provides instructors with answers to all exercises in the handbook as well as a variety of pedagogical and teaching materials and is available in MindTap.

MindTap

MindTap® English for Glenn / Gray, *Harbrace Essentials* is the digital learning solution that powers students from memorization to mastery. It gives you complete control of your course—to provide engaging content, to challenge every individual, and to build their confidence. Empower students to accelerate their progress with MindTap. MindTap: Powered by You.

MindTap gives you complete ownership of your content and learning experience. Customize the interactive assignments, emphasize the most important topics, and add your own material or notes in the eBook.

- Interactive activities on grammar and mechanics promote application to student writing.
- An easy-to-use paper management system helps prevent plagiarism and allows for electronic submission, grading, and peer review.
- A vast database of scholarly sources with video tutorials and examples supports every step of the research process.
- Professional tutoring guides students from rough drafts to polished writing.
- Visual analytics track student progress and engagement.

- Seamless integration into your campus learning management system keeps all your course materials in one place.
- A collection of vetted, curated student writing samples in various modes and documentation styles to use as flexible instructional tools.

MindTap® English comes equipped with the diagnostic-guided JUST IN TIME PLUS learning module for foundational concepts and embedded course support. The module features scaffolded video tutorials, instructional text content, and auto-graded activities designed to address each student's specific needs for practice and support to succeed in college-level composition courses.

Available as a downloadable PDF in the MindTap learning path, College Workbook covers grammar, punctuation, usage, style, and writing. This workbook provides supplemental exercises and includes clear examples and explanations.

The Resources for Teaching folder provides support materials to facilitate an efficient course setup process focused around your instructional goals: the MindTap Planning Guide offers an inventory of MindTap activities correlated to common planning objectives so that you can quickly determine what you need. The MindTap Syllabus offers an example of how these activities could be incorporated into a 16-week course schedule. The Instructor's Manual provides suggestions for additional activities and assignments. The Answer Key for the College Workbook is also included.

Acknowledgements

We would like to thank our colleagues who reviewed this handbook during the course of its development. Their astute comments and thoughtful suggestions helped shape this third edition: David Cirillo, *St. Charles Community College*; Gina Claywell, *Murray State University*; Judy Cormier, *Imperial*

Valley College; Dick Costner, *Georgia Northwestern Technical College*; Wes Davis, *Dalton State College*; Eric Jurgens, *College of Menominee Nation*; Jessica Lindberg, *Georgia Highlands College*; Amanda Moras, *Sacred Heart University*; Nick Obradovich, *Elgin Community College*; Pam Reid, *Copiah-Lincoln Community College*; Lisa Russell, *Georgia Northwestern Technical College*; P. Wayne Stauffer, *Houston Community College*; Bruce Swanland, *Santa Ana College*; Marjorie Thrash, *Pearl River Community College*; and Justin Williamson, *Pearl River Community College*.

W

WRITING

Visit the MindTap® for this book for additional information and resources.

1 Writing and Reading Rhetorically

Whether you are reading textbooks or e-mails, writing assignments for class, text messaging your friends, or composing with words or visuals, you are actively using your knowledge of **rhetoric**, the purposeful and effective use of language (whether verbal or visual). In fact, you are intentionally using language to address your **rhetorical situation**, the set of circumstances within which a person writes or reads a text.

1a Understanding the rhetorical situation

You already intuitively know the basic elements of the rhetorical situation: **opportunity**, **writer**, **audience**, **message**, **stance**, and **context**. To communicate effectively, writers must analyze their particular situation and respond appropriately to their intended audience. Therefore, in academic and other formal rhetorical situations, you will want to allow time to consider the basic elements of the situation:

- **Opportunity.** What problem or issue is the writer (or you) taking the opportunity to resolve or address through language or images?
- **Writer.** What do you know about the writer (or author) and the writer's values, whether yourself or the person whose work you are reading?
- **Audience.** Who is the writer's audience? What values does the audience hold? How might this audience help the writer resolve or address the problem? Will the audience understand, be influenced (to change behavior or opinion), be entertained?

- **Purpose.** How does the writer's purpose connect with the interests of the audience? Does the writer want to entertain, inform, explain, describe, or argue a point? How does the purpose connect with the opportunity?
- **Message.** What specific assertions, examples, and support does the writer use? How is the message delivered—via a visual text, a verbal text, or a combination? Is it print, spoken, or electronic? In what ways are both the content and the delivery of the message appropriate for the audience?
- **Stance.** What opinions, hopes, or experiences does the writer connect with the purpose and the message itself? How does the writer's stance translate into the **thesis statement** (the central point or main idea of the text)?
- **Context.** In what context is the communication between writer and audience taking place? Context includes the time and place, the writer and audience, the medium of delivery—as well as the social, political, historical, geographical, and cultural factors that influence the context, whether helping or hindering successful communication.

1b Applying rhetorical knowledge

When you write rhetorically, you consider the best ways of reaching your audience—the best way to deliver an appropriate, purposeful, and convincing message. When you read rhetorically, you allow yourself to consider the writer's message. Before making a decision, you want to understand the message the writer is sending. Rhetorical readers read critically (asking questions and weighing evidence). They often begin with a **preview**, skimming over the message to locate its major points (title and headings, for example), and then they read through it carefully (including author biography, preface, index, and bibliography) to determine the credibility and reputation of the author as well as the amount of research that went into the message itself. During the preview and close reading, rhetorical readers watch for **transitional** words that indicate important points of purpose, result, summary, causation, repetition, exemplification, or intensification (**3d**).

1c   Academic writing

Academic writing, the writing expected of you as a student, will vary according to the assignments you receive within various academic disciplines. Much academic writing, though, shares several features: a thesis statement, purposefully organized supporting details and examples (often drawn from outside sources), and conventional grammar, spelling, punctuation, and mechanics. In other words, academic writing is carefully planned out and seriously delivered—unlike casual, social writing.

(1) Expectations for academic writing

Although assignments across courses and disciplines may differ, the expectations for academic writing remain fairly constant. Academic writing demonstrates an essential set of skills, including your ability to:

- respond appropriately to the assignment
- think critically (asking questions and weighing evidence while reading and writing)
- apply outside sources (your research, practice, observations, readings) as you join the scholarly conversation
- organize and develop your material effectively and logically
- communicate with clarity, purpose, and a sense of audience
- edit and proofread with an eye to conventions of formatting, documentation, grammar, punctuation, mechanics, and tone (or level of formality)
- deliver your knowledge and researched information in a number of ways (orally, visually, electronically, verbally)

(2) Analysis of assignments

To meet the expectations for academic writing, you need to understand every assignment. Ideally, assignments will be communicated in writing and explained and discussed in class. For each assignment, make sure you understand the following requirements. Ask your instructor questions in the case you do not understand.

- **Task.** What task does the assignment ask you to complete? What verb does the assignment use? The imperative verb (*argue*, *describe*, *explain*) should direct you toward the expected purpose. Are you to solve a problem, research an issue, answer a question, remember and retell a significant event, support a thesis, explain a process, define a concept?
- **Role and audience.** What stance are you expected to or allowed to take with regard to your audience? Are you being asked to assume the role of expert, explainer, questioner, arguer? Are you writing from a position of knowledge and power, from that of a learner, or from an opposing point of view?
- **Format.** What are the instructor's expectations with regard to length, manuscript form (electronic or print? verbal or visual?), documentation style, and so on? What manuscript format should you follow (that of a report, an essay, an oral delivery)?
- **Process to be followed.** Are you expected to conduct library or laboratory research? What is the schedule for completion of research, drafts, peer reviews, workshops, revisions, and so forth? Are you expected to submit your rough drafts with the final draft?
- **Criteria for evaluation.** How will the final product be graded? What are the criteria for success?

Keep in mind that these same criteria can be applied to workplace writing assignments. They are also helpful criteria for you to use when writing for personal, political, or civic reasons.

1d Genres and formats of academic writing

You may already be familiar with many of the genres of academic writing. A **genre** is a type of writing categorized by a well-established format with familiar features. Writers deliberately choose a single genre or purposeful combination of genres in order to reach a specific audience. Think of the personal essay, letter, memoir, case study, lab report, petition, résumé, job application letter, profile, evaluation, argument, proposal, investigative report, or research essay. Each of these genres has a distinctive purpose, format, and tone.

Once you settle on the appropriate genre and format for your writing, you can choose the best **medium** of delivering that message or some purposeful combination of oral, visual, verbal, digital, or print **media**. Just as your choice of medium shapes how you produce your message, that choice also offers you opportunities for experimenting with its delivery and reach. You are no doubt familiar with how to deliver a print message to your instructor. However, there may be occasions when you want to write specifically for online media so you can extend the range of your project by including visuals, animation, charts, graphs, and sonic elements, thereby reaching a wider audience outside your classroom and campus.

(1) Web pages

Writing material for a web page is different from writing a traditional academic essay or report. Web material requires a rethinking of organization, design, and style. The writer must determine a hierarchy of content emphasis (with related links to additional information); develop a clear, pleasing organization; and include useful links and other tools for navigation.

(2) Blogs

Writing a blog requires you to aim toward a specific, often limited, audience who will be receptive to your topic(s), your stance (your attitude toward your subject and your audience), and your ability to engage intelligently and frequently.

(3) Twitter

Limited to 140 characters, posts (or tweets) demand that you catch your readers' attention and get to the point. Your purpose is to spark conversation.

(4) Wikis

Wikis—collaborative online texts—allow you to share huge amounts of information with colleagues. All wiki writers expect to receive both positive and negative feedback from one another.

(5) Audio and video

The possibilities of audio and video delivery allow you to compose podcasts, YouTube videos, documentaries, and short films—all sorts of multimedia genres, including mash-ups that integrate music, visuals, information, and data. You can use these media to enhance your print texts or as stand-alone compositions.

All of these media of delivery are also used professionally, personally, and politically.

2 Planning and Drafting Essays

Writing is a process, a series of manageable steps. Effective writers know they cannot possibly do everything at once, so they generate, organize, develop, and clarify their ideas as well as polish their prose in separate—but often overlapping—stages.

2a Stages of the writing process

Prewriting is the initial stage of the writing process. Consider your intended audience, purpose, and context. Then jump-start your thinking about a suitable topic by talking with others working on the same assignment, keeping a journal, freewriting, or questioning.

Drafting involves writing down as much as you can with regard to your topic. Academic writing calls for evidence to support your assertions and your opinions. At this stage, then, you will need to determine the kinds of evidence your writing calls for (facts, testimony, personal experience, library, archival, laboratory, and/or field research) and set about collecting that evidence. The more information you get down, the more options you will have as you begin to clarify your thesis (or guiding question) and purpose for writing. Ironically, you will generate ideas at the same time that you focus them. Progress is your goal at this stage, not perfection.

Revising offers you the opportunity to focus your purpose for writing, establish a clear thesis statement or governing idea, and organize your ideas accordingly. During revision, you work to stabilize the overall structure of your essay and individual paragraphs. You also shape your introduction and conclusion. Revising often means producing another draft for yet further revision and editing.

Editing and **proofreading** focus on deep and surface features, ranging from organization and use of topic sentences to punctuation, spelling, word choice, sentence structure, and all the rest of the details of academic English (**4d**).

CHECKLIST FOR ASSESSING A TOPIC

- Why are you interested in the topic?
- What audience might be interested in the topic? How is the topic appropriate for your audience?
- What is your purpose in writing about this topic to your intended audience?
- How can you do justice to the topic in the time and space available to you? Should you narrow it, expand it, or give it a specific slant?
- Do you have all the information you need to address this topic? If not, what additional information might you need?

2b Developing a thesis statement

Once you decide on a topic (or a focus on an assigned topic), ask yourself what you would like to say about it—and why. By combining your topic (for example, studying another language) with your point about that topic (it's important because it prepares students to participate in a global economy), you will create a thesis statement, an explicit declaration of the overarching idea of your paper. A thesis statement keeps your writing on target, unifies your writing, and guides your readers through the content that follows at the same time that it showcases your originality.

To bring your topic into focus, consider your individual interests, your purpose, the needs of your audience, and the time and space available. Look over your prewriting and drafting to determine where, exactly, your interests took hold. Often, your interest provides the most fruitful site for sharpening your focus, developing a tentative thesis, and then drafting an essay.

TIPS FOR DEVELOPING A THESIS STATEMENT

- Decide which feature of the topic interests you most, which feature opens up a rhetorical opportunity that your words might resolve or a change they might bring about.
- Write down your point of view, opinion, or assertion about it.
- Draft a thesis statement that includes the topic and your assertion about it.
- Mark the passages in your rough draft that support your position to see how well this thesis fits with ideas you've been developing.
- Ask yourself whether your thesis is too broad or too narrow to be sufficiently developed given the constraints of your project.
- After completing a draft, ask yourself whether the scope of your thesis should be adjusted to reflect the direction your essay has taken. Qualify your thesis if necessary, acknowledging any conditions where your assertion may not hold up.
- If you are still unhappy with your thesis, start again with the first tip and be even more specific.

Whether you are writing for work or the community, you will most often need a thesis statement that indicates your position.

2c   Creating an Outline

Many writers need a working plan to direct their ideas and keep their writing on course. Others rely on outlines to organize their writing, as in this example:

TENTATIVE THESIS STATEMENT: Students who study another language become better communicators, both in their own language and with people from other cultures.

I. Many Americans don't think they need to learn another language.

    A. English is the language of global communication.

    B. English speakers always have an advantage in intercultural communication.

II. English-only speakers miss out on benefits of learning another language.

    A. Learning another language is not just about being able to talk to people in different countries.

    B. Studying another language increases a student's knowledge of another culture and so promotes tolerance and understanding.

    C. Knowing the language enriches a student's stay in a foreign country.

III. Students who take another language do better on standardized tests.

    A. Students can compare grammars to better remember the rules of their own language.

    B. Studying another language opens up a student's mind to different ways of speaking and expressing ideas.

    C. Studying another language helps students acquire better reading skills.

3 Developing Paragraphs

You compose a draft by developing the information that will constitute the individual paragraphs of your essay. Every paragraph serves a purpose: whether it is the introduction, the support for a main point, or the conclusion, each paragraph guides your reader through your piece of writing. For these reasons, paragraphs have no set length: sometimes, you will need a longer one; other times, a short one will provide an important transition or make a point.

3a Stating the main idea

Effective paragraphs are unified around one main idea, often stated in a topic sentence. A **topic sentence** states the main idea of the paragraph clearly, and all the other sentences in the paragraph relate to that idea. Topic sentences often appear at the start of a paragraph to focus readers on what the paragraph is about. At other times, they appear as the last sentence of the paragraph, as a summation. Whether a paragraph is long or short, it should focus on one main idea or point.

In the following paragraph about business at Hollywood movie studios in the late 1960s, the topic sentence appears at the beginning of the paragraph. The support sentences mention the consequences of the event described in the topic sentence.

> *Between August 1964 and March 1965, four new movies sold so many tickets and made so much money that, collectively, they pointed toward a dramatic shift in the tastes of American moviegoers and suggested an entirely new way for the studios to do business.* Hollywood did not react well. Historically, the only event more disruptive to the industry's ecosystem than an unexpected flop is an

unexpected smash, and, caught off guard by the sudden arrival of more revenue than they thought their movies could ever bring in, the major studios resorted to three old habits: imitation, frenzied speculation, and panic.

—MARK HARRIS, *Pictures at a Revolution*

3b Developing the main point

(1) Using details

The following well-developed paragraph uses details to bring an idea to life:

> *This reminds me of how I learned to drive growing up in western Kansas: my parents and grandparents turned me loose behind the wheel of grandpa's old blue Ford pickup in the big, open cow pasture behind their farm house, gave me some basic instructions of gears, clutches, brakes, accelerator—and then let me go.* It was exhilarating to get the feel of the thing, bumping along over gopher holes with dried cow patties flying behind me, creating a little dust cloud to mark the path I had taken, and not worrying about which way I should turn or go next. And I learned well the basics of the machine and its movements by driving this way. But soon I wanted more: a road to travel, a radio that actually worked, a destination and a goal, a more finely tuned knowledge of navigation involving blinkers, lights, different driving conditions, and—most of all—the ability to travel and negotiate with others also on the road.
>
> — BRENDA JO BRUEGGERMANN, "American Sign Language and the Academy"

(2) Providing examples

Like details, examples contribute to paragraph development by making specific what otherwise might seem general and hard to grasp. The author of the following paragraph uses both details and examples:

> *I was in fourth grade and in trouble.* The students of Wildwood Elementary School in Burlington, Massachusetts, shifted in their uncomfortable metal seats as they waited for me to say

my next line. A dog rested in my arms and an entire musical rested on my shoulders. I was playing Dorothy in *The Wizard of Oz*, and it was my turn to speak. Dorothy is *Hamlet* for girls. Next to Annie in *Annie* and Sandy in *Grease*, it is the dream role of every ten-year-old. *Annie* taught me that orphanages were a blast and being rich is the only thing that matters. *Grease* taught me being in a gang is nonstop fun and you need to dress sexier to have any chance of keeping a guy interested. But *The Wizard of Oz* was the ultimate. It dealt with friendship and fear and death and rainbows and sparkly red shoes.

—AMY POEHLER, *Yes Please*

3c Choosing methods for developing paragraphs

When drafting an essay, you can develop paragraphs using various **rhetorical methods**. The method you choose will depend on how you want to achieve the purpose of your paragraph. Your paragraph might make sense of a person, place, or event (narration and description); think critically about a process (process analysis or cause-and-consequence analysis); investigate similarities or differences (comparison or contrast); organize concepts (classification and division); establish boundaries (definition); or convince someone (argument). These rhetorical methods are already second nature to you. You use them every day to understand the world around you.

By using these rhetorical methods of development, you will make your writing more understandable to your audience. Take care to use the one(s) best suited to supporting your thesis, fulfilling your purpose, and reaching your audience. As you draft and revise, check to see that each paragraph is anchored in your thesis statement.

(1) Narration

A **narrative** discusses a sequence of events, normally in **chronological** order (the order in which they occur), to develop a particular point or set a mood. Narrative often includes a setting, characters, dialogue, and description and makes use of transition words or phrases such as *first, then, later, that evening,* and so forth to guide readers from one incident to the next. Whatever its length, a narrative must remain focused on the main idea. The narrative in this paragraph traces Amy Poehler's role as Dorothy in the tornado scene:

> In the second and final performance of *The Wizard of Oz*, I decided to take control during the tornado scene. I paused, put the blinking dog down on the stage, and walked a few feet away from it. "Toto, Toto! Where are you?" I said, pretending to look for my lost dog in the fearsome storm. The dog froze and played it perfectly. I got laughter and some light applause for my efforts. I had improvised and it had worked. One could argue that it worked because of the dog. A good straight dog can really help sell a joke. Whatever. I have been chasing that high ever since.
>
> —AMY POEHLER, *Yes Please*

(2) Description

Descriptions make your writing come alive. Predominantly visual, descriptions can also include the details of what you hear, smell, taste, and touch; that is to say, descriptions appeal to your senses. In the following paragraph, Supreme Court Justice Sonia Sotomayor employs vivid descriptive details to convey how her working-poor Puerto Rican immigrant mother strived to comfort her children:

> One memory of my mother's comforting sneaks up on me in the night sometimes. The bedroom I shared with Junior on Watson Avenue, with its one little window, was not just tiny but unbearably hot in summer. We had a little electric fan propped up on a chair, but it didn't help much. Sometimes I would wake up miserable in the middle of the night, with the pillow and sheets drenched in sweat, my hair dripping wet. Mami would come change the bed, whispering to me quietly in the dark so as not to wake Junior. Then she'd sit beside me with a pot of cold water and washcloth and sponge me down until I fell asleep. The cool damp was so delicious, and her hands so firmly gentle—expert nurse's

hands, I thought—that a part of me always tried to stay awake, to prolong this blissful taken-care of feeling just a bit longer.

—SONIA SOTOMAYOR, *My Beloved World*

(3) Process analysis

In explaining how something is done or made, process paragraphs often use both description and narration. You might describe the items used in a process and then narrate the steps of the process chronologically. See how Sam Swope explains the process by which an elementary school assistant principal tried (unsuccessfully) to intimidate students into snitching on a fellow student.

Later that day, a frowning assistant principal appeared in the doorway, and the room went hush. Everyone knew why he was there. I'd known Mr. Ziegler only as a friendly, mild-mannered fellow with a comb-over, so I was shocked to see him play the heavy. His performance began calmly, reasonably, solemnly. He told the class that the administration was deeply disappointed, that this theft betrayed the trust of family, teachers, school and country. Then he told the children it was their duty to report anything they'd seen or heard. When no one responded, he added a touch of anger to his voice, told the kids no stone would go unturned, the truth would out; he vowed he'd find the culprit—it was only a question of time! When this brought no one forward, he pumped up the volume. His face turned red, the veins on his neck bulged, and he wagged a finger in the air and shouted, "I'm not through with this investigation, not by a long shot! And if any of you know anything, you better come tell me, privately, in private, because they're going to be in a lot of trouble, *a lot of trouble!*"

—SAM SWOPE, "The Case of the Missing Report Cards"

(4) Cause-and-consequence analysis

Writers who analyze cause and consequence raise the question *Why?* and must answer it to the satisfaction of their audience. In this type of analysis, writers often differentiate the **primary cause** (the most important one) from **contributory causes** (which add to but do not directly cause an event or situation) and the **primary consequence** (the most important result) from **secondary consequences** (which are less important). Writers who analyze cause and consequence also usually link a sequence of events along a timeline, always keeping in mind that just because one event happens before—or after—another event does not necessarily make it a cause or consequence of that event. In the following paragraph, journalist Christopher Hitchens analyzes the consequences of his chemotherapy.

It's quite something, this chemo-poison. It has caused me to lose about 14 pounds, though without making me feel any lighter. It has cleared up a vicious rash on my shins that no doctor could ever name, let alone cure. . . . Let it please be this mean and ruthless with the alien and its spreading dead-zone colonies. But as against that, the death-dealing stuff and life-preserving stuff have also made me strangely neuter. I was fairly reconciled to the loss of my hair, which began to come out in the shower in the first two weeks of treatment, and which I saved in a plastic bag so that it could help fill a floating dam in the Gulf of Mexico. But I wasn't quite prepared for the way that my razorblade would suddenly go slipping pointlessly down my face, meeting no stubble. Or for the way that my newly smooth upper lip would begin to look as if it had undergone electrolysis, causing me to look a bit too much like somebody's maiden auntie. (The chest hair that was once the toast of two continents hasn't yet wilted, but so much of it was shaved off for various hospital incisions that it's a rather patchy affair.) I feel upsettingly de-natured. If Penélope Cruz were one of my nurses, I wouldn't even notice. In the war against Thanatos, if we must term it a war, the immediate loss of Eros is a huge initial sacrifice.

—CHRISTOPHER HITCHENS, "Topic of Cancer"

(5) Comparison and contrast

A **comparison** points out similarities, helping readers see a relationship they might otherwise miss, whereas a **contrast** points out differences, establishing useful distinctions to better

18

understand an issue or make a decision. Comparison and contrast can be arranged in at least two ways: The paragraph can discuss all the details about one subject and then cover similarities or differences of the other. Or the paragraph might shift back and forth to discuss both subjects, point by point. In the following paragraph, the Silicon Valley GOP (Republican) organization uses details to compare and contrast the positions the Republican and Democratic political parties take toward immigration and, thus, help potential voters make their decisions at the polls.

> **Republicans** recognize that our nation is enriched by immigrants seeking a better life. In many cases immigrants have fled violence and oppression searching for peace and freedom. All suffered and sacrificed but hoped for a better future for their children in America. Republicans agree that the lack of security along our borders has contributed to the flow of narco-trafficking, gang violence, and the yearly forced servitude and slavery of over 50,000 women and children from foreign countries by human smugglers. While our nation has been enriched by the determination, energy, and diversity of immigrants, Republicans believe that in this nation of laws, immigration policies should be followed and that securing our borders is vital to ensuring the safety of our citizens. Democrats believe that as the world superpower, it is a fundamental right for the United States to provide unconditional aid and comfort to the citizens of other nations. **Democrats** believe in open borders, unconditional amnesty, and that the laws of this nation be curtailed to provide non-emergency assistance and legal forms of identification to foreign nationals.
>
> —SILICON VALLEY GOP

Another kind of comparison is the **analogy**, which compares two subjects that may seem dissimilar or compares an unfamiliar subject or item with a familiar one, as in the following paragraph:

> And she was happy right now, it was true. Jane Houlton, shifting slightly inside her nice black coat, was thinking that, after all, life was a gift—that one of those things about getting older was knowing that so many moments weren't just moments, they were gifts.
>
> —ELIZABETH STROUT, *Olive Kitteridge*

(6) Classification and division

Classification is a way to understand or explain something by establishing how it fits within a category or group. Book classifications, for instance, include such categories as reference, fiction, and nonfiction. And those same classifications can be further broken down with fiction subclassified into historical, suspense, mystery, Western, literary, and so on. **Division**, in contrast, separates something into component parts and examines the relationships among them. Thus, classification and division offer two different perspectives: classify things into groups or divide things into subclasses, as the following paragraph illustrates. Both classification and division are used to differentiate among the range of human skin pigmentation. Like many paragraphs, this one mixes rhetorical methods: the writer uses description, comparison and contrast, and cause-and-consequence analysis to support her major point of classification. Notice that the classification itself has a medical purpose: to evaluate the risk of skin cancer.

> In medicine, the classification of skin color has stemmed primarily from the need to quickly and reliably evaluate the risk of skin cancer in light-skinned patients, in the setting of a doctor's office. Because lightly pigmented people differ in their ability to tan and are not equally susceptible to sunburn and skin cancer risk, the method of skin phototyping, developed in 1975, helps physicians accurately predict a person's reaction to moderate sun exposure. According to this classification system, there are six skin phototypes: three are referred to as "melanocompromised" (phototypes I–III) and three are considered "melanocompetent" (phototypes IV–VI). The definition of sun exposure in this system is thirty minutes of unprotected exposure without sunscreen at peak (summer) UVR levels.
>
> —NINA G. JABLONSKI, *Skin: A Natural History*

(7) Definition

By defining a concept or term, you efficiently clarify your meaning and so develop an idea. You also immediately connect with your readers when they know what you are and are not talking about. Definitions are usually constructed in a two-step process: the first step locates the term by placing it in a class or general category; the second step differentiates this particular term from other terms in the same class. The following paragraph defines volcanoes by placing them into a class ("landforms") and then distinguishes them ("built of molten material") from other members of that class. The definition is clarified by examples.

> Volcanoes are landforms built of molten material that has spewed out onto the earth's surface. Such molten rock is called lava. Volcanoes may be no larger than small hills, or thousands of feet high. All have a characteristic cone shape. Some well-known mountains are actually volcanoes. Examples are Mt. Fuji (Japan), Mt. Lassen (California), Mt. Hood (Oregon), Mt. Etna and Mt. Vesuvius (Italy), and Paricutín (Mexico). The Hawaiian Islands are all immense volcanoes whose summits rise above the ocean, and these volcanoes are still quite active.
>
> —JOEL AREM, *Rocks and Minerals*

3d   Making paragraphs unified and coherent

When a paragraph flows, sentences and details are arranged in a way that is easy for readers to follow. When every sentence relates to the main idea, the paragraph is **unified**.

TIPS FOR STRONG, UNIFIED PARAGRAPHS

Identify   Identify the topic sentence, if there is one, making sure that it both highlights the main idea of the paragraph and connects the paragraph to the thesis statement. If the main idea is not stated in a topic sentence, what is the implied main idea of the paragraph?

Relate   Read each sentence in a paragraph and determine how it relates to and develops the main idea.

TIPS FOR STRONG, UNIFIED PARAGRAPHS

Eliminate   Eliminate any sentence that does not relate to the main idea or violates the unity of the paragraph. Or consider adding clarifying details or a transitional word or phrase to make the relationship clear.

Connect   Check to see how your sentences fit together. What specific words or phrases help your reader move from one idea to the next?

Clarify   Clarify the relationship between each sentence and the main idea by using details, examples, and other evidence that bring the main idea of the paragraph to life. Without details and examples, broader statements in the paragraph can seem abstract or hollow.

Rewrite   If more than one idea is conveyed in a single paragraph, either split the paragraph in two or rewrite the paragraph so that it establishes a relationship between both ideas.

(1) Using patterns of organization

When sentences are arranged in such a way that the relationship among ideas is clear as is the progression of those ideas, then the paragraph is **coherent**. The following patterns of organization are useful for creating unity and coherence.

- **Chronological order** (particularly useful in narration) arranges ideas according to the order in which things happened.
- **Spatial order** (effective in description) orients the reader's focus from right to left, near to far, top to bottom, and so on.
- **Emphatic order** (useful in expository and persuasive writing) arranges information in order of importance, usually from least to most important, which helps readers understand logical relationships.

- **Logical order** presents information from specific to general or from general to specific, as in the following paragraph.

> Whether one reads for work or for pleasure, comprehension is the goal. Comprehension is an active process; readers must interact and be engaged with a text. To accomplish this, proficient readers use strategies or conscious plans of action. Less proficient readers often lack awareness of comprehension strategies, however, and cannot develop them on their own. For adult literacy learners in particular, integrating and synthesizing information from any but the simplest texts can pose difficulties.
> —MARY E. CURTIS AND JOHN R. KRUIDENIER, "Teaching Adults to Read:
> A Summer of Scientifically Based Research Principles"

(2) Using pronouns

Instead of repeating names or key words, use pronouns such as *both*, *their*, and *they* to keep references within a paragraph clear.

> Jim Springer and Jim Lewis were adopted as infants into working-class Ohio families. **Both** liked math and did not like spelling in school. **Both** had law enforcement training and worked part-time as deputy sheriffs. **Both** vacationed in Florida; **both** drove Chevrolets. Much has been made of the fact that **their** lives are marked by a trail of similar names. **Both** married and divorced women named Linda and had second marriages with women named Betty. **They** named **their** sons James Allan and James Alan.

(3) Using repetition

Repeating words, phrases, structures, or ideas can help you link a sentence to those that precede it. Here the repetition of the pronoun *they* and references to *No Child Left Behind* link sentences.

> I recently encountered a mother who told me that her school "had some of those **Nickleby** kids" . . . in reference to **No Child Left Behind** kids. **NCLB**. It was said in a derogatory way, like the school was being dragged down because of these children.

So who are these "**Nickleby**" kids? The voiceless ones who slipped through the system because **they** were someone else's problem. **They** were in someone else's school. But you know what? **They** weren't. And aren't. **They** are in almost every school. Your child's school. My daughters' schools. And **they** are gifted young people with much to offer our communities, our country, and our world.

—MARGARET SPELLINGS, "Spellings Addresses PTA Convention"

(4) Using transitions

Even if your sentences are arranged in a seemingly clear sequence, they may be hard for readers to follow without transitions and other necessary connections.

Conjunctions and other transitional words or phrases indicate the logical relationship between ideas.

➤ The athlete stretched, **and** she studied him carefully.

➤ The athlete raced **while** she filmed him with her iPhone.

➤ The athlete frowned **because** she was making him nervous.

➤ The athlete shouted out, **so** she walked away.

➤ The athlete won the next race; **later**, she was glad she had left the track.

COMMONLY USED TRANSITIONS	
Addition	again, also, and, and then, besides, equally important, further, furthermore, in addition, in the same way, not to mention, too
Alternative	conversely, either, neither, nor, or, on the other hand, otherwise
Comparison	in like manner, in the same manner, just as, likewise, similarly
Concession	although this may be true, at the same time, even so, in any event, nevertheless, nonetheless, notwithstanding, still, that said, without doubt

(Continued on page 24)

COMMONLY USED TRANSITIONS *(Continued)*

Contrast	but, however, in contrast, on the contrary, or, yet
Exemplification	as an illustration, for example, for instance, in the case of, specifically
Emphasis	especially, even more so, even more important, indeed, important to realize, in fact, moreover, to be sure, to clarify, to emphasize, to point out, significantly
Place	across, adjacent to, beyond, here, farther, nearby, on the opposite side, opposite to
Purpose	due to, for this purpose, given that, in case, in order to, so that, to this end, with this in mind, with this objective
Repetition	as has been noted, as I have said, as previously stated, in other words, that is
Result or cause	accordingly, as a result, because, consequently, for, hence, so, then, therefore, thereby
Sequence	afterward, finally, first, from time to time, in the first place, in the meantime, in the second place, last, later, next, second, sooner or later, then, third, until now, whenever
Summary	in brief, in short, in sum, on the whole
Time	after a few days, during, in the meantime, in the past, following, meanwhile, simultaneously, since, so far, soon, subsequently, while

4 Revising and Editing Essays

Revising entails reviewing your writing in light of your overall purpose: your success at addressing your audience, the clarity of your thesis, the effectiveness of your arrangement, and the development and detailed support of your assertions. When you are **editing**, you are polishing your writing: choosing precise words, shaping distinct prose, and structuring effective sentences. When you are **proofreading**, you focus even more: you eliminate surface errors in grammar, punctuation, and mechanics, and you check the formatting and documentation of your sources. If you set aside your writing for twenty-four hours, you will more likely return to it with a critical eye.

CONCERNS FOR REVISION

Look at your draft with a critical eye, considering the following areas closely.

- **Opportunity for writing.** Why are you writing on this topic in the first place?
- **Audience and purpose.** How does your purpose align with your audience?
- **Introduction.** How does it grab the reader?
- **Thesis statement.** How do you declare your purpose?
- **Organization.** According to what specific purpose is your information arranged?
- **Reasons and evidence.** What reasons, evidence, examples, and details do you use to support or extend your thesis?
- **Transitions.** How do you move your reader from one point to the next?

(Continued on page 26)

CONCERNS FOR REVISION   *(Continued)*

- **Conclusion.** How do you describe the consequences of your argument in a final attempt to encourage your audience to consider (if not commit to) a particular course of action?

4a   Revising for unity and coherence

When revising the body of an essay, writers are likely to discover ways to make the essay itself more **unified** by relating the assertions and support of each individual paragraph to the thesis statement. After deleting, expanding, or compressing the information in each paragraph accordingly, writers concentrate on **coherence**, ordering their paragraphs purposefully (chronologically, spatially, emphatically, logically) so that a reader can easily follow the connections from one idea, sentence, and paragraph to the next (**3d**).

4b   Revising and editing paragraphs

Just as every paragraph should align itself with the thesis statement, each paragraph should have its own main idea, which often appears as a topic sentence (**3a**). Every sentence in a paragraph should then align with the main idea or topic sentence. Sometimes, the main idea is implied by the cumulative effect of all the sentences in the paragraph. More often, writers open their paragraphs with an explicit topic sentence. Still, strong paragraphs can end with a topic sentence as well, as in the following paragraph:

> The first time I visited Texas, I wore a beige polyester-blend lab coat with reinforced slits for pocket access and mechanical-pencil storage. I was attending a local booksellers' convention, having just co-written a pseudo-scientific book . . . , and my publicist suggested that the doctor getup would attract attention. It did. Everyone thought I was the janitor. *Lesson No. 1: When in Texas, do not dress down.*
>
> —PATRICIA MARX, "Dressin' Texan"

CHECKLIST FOR REVISING PARAGRAPHS

For more advice about developing and editing strong paragraphs, see chapter **3**.

- Does each paragraph include a topic sentence that states (or clearly implies) the main idea of the paragraph?
- Does every sentence in the paragraph align with the paragraph's main idea? Eliminate those that do not relate or consider using them elsewhere.
- Check the detailed support in each paragraph. Are the reasons, evidence, examples, and details effective? What kinds of detailed support might be missing?
- What method or methods have been used to develop the paragraph? What other methods might also be effective, maybe more effective?
- What effective transitions are used to connect sentences?

4c Getting response

Before you submit your work to an instructor, take advantage of other opportunities for getting response to it. Consult with readers—at the writing center, in your classes, or in online writing groups—asking them for responses to your writing. The following questions will help your readers focus their responses as they read your draft closely.

- How does the draft fulfill every single criterion of the assignment?
- What rhetorical opportunity does the draft address?
- Who is the specific audience? How is that audience appropriate for the assignment?
- How is the tone appropriate? How does it align with the draft's audience and purpose? Is the stance on the topic made clear?

- What is the thesis statement? How is it focused? What assertions support the thesis statement? What evidence, examples, and details are used?
- What makes the arrangement of paragraphs effective? How might the organization be improved?
- What specifically makes the introduction effective? How is it engaging?
- How is the conclusion appropriate? How does it draw the draft together?

4d   Editing and proofreading

If you are satisfied with the revised structure of your essay and the content of your paragraphs, you can edit individual sentences for clarity, effectiveness, and variety. Once you have revised and edited, then you must proofread the entire draft, making sure the final product is free from error.

CHECKLIST FOR EDITING SENTENCES

Sentences

- What is the unifying idea of each sentence (23)?
- How have you varied the lengths of your sentences? If your sentences tend to be the same length (whether long or short), revise them for variation (27a).
- How many of your sentences use subordination? Coordination? If you overuse any one sentence structure, revise for variation (24).
- Which sentences might be strengthened with parallel structure? Check that lists and series are in parallel form (25).
- Check that each verb agrees with its subject (20f). Check that every pronoun agrees with its antecedent (21c). Reread your sentences with these agreement issues in mind, revising accordingly.

CHECKLIST FOR EDITING SENTENCES

Diction

- Check that any repeated words are intentionally repeated (**30**).

- Which general words can you make more specific (**29**)?

- How exactly is the vocabulary you have chosen appropriate for your audience, purpose, and context?

- Which technical or unfamiliar words have you defined for your audience?

CHECKLIST FOR PROOFREADING

Spelling

- Have you double-checked the words you frequently misspell and any the spell checker may have missed (**36**)? For example, check for misspellings that still form words (such as *form* for *from*).

- If you used a spell checker, did it overlook homophones (such as *there/their, who's/whose,* and *it's/its*)?

- Have you double-checked the spelling of all foreign words and all proper names?

Punctuation and Capitalization

- Check that each sentence has appropriate closing punctuation. Check that you use only one space after each end punctuation mark (**35**).

- Check that all punctuation within sentences—commas, semicolons, apostrophes, hyphens, and dashes—is used appropriately and placed correctly (**31**, **32**, **33**).

- Are direct quotations carefully and correctly punctuated (**34a**)? Where have you placed end punctuation with a quotation (**34c**)? Are quotations capitalized properly?

- Are all proper names, people's titles, and titles of published works correctly capitalized (**37**)?

- Are titles of works identified with quotation marks (**34b**) or italics (**38a**)?

5 Critical Reading and Textual Analysis

In your academic work, you will be called on to read a variety of complex visuals and texts that make arguments to support a position. You will need to identify the argument, the claims it makes, and the evidence it uses. To engage these texts fully, you must learn to read them actively and critically.

5a Critical reading

Because you cannot always take a message at face value, you must read critically. Critical reading is *not* negative reading; it is *not* finding fault. Rather, critical reading is composed of concentrating on asking good questions and commenting thoughtfully on or about the text itself. Whether the text is print, electronic, spoken, visual, or some combination, you need to interpret it critically.

You already use this skill in your personal life when you are considering a friend's text message, a child's excuse, or a popular movie. For example, when you go to see *La La Land*, you watch the complex plot quickly unfold, asking yourself how the Los Angeles freeway traffic jam, the run-down jazz club, and the lavish Hollywood party all connect with Mia, with Sebastian, and with the performing arts. All during the movie, you use similar critical skills, posing questions and making comments to yourself as you figure out the connections. In your academic life, you use the same questioning and commenting skills, whether you are reading finance problem sets, your political science textbook, or a speech class podcast.

Reading critically helps you establish what you already know about a topic or author, what you are likely to learn from the text, and what information is lacking. Reading critically also helps you gauge the expertise and credibility of the writer. In addition, the process helps you distinguish between actual content and your expectations for that content, a process that prepares you to handle a heavy academic reading and writing load.

CHECKLIST FOR CRITICAL READING

- **Consider your purpose.** What is your purpose for reading? Pleasure? Assignment?
- **Preview the text.** What information does the title convey? What do you already know about the topic? What opinions do you hold about the topic?
- **Consider the author.** What do you know about the credibility of the author or creator? What is the author's purpose?
- **Read the text.** Identify the key parts of the text itself. How do they relate to one another? What parts do you find informative? Confusing?
- **Annotate.** Identify the key terms or characters in the text. How do they contribute (or not) to your understanding of the text?
- **Analyze the text.** With what parts of the text do you agree? Disagree? Does the author achieve his or her purpose? Why or why not?
- **Consider the effects of the text.** What parts of the text reinforced what you already knew? What you already value? What parts of the text surprised you? Why? What else would you like to know?

5b Textual analysis

When you analyze, you take care to evaluate the claims and positions of written and visual texts, whether they are advertisements, accounts of current events, or excuses for breaking a date (6c). Textual analysis is an intellectual skill closely aligned with argumentation in that it serves as a mechanism for recognizing and examining the arguments of others as well as for formulating and then examining your own. Most communication is to some extent an argument intended to influence the attitudes or actions of an audience. Writing is recognized as argumentative when it clearly supports a position. A résumé is an argument for a job interview, just as a warm welcome is an argument for you to enjoy an evening with friends.

Effective arguments are well developed and broken into strong assertions that are supported by intelligent and appropriate **evidence**. Effective arguments also take into consideration the **reasons** others might disagree. For readers to take the ideas in an argument seriously, the writer must communicate the reasons that have led to a position as well as the values and **assumptions** (assumed shared beliefs, often unstated) that underlie the writer's thinking.

Although many arguments are based on the use of assertions and support, some, like those of Stephen Toulmin, are rooted in a logical progression. The Toulmin method for understanding an argument provides yet another way for you to consider the elements of an argument for analysis.

FEATURES OF A TOULMIN ARGUMENT

The philosopher Stephen Toulmin defined **argument** as a logical progression, from the **reasons** (accepted evidence or **data** that support a claim), to the **claim** (an arguable statement of fact, opinion, or belief; a **thesis**) based on **assumptions** (the underlying, often unstated **warrants** that connect the claim and the reasons for the claim). If the assumption is controversial, it requires **evidence** (the independent support or justification that Toulmin refers to as **backing**).

Starting with a general statement and then reasoning toward a conclusion, Toulmin's method establishes a reasonable relationship

FEATURES OF A TOULMIN ARGUMENT

among the reasons, the claim, and the evidence, as in the following argument:

➤ Given that nearly one hundred American high school football players received catastrophic head injuries over a thirteen-year period, with 71 percent of them suffering a previous concussion during the same season, and 39 percent of them playing with residual symptoms, younger players, with even more vulnerable brains, should not play full-contact football.

Reasons (or Data support)	Older, stronger players are regularly hurt, but the physiology of children leaves them even more prone to collision-induced trauma than is the case with older players.
Thesis (or Claim)	In light of the obvious dangers and threats, we should ban full-contact football for players younger than high school age.
Assumption (or Warrant)	Safety is the first priority of team sports.

TIPS FOR ANALYZING AN ARGUMENT

- Read through the argument carefully. Determine the author's thesis or claim.
- Map out the supporting evidence that the author uses to support that thesis.
- Identify the kinds of sources the author uses. How reliable, current, and effective are they?
- Determine the author's qualifications, assumptions, and values. Identify evidence that supports the credibility (or lack thereof) of the author.

(Continued on page 34)

TIPS FOR ANALYZING AN ARGUMENT   *(Continued)*

- Weigh your opinions against the author's, identifying places you agree and disagree with the author, assumptions you share and do not share.

- Evaluate the quality of the supporting examples or evidence the author uses to reinforce the position. Whether visual, verbal, or a combination, the reasons should be good ones, reasonable, practical, and ethical. What objections might be made to this series of good reasons?

- Identify the assumptions the author makes about the intended audience. How does the author reach out to that audience?

- Consider your overall impression of the argument. What does the author want readers to do in response to the argument? If you were successfully, partially, or unsuccessfully persuaded by this argument, identify the passages that were effective or weak. How might the author strengthen those passages?

5c   Basic appeals in an argument

Effective arguments always incorporate a combination of persuasive strategies, which include three general types of **appeal**.

(1) Ethical appeals

The most important appeal is the **ethical appeal** because it establishes the writer's ethos (credibility and trustworthiness). An ethical appeal demonstrates goodwill toward the audience, good sense or knowledge of the subject at hand, and good character. To identify the ethical appeal, look for the way the writer strives to establish common ground with readers in the introduction. Then, look for ways that the writer demonstrates a thorough knowledge of the topic to establish credibility. Also check biographical information that may accompany the text for personal and professional information about the author (qualifications, credentials, and experiences), all of which help establish good sense and moral character.

(2) Logical appeals

By providing good reasons (practical, moral, even aesthetic reasons) in the body of a text, an author establishes the **logical appeal**. Evidence, examples, statistics, comparisons, facts, expert opinions, and personal experiences or observations all constitute good logical appeals—if they are trustworthy, effective, and judicious. Evaluate these pieces of evidence and check facts; you cannot assume that all logical appeals are built on valid facts and sources.

(3) Emotional appeals

An **emotional appeal** connects the writer's beliefs and feelings with those of the audience. To identify an emotional appeal, look for language (examples, narratives, possible consequences, and so on) designed to stir emotions, build connections, and invoke shared values. Like the ethical and logical appeals, emotional appeals should also be trustworthy, never manipulative. Neuroscientists claim that the emotional appeal is actually more important than that of logic, maybe even more than ethos.

5d   Avoiding rhetorical fallacies

Logical reasoning fortifies the overall effectiveness of an argument as well as builds the ethos of the speaker or writer. Constructing an argument effectively means avoiding errors in logic known as rhetorical fallacies, which weaken an argument as well as the writer's ethos. These fallacies signal to your audience that your thinking is not entirely trustworthy and that your argument is not well reasoned or researched.

These are some of the most commonly used rhetorical fallacies.

(1) *Non sequitur*

A *non sequitur* (Latin for "it does not follow"), the basis for most of the other rhetorical fallacies, attempts to make a connection where none actually exists. Just because the first part of a statement is true does not mean that the second part is true, will become true, or will necessarily happen.

Faulty   Heather is married and will start a family soon.

This assertion is based on the faulty premise that *all* women have children soon after marrying.

(2) *Ad hominem*

The *ad hominem* (the Latin phrase translates to "toward the man himself") fallacy refers to a personal attack that draws attention away from the issue under consideration.

Faulty   With his penchant for expensive haircuts, that candidate cannot relate to the common people.

The fact that a candidate pays a lot for a haircut may say something about his vanity but says nothing about his political appeal.

(3) Bandwagon

The bandwagon fallacy argues that everyone is doing, saying, or thinking something, so you should, too. It makes an irrelevant and disguised appeal to the human desire to be part of a group.

Faulty   Everyone texts while driving, so I do, too.

Even if the majority of people text while driving, doing so has proven to be dangerous. The majority is not automatically right.

(4) Equivocation

The rhetorical fallacy of equivocation falsely relies on the use of one word or concept in two different ways.

Faulty   Today's students are illiterate; they do not know the characters in Shakespeare's plays.

Traditionally, *literacy* has meant knowing how to read and write, how to function in a print-based culture. Knowing about Shakespeare's characters is not the equivalent of literacy; someone lacking this special kind of knowledge might be characterized as uneducated or uninformed but not as illiterate.

(5) Hasty generalization

A hasty generalization is a conclusion based on too little evidence or on exceptional or biased evidence.

Faulty	Ellen is a poor student because she failed her first history test.

Ellen may be doing well in her other subjects.

(6) Red herring

Sometimes called *ignoring the question*, the red herring fallacy dodges the real issue by drawing attention to a seemingly related but irrelevant one.

Faulty	Why worry about violence in schools when we ought to be worrying about international terrorism?

International terrorism has no direct relationship with school violence.

(7) Slippery slope

The slippery slope fallacy assumes that one thing will inevitably lead to another—that if one thing is allowed, it will be the first step in a downward spiral.

Faulty	Handgun controls guarantee that only criminals will have guns.

Handgun control has not led to more criminals with guns in other countries (England, for example).

6   Writing Arguments

If everyone agreed on everything, there would be no need for **argument**, for taking a position, whether gently or forcefully. Therefore, a good deal of the writing you will do in school, at home, or at work will require you to take an arguable position on a topic. Arguments serve three basic purposes: (1) to analyze a complicated issue or question an established belief, (2) to express or defend a point of view, (3) and to invite or convince an audience to change a position or adopt a course of action.

6a   Considering differing viewpoints

Behind any effective argument is a question that can generate more than one reasonable answer. Answers differ because people approach questions with various backgrounds, experiences, and assumptions, and they are often tempted to use reasoning that supports what they already believe. As a writer, employing such reasoning is a good place to start. However, as you expand your argument, you will want to demonstrate not only that you are knowledgeable about your topic but also that you have given fair consideration to other views about it.

When you choose a topic for argumentation, you will want to take a stance that provides you with a reason for writing, a problem to address or resolve (chapter **1**). At the same time, you must establish **common ground** with your audience, stating a goal toward which you both want to work or identifying a belief, assumption, or value that you both share. First, focus on a topic, on the part of some general subject that you will address in your essay, and then pose a question about it. Consider what you know about the topic and the following:

- your own values and beliefs with respect to the question
- how your assumptions might differ from those of your intended audience
- how you might establish common ground with members of your audience while respecting any differences between your opinion and theirs

The question you raise will evolve into your **thesis**, an arguable statement. To determine whether a topic might be suitable, make a statement about the topic.

"I believe strongly that . . . ."

"My view is that . . . ."

Then check to see if that statement can be argued.

6b Distinguishing between fact and opinion

When you develop your thesis statement into an argument, you use both facts and opinions. **Facts** are reliable pieces of information that can be verified through independent sources or procedures. **Opinions**, on the other hand, are assertions or inferences that may or may not be based on facts. Opinions that are widely accepted may seem to be factual when they are not; rather, they are assumptions. Facts are significant only when they are used responsibly to support a claim; otherwise, a thoughtful and well-informed opinion might have more impact and forge a stronger connection with your audience.

6c Taking a position or making a claim

When making an argument, a writer takes a position (called the **claim**) on a particular topic, which clearly states what the writer wants the audience to do with the information being provided. The central claim is the thesis for your argument and is articulated in your thesis statement.

Claims can be absolute or moderate, large or limited. Absolute claims assert that something is always true or false ("The sun will rise tomorrow"), completely good or bad ("All professional athletes dope"); moderate claims make less sweeping assertions ("It looks like rain" or "Unfortunately, some professional athletes have admitted to doping").

ABSOLUTE CLAIM   All full-contact football is dangerous and should be banned.

MODERATE CLAIM   Because full-contact youth football is dangerous, players should play flag or touch football until they get older.

The stronger the claim, the stronger the evidence needed to support it. Be sure to consider the quality and the significance of the evidence you use—not just its quantity.

A **substantiation claim** may assert that something exists or is evident. Without making a value judgment, such a claim makes a point that can be supported by evidence.

➤ The job market for those with only a high school diploma is limited.

➤ The post office is raising rates again and losing money again.

Evaluation claims may assert that something has a specific quality or is good or bad, effective or ineffective, attractive or unattractive, successful or unsuccessful.

➤ The high graduation rate for athletes at Penn State is a direct result of the school's supportive academic environment.

➤ The public transportation system in Stockholm is reliable and safe.

Policy claims may also call for a specific action.

➤ We must establish the funding necessary to hire the best qualified high school teachers.

➤ We need to build a light-rail system linking downtown with the airport and the western suburbs.

6d Providing evidence for an effective argument

(1) Establishing reasons for the claim

If you want readers to take your ideas seriously, you must communicate the reasons that have led to your position as well as the values and **assumptions** (the underlying beliefs) of your thinking. When you are exploring your topic, make a list of the reasons that have led to your belief. If it is likely that your readers will not share an assumption, consider giving your reasons and offer supporting evidence. For example, when Billy Lucas was working on his argumentative essay (**6g**), he listed the following reasons for his belief that full-contact football should be banned for players younger than high school age:

1. Professional and college leagues admit the dangers of full-contact football based on medical research findings.
2. Both leagues have already set regulations in place to protect "defenseless" players.
3. Young players, whose brains and spines are particularly vulnerable, regularly sustain hard, damaging hits.
4. Scientific research continues to reveal the progressive brain damage caused by full-contact football, particularly for young players.

Although it is possible to base an argument on one good reason (such as "The brains and bodies of young players are too vulnerable for full-contact football"), doing so can be risky. When you show that you have more than one reason for believing as you do, you increase the likelihood that your audience will find some measure of merit in your argument. Sometimes, however, one reason is more appropriate than several others you could advance. To develop an argument for which you have only one good reason, explore the bases underlying your reason: the assumptions that led you to take your stand.

Whether you have one reason or several, be sure to provide sufficient evidence from credible sources to support your claim: facts, statistics, examples, and testimony from personal experience or professional expertise. This evidence must be accurate, representative, and sufficient. Accurate information should be verifiable by others. Recognize, however, that even if the information a writer provides is accurate, it may not be representative or sufficient if it was drawn from an exceptional case, a biased sample, or a one-time occurrence. Whatever form of evidence you use, you need to make clear to your audience exactly *why* and *how* the evidence supports your claim.

(2) Responding to diverse views

Effective arguments consider and respond to other points of view fairly and respectfully. The most common strategy for addressing opposing points of view is **refutation**: you introduce diverse views and then respectfully demonstrate why you disagree with or accept each of them. When you find yourself agreeing with a point that supports another side of the issue, you can benefit from offering a **concession**, which can demonstrate your fairmindedness. If you admit that others are partially right, they are more likely to admit that you could be partially right as well.

(3) Using visuals

Visuals, such as tables, charts, graphs, photographs, and maps, can strengthen your argument by offering evidence, as well as organizing and describing facts and data.

TIPS FOR THINKING CRITICALLY ABOUT VISUALS

Before you incorporate a visual into your project, analyze the argument it makes and its purpose.

- Study the visual until you understand its claim.
- Determine the trustworthiness and accuracy of the visual. How does the creator of the visual establish credibility? What sources are used? Are they current and reliable?

TIPS FOR THINKING CRITICALLY ABOUT VISUALS

- Determine if—and how—the visual incorporates rhetorical appeals: ethical, logical, or emotional (5c).

- Determine the purpose of the visual: to organize facts, present data, illustrate a piece of background, demonstrate authority.

- Identify the intended audience. What assumptions does the visual make about viewers? What background knowledge or attitudes would the audience likely have?

- If the visual includes words and images, consider how they work together. How do the words and visual elements relate to one another?

- Look closely at composition and the design of the visual. What colors, lines, shapes, positions of objects, or expressions of people do you notice? How do these elements relate to one another to make a point or serve the purpose of the visual?

Make clear how the visual supports the claim you are making in your text. Check the disciplinary conventions and models in your field for the kinds of visuals that are considered appropriate.

6e Using appeals to ground your argument

Effective arguments always incorporate a combination of three persuasive strategies: the **appeals** of ethos, logos, and pathos (5c). **Ethos** (an ethical appeal) establishes the speaker's or writer's credibility and trustworthiness. An ethical appeal demonstrates goodwill toward the audience, good sense or knowledge of the subject at hand, and good character. Establishing common ground with the audience is another feature of ethos. **Logos**, a logical appeal consisting of good reasons, demonstrates an effective use of reason and judicious use of evidence, whether that evidence consists of facts, statistics, comparisons, anecdotes, expert opinions, personal experiences, or observations. Good reasons should be practical, moral, and aesthetic (meaning they should have a pleasing outcome). You employ your good reasons in the process of supporting claims, drawing reasonable conclusions, and avoiding rhetorical fallacies (**5d**). **Pathos** (an emotional appeal) involves using language that will engage (not manipulate) the feelings of the audience by establishing empathy and authentic understanding. The most effective arguments combine these three persuasive appeals responsibly and knowledgeably.

6f   Organizing an effective argument

No single organization is right for every written argument. The decisions you make about arrangement should be based on several factors: your topic, your audience, and your purpose. You can develop a good plan by listing the major points you want to make, deciding what order to put them in, and determining where to include refutation or concession. You must also decide where to place your thesis statement or claim.

Your conclusion should move beyond what has already been stated to reinforce your rhetorical purpose: the course of action you want your audience to take, an invitation to further understanding, or the implications of your claim.

FEATURES OF THE CLASSICAL ARRANGEMENT

One way to organize your argument is to use classical arrangement, which assumes that an audience is prepared to follow a well-reasoned argument.

Introduction	Introduce your issue and capture the attention of your audience. Begin establishing your credibility (using ethos) and common ground with your audience.

FEATURES OF THE CLASSICAL ARRANGEMENT

Background information	Provide your audience with a history of the situation and state how things currently stand. Define any key terms. Draw the attention of your audience to those points that are especially important and explain why they are meaningful.
Proposition	Introduce the position you are taking: present the argument itself and provide the basic reasons for your belief. Frame your position as a thesis statement or a claim.
Proof or confirmation	Discuss the reasons that have led you to take your position. Each reason must be clear, relevant, and representative. Provide facts, expert testimony, and any other evidence that supports your claim.
Refutation	Recognize and disprove the arguments of people who hold a different position and with whom you continue to disagree.
Concession	Concede any point with which you agree or that has merit; show why this concession might affect yet does not damage your own case.
Conclusion	Summarize your most important points and appeal to your audience's feelings, making a personal connection. Describe the consequences of your argument in a final attempt to encourage your audience to consider (if not commit to) a particular course of action or belief.

6g Sample argument

As you read the following essay by Billy Lucas, note his use of ethical, logical, and emotional appeals; reasoning; and arrangement. Also, identify the kinds of evidence he uses (facts, examples, testimony, or authority).

Billy Lucas

Professor Pisani-Babich

English 138T

14 April 2017

Friday Night Fright: Banning Kids' Tackle Football

Eleven-year-old Donte Goss lies in his hospital bed, his head wrapped with attached electrodes, his eyes dazed. Donte's mother, tears in her eyes, turns to *Friday Night Tykes* cameraman and tells him that Donte had looked at her and said, "I don't know you; leave me alone" ("Now They're Playing Scared"). So begins the third episode of this season's new reality show, *Friday Night Tykes*, a glorification of kids' football in this "Friday Night Lights" country of Texas. Donte, tackled and knocked unconscious the day before, has suffered a severe concussion. Visibly shaken, Donte's parents assure the television viewing audience (nearly half of whom support tackle football) that Donte will return to the field again—when the doctors clear him. Still, these parents have limits: after his third concussion, Donte will no longer be allowed to play football.

In the Texas Youth Football Association (TYFA), what with its rivalries, aggressive parents, and wildly competitive coaches, Donte's parents shine as reasonable beings. In their world, tackle football begins at age six, on-field head injuries are ignored, and game-time medical assistance goes unprovided ("TYFA Football Programs").

Billy opens his essay with a concrete example to "hook" his readers and set up his argument against youth football tackling.

Billy's second paragraph provides a historical overview of the situation.

Lucas 2

Physical peril and extreme competitiveness are celebrated while the medical profession as well as the public speak of the long-term dangers of repetitive concussions. According to medical researchers David Xavier Cifu and Craig C. Young, American high school football players demonstrated "94 catastrophic head injuries (significant intracranial bleeding or edema) over a 13-year period" and "seventy-one percent of high school players suffering such injuries had a previous concussion in the same season, with 39 percent playing with residual symptoms." With still so much to learn about brain injuries, why do we continue to expose ever-younger children to the risks of tackle football? In light of the obvious dangers and threats, we should ban full-contact football for prehigh school kids.

The national debate over the danger of concussions and brain injuries in football began in earnest fifteen years ago when the National Football League (NFL) acknowledged those dangers by enacting changes to rules and equipment and by sponsoring studies of players' health and sports concussions. Following suit, the National Collegiate Athletic Association (NCAA) has also enacted rules to better protect its players from helmet-to-helmet injuries leading to concussions (Roling).

Regardless of the strides the NFL and NCAA have taken to protect our nation's best professional and college players, no such safeguards have been taken for youth football. Unlike the pro and collegiate teams, no single governing body regulates high school

Billy uses medical research findings to support the idea that will become his thesis.

Billy ends his second paragraph with his arguable thesis statement.

Billy uses the following paragraph, too, to demonstrate the care he has taken to research and build an ethical, logical argument.

Lucas 3

Billy sticks to his guns, conceding that football—at all levels—is a truly popular sport but invoking the dangers to the youth, thereby establishing common ground: we all agree that young players should be kept safe.

football, let alone youth football in the United States. Yet, even if there were a governing body, that body—either through laws or equipment—could not undo the high risk of concussion on the youth level, risks much higher than those for older players. No regulation short of prohibition could adequately protect the millions of young players involved in full-contact football.

The dangers of concussions and brain injuries are significant for NFL, college, and high school football players, but the risks for younger players are even greater due to their stage of physical development. Simply put, the physiology of children leaves them more prone to collision-induced trauma than is the case with older people. As Dr. Mark Hyman explains, a child's head is similar in size to that of an adult, but the neck is "much weaker than an adult's neck. The combination creates a danger. When a child takes a hard blow . . . it is more difficult to keep the head steady. The result is greater force to the brain from being jerked inside the skull." And neurologist Larry Robbins refers to younger children as "bobbleheads," whose brains take the entire shock of an impact. He argues that even minor impacts, even single hits, are major head traumas for those immature developing brains, creating an extremely risky and dangerous situation for those players.

In this paragraph, especially, Billy establishes common ground: we must keep our youth players safe.

When we know so much about the risks and dangers involved—and know that there is still much we do not understand—why do we continue to allow children to play

Lucas 4

full-contact football? Proponents of youth football offer a number of arguments for full-contact football, the single most popular sport in the United States.

The first argument is that young players need to play full contact to learn the sport. Supporters argue that kids must be pushed, that they themselves wish they had played full-contact football at an early age, that life is tough. While it is true that learning to play early can be an advantage, youth footballers can learn all the fundamental skills of the game without engaging in full contact. Younger football players can learn the basic skills of running, passing, defending, and game strategies through flag football. Even Hall of Fame quarterback Tom Brady waited until high school to play organized tackle football because his parents found full-contact football too dangerous.

The second reason proponents give for continuing full-contact youth football is that other sports with even greater risk of injury face no bans. Indeed, concussions are a danger in other youth sports, like soccer and hockey, and no reforms have been laid down for those sports. But just because they haven't made changes doesn't mean they shouldn't. To prevent concussions and brain injuries, young soccer players should not be permitted to "head" the ball, nor should youth hockey players be permitted to engage in full contact. Concussions in soccer and other sports are caused primarily by single-impact incidents, not by the continual head hits of

In the following paragraphs, Billy lays out specific opposing arguments, carefully considering them without losing his focus on his own argument or alienating his readers.

Billy's refutation of opposing arguments is always fair-minded, and he constantly makes the concession that football is, indeed, a popular sport.

Lucas 5

football. And as journalist Gregg Easterbrook points out, the medical profession is only just learning of the long-term dangers of continual and numerous hits over a football season, especially for young players (162). Football—not other sports—carries the greatest risks.

The third argument supporters use is that improved equipment decreases the risks of tackle football. But not even helmet technology and other protective measures can prevent concussions, especially among youth footballers, according to Brian L. Mahaffey, a physician and sports medicine specialist (436). Concussions do not result from external contact from a head hit but result from the movement of the brain inside the skull that happens on contact. Therefore, there is no indication that the new technology will help reduce the risks of concussions at the youth level.

Football is the most popular sport in the United States. Its stars are venerated, its toughest plays admired by kids and their parents alike. Little wonder, then, that support for full-contact football for all ages is strong. But given our increasing understanding of the serious risks of football-related brain injuries, maybe it is time to consider viable alternatives, modified versions of the game (like flag football) that will allow our kids to play and compete without significant health risks. When they have matured physically and mentally, then they will be better prepared to engage in full-contact tackle football. The NFL, the NCAA, and other sports-related organizations should support this critical decision, overriding the opinions of parents, youth coaches, and fans of *Friday Night Tykes*.

Billy again concedes the popularity and value of football. He artfully offers replacements for the "tackle" in the youth league.

Billy takes his readers further than a mere summary of all his arguments; rather, he prepares them for the football these youth will play when they get older.

Lucas 6

Works Cited

Cifu, David Xavier, and Craig C. Young. "Repetitive Head Injury
    Syndrome." *Medscape Reference.* WebMD, 27 Mar. 2014,
    emedicine.medscape.com/article/92189.

Easterbrook, Gregg. *The King of Sports: Football's Impact on
    America.* St. Martin's, 2013.

Hyman, Mark. "Why Kids Under 14 Should Not Play Tackle
    Football." *Time*, 6 Nov. 2012, ideas.times.com/2012/11/06/
    why-kids-under-14-should-not-play-tackle-football/.

Mahaffey, Brian L. "Concussions in High School Sports: Are They
    Worth the Risk? Should School Football Be Banned?" *Missouri
    Medicine*, vol. 109, no. 6, 2012, pp. 445-49.

"Now They're Playing Scared." *Friday Night Tykes*, Esquire Network,
    21 Jan. 2014.

Robbins, Larry. "Let's Ban Tackle Football Under Age 18."
    RealClearSports, 6 Dec. 2012, www.realclearsports.com/
    articles/2012/12/06/lets_ban_tackle_football_until_
    age_18_97818.html.

Roling, Chris. "College Football Rule Changes 2013: Breaking Down
    Most Important New Rules." *Bleacher Report*, 29 Aug. 2013,
    bleacherreport.com/articles/1754276-college-football-rule-
    changes-2013-breaking-down-most-important-new-rules.

"TYFA Football Programs." *Texas Youth Football & Cheer Association*,
    29 Mar. 2015, www.tyfa.com/tyfa-football-programs.

7 Designing Documents

Consistent, thoughtful use of design and effective visual elements in your writing—whether reports, essays, articles, or news stories, whether online or in print—can enhance your message, engage your readers, and thus create an appropriate overall impression. The elements of design include typeface, layout, lists, headings, and color. The visual elements of writing can include tables, pie charts, line graphs, bar graphs, diagrams, photographs, maps, and even cartoons. For academic writing, be sure to check the formatting guidelines for your discipline. This handbook provides advice for formatting essays and other projects using style guides sponsored by the Modern Language Association (MLA), the American Psychological Association (APA), the *Chicago Manual of Style* (CMS), and the Council of Science Editors (CSE). If you are unsure of which style to follow, check with your instructor.

7a Elements of design

No matter what you compose, your first design decisions center on layout and typeface. Other choices, from those of headings to use of color, come later.

(1) Layout

Layout, also referred to as *formatting*, is the arrangement of the text on a page or screen, the **spacing**, and the **margins**. Final drafts of your academic projects will often be double-spaced with indented paragraphs (usually one-half inch or five spaces, following the style of your discipline). Other documents, including lab reports and business documents (such as memos, résumés, and letters) will be single-spaced and use an extra line space to indicate a new paragraph instead of indentation. Texts you create to be read online should also be single-spaced.

Appropriate use of margins and white space in your document guides readers and creates a sense of control and readability. Most of the writing (essays and reports) you do in school will be formatted for 8½-by-11-inch paper, usually with one-inch margins throughout. Use additional space around block quotations (often indented one inch from the left margin), headings, and visuals, such as graphs and tables. MLA, APA, and other documentation styles offer specific guidelines for margins and the amount of space around block quotations, headings, and other visuals.

(2) Fonts or typefaces

The fonts and sizes of type used in a document can greatly affect readability. For most of your academic essays, professional reports, and other print documents, use serif fonts, such as Times New Roman, Garamond, or Century. (Bookman Old Style is quickly becoming another popular font, as it is considered the "most trustworthy" looking.) Regarded as most readable for printed works (including in this book, which uses Times New Roman), these fonts include serifs, those little tails that elongate the tips of most of the letters. Fonts without serifs (sans serif fonts), such as **Arial**, **Lucida Sans**, and Calibri, are said to be easier to read on the screen, so they are the popular typeface choice for web texts. For print documents using multiple fonts, sans serif fonts are effective when used in headings, subheadings, or captions.

For most academic work, you will use 10-, 11-, or 12-point type. A wide variety of fonts are available. Use the decorative or amusing ones (such as **ALGERIAN**, *Blackadder*, and Curlz MT) sparingly because they are difficult to read in large passages.

Use **bold**, *italicized*, or <u>underlined</u> text options for emphasis. For example, bold can be useful to distinguish headings, and italic type is used to set off titles and words being defined. Your use of type style often depends on your academic discipline, so be sure you follow the appropriate formatting rules—MLA, APA, CMS, or CSE—for your field.

(3) Headings

Headings provide visual signposts for your audience that offer help navigating your text and understanding its organization. Consider the wording of your headings carefully, making sure they are concise and consistent throughout your document. Word your headings informatively so they relay the essence of the text they accompany. Use grammatically parallel structures, either a noun (*Immigration*), phrases with gerunds (*Restricting Immigration*), or questions (*How Can the United States Manage Immigration?*). In many cases, the wording of headings will be dictated by the documentation style you use (for example, *Abstract* or *References* in APA style).

Your discipline may also have guidelines for the placement and format of your headings, for example, requiring that they be centered. (APA style offers specific instruction for the style and placement of headings.) In most academic writing, you might

Center and Use Boldface for Your First-Level Heading

Align Left Your Second-Level Heading or Subheading

<u>Underline and Merge Your Third-Level Heading</u> with the paragraph information that follows. However you use headings, position them consistently and follow the guidelines of your discipline

(4) Lists and examples

Purposeful lists and examples also enhance your design. Many writers use bullets, numbers, or letters to highlight lists and examples. Choose bulleted lists when the items are related but may appear in any order. Use numbered or lettered lists when the sequential order of items is important (as in "first, do this; second, do that"). Lists are always indented, at least one-half inch, and single-spaced. Leave white space around your list, on both sides as well as above and below.

(5) Color

To use color appropriately in your documents, first consider the conventions in your discipline and assignment, along with your purpose and audience. Use of color helps you draw attention to headings or to other elements on a page, including graphs, charts, or other visuals. Position colors thoughtfully, keeping the number of colors to a minimum, and use them consistently throughout. Choose legible colors that offer contrast, and check that colors you choose will work well in the final product. Color combinations that are strong and legible on your screen may look different to your readers when printed or projected.

7b Use of visuals

Many academic and professional documents that are primarily composed of text also make substantial use of visuals, or **graphics**, to clarify written material. Because they are fully integrated into the overall argument of the text, such visuals are much more than decoration. Used purposefully, they organize and clarify evidence or establish credibility. All visuals should be cited carefully and used ethically.

Figures, or illustrations, consist of artwork (photographs, drawings, maps, charts, and so on), whereas **tables** consist of alphanumeric lists, columns, and rows.

TIPS FOR USING VISUALS EFFECTIVELY

- Choose images that have a clear purpose and that relate clearly to a point you are making in your text.

- Insert visuals following or near the text that refers to them. Give each visual a number (*Figure 1* or *Fig. 1*) and number tables separately. The word *Figure* is not italicized. Include a title for each.

- Identify the visual in your text, clarifying the connection or purpose for including it (*Fig. 2 presents the number of children with high lead levels over time*). The caption for the figure is not italicized.

- Following the rules of your discipline, include documentation for each visual in your bibliography. For visuals that you create using data or information in a source, you must cite the source of that information.

- Obtain permission to include visuals from other sources if you plan to publish your work online or outside your course.

- Resize, crop, and edit images if necessary, taking care not to alter meaning or distort the original point of a visual you find in another source. Check to be sure for any maps, charts, diagrams, or graphs that all elements of the graphic and its labels are clear so that readers will understand the information.

---

(1) Tables

Tables use a row-and-column arrangement to organize data (numbers or words) spatially. They are especially useful for presenting great amounts of numerical information in a small space, enabling the reader to draw direct comparisons among pieces of data or even to locate specific items. When you design a table, be sure to label all of the columns and rows accurately and to provide both a title and a number for the table. The table number and title traditionally appear above the table body, as table 7.1 demonstrates, and any notes or source information should be placed below it.

(2) Charts and graphs

Charts and graphs display relationships among statistical data in visual form by using lines, bars, or other visual elements rather than just letters and numbers. **Pie charts** are especially useful for showing the relationship of parts to a whole (see fig. 7.1), but they can be used to display only sets of data that add up to 100 percent (a whole).

Table 7.1. This table makes it easy to see the increasing amount of time Americans spend each day using various media.

AVERAGE TIME SPENT PER DAY WITH MAJOR MEDIA BY US ADULTS, 2010-2013

hrs:mins

	2010	2011	2012	2013
Digital	3:14	3:50	4:31	5:09
—Online*	2:22	2:33	2:27	2:19
—Mobile (nonvoice)	0:24	0:49	1:33	2:21
—Other	0:26	0:28	0:31	0:36
TV	4:24	4:34	4:38	4:31
Radio	1:36	1:34	1:32	1:26
Print**	0:50	0:44	0:38	0:32
—Newspapers	0:30	0:26	0:22	0:18
—Magazines	0:20	0:18	0:16	0:14
Other	0:42	0:36	0:20	0:14
Total	10:46	11:18	11:39	11:52

Note: ages 18+; time spent with each medium includes all time spent with that medium, regardless of multitasking; for example, 1 hour of multitasking online while watching TV is counted as 1 hour for TV and 1 hour for online; *includes all internet activities on desktop and laptop computers; **offline reading only

Source: eMarket.com

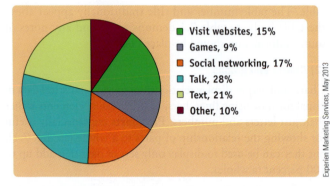

Experien Marketing Services, May 2013

Figure 7.1. On average, US smartphone owners spend 58 minutes daily on their phones.

Bar charts show correlations between two variables that do not change smoothly over time. For instance, a bar chart might illustrate the relative speeds of various computer processors or statistics about the composition of the US military (see fig. 7.2).

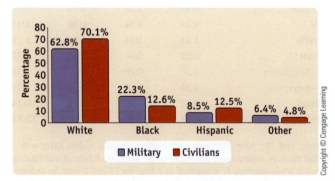

Copyright © Cengage Learning

Figure 7.2. Bar chart illustrating the composition of the US military.

(3) Maps

Historical, economic, and geographic accounts often call for the use of maps (see fig. 7.3).

Figure 7.3. 2016 presidential election electoral vote results.

Source: Tim Eagan / Cagle Cartoons

Figure 7.4. Cartoon (*Our Moral* by Tim Eagan) illustrating a political idea.

(4) Cartoons

Sometimes a cartoon can enhance your writing as political, medical, and educational humor often brings home a point even better than words do. In the cartoon shown in fig. 7.4, the reader is asked to separate the alleged policies from the message itself.

7c   Effective use of pictures

Pictures include photographs, sketches, technical illustrations, paintings, icons, and other visual representations. Photographs are often used to reinforce textual descriptions or to show a reader exactly what something looks like. But photographs are not always the most informative type of picture. Compare the two images in fig. 7.5. Although the photograph is a more realistic image of a small wind turbine, the illustration more clearly shows the wind turbine's important features: rotor, gearbox, generator, and so forth. Line drawings enable the designer of a document to highlight specific elements of an object while de-emphasizing or eliminating unnecessary information.

Figure 7.5. A photo and a drawing of a small wind turbine

R

RESEARCH

Visit the MindTap® for this book for additional information and resources.

8   Planning Research

Research is much more than the act of searching for information. It consists of posing intriguing, challenging questions. Seeking information is a response to these questions. In fact, thinking of research as **inquiry**, as asking questions and finding answers, will help you to craft a research question, or a set of related questions, as well as to create a plan that focuses your attention and makes your work efficient.

8a   Considering your assignment

When you are given an assignment that calls for research, begin by asking yourself why you are doing this research and who will benefit from your research findings. Common purposes for doing research include the following:

- **To inform an audience.** The researcher reports current thinking on a specific topic, including opposing views, factual information, and credible evidence.
- **To analyze and synthesize information and then offer possible solutions.** The researcher analyzes a topic and synthesizes the available information about it, looking for points of agreement and disagreement and for gaps in coverage. Sometimes the researcher offers possible ways to address any problems found.
- **To convince an audience.** The researcher states a position and backs it up with data, statistics, testimony, corroborating texts or events, or supporting arguments. The researcher's purpose is to persuade readers to take the same position.

- **To invite readers to debate.** Instead of trying to convince others of a particular point of view or persuade them to take action, the researcher asks readers to discuss an issue and search for common ground.

Sometimes a researcher has to consider more than one purpose. For example, in the introduction of a lab report, a researcher analyzes and synthesizes previous work on a topic and locates a research niche—an area in need of further study. The researcher then attempts to convince the readers that his or her current study will address this need. The body of the report is informative: it describes the materials used, explains the procedures followed, and presents the results. In the conclusion, the researcher may try, given the results of the experiment or study, to persuade the audience to take some action (such as giving up smoking, eating fewer carbohydrates, or funding future research).

Next, consider your audience. Who are your readers, and what do they most need to know? What kinds of sources and evidence will they find reliable? Also important is consideration of your stance (or attitude). Will you be able to keep an open mind as you do your research? Will you be able to take into account multiple points of view?

Before you start to write, be sure you understand your instructor's expectations for length, format, due date, and other practical matters. Creating a research plan will help you meet these expectations and complete your work on time (8d).

8b Formulating research questions

Research questions often arise when you try to relate what you are studying to your own experience. For instance, you may start wondering about voting regulations while reading about past elections for a history class and, at the same time, noticing news stories about the role technology plays in current elections or the unfair practices reported in some states. Each of these observations may give rise to a different question. Focusing on the influence of technology may prompt you to inquire, "What are the possible consequences of having only electronic ballots?" However, if you focus on unfair voting practices, you may ask, "How do voting procedures differ from state to state?" Because you can ask a variety of research questions about any topic, choose the one that interests you the most and allows you to fulfill your assignment.

To generate useful research questions, you may find it helpful to ask yourself about causes, consequences, processes, definitions, or values.

Does smoking cannabis cause cancer?

What are the consequences of taking selective serotonin reuptake inhibitors (SSRIs) for a long period of time?

How do musicians decide whether to charge for access to their music online?

Do psychiatrists agree on a definition for Internet addiction?

Should the federal minimum wage be raised?

Although choosing just one question will make your research efficient, you may find it beneficial to answer more than one question when you write your paper. For example, if you explain the debate over the minimum wage, you may also decide to define *federal minimum wage*. Regardless of how many questions you ask, the best research questions are challenging, focused, and connected to current facts or events. A question such as *Do psychiatrists agree on a definition for Internet addiction?* is much more focused than *What is Internet addiction?*

Another way to generate and situate a research question is to find a claim (or assertion) made in a text you are currently reading and pose a question related to that claim:

> In "School Should Be about Learning, Not Sports," journalist Amanda Ripley states that the allure of high school competitive sports is "a fantasy with a short shelf life." She worries that when students

believe in this fantasy, they do not take their academic courses seriously and may inadvertently sabotage their future in a culture and economy that values highly educated workers. However, while Ripley points out problems caused by competitive sports, she fails to acknowledge any benefits that students might gain from them. *Are there any advantages to having competitive sports teams in high school? If there are, do they offset the drawbacks mentioned by Ripley?*

When you start by addressing a claim, you acknowledge that research is an ongoing conversation. As a participant in this conversation, you recognize the contributions of others before asking questions or offering comments and suggestions.

TIPS FOR FINDING A CHALLENGING RESEARCH QUESTION

First find a topic.

- What problem or issue from one of your classes would you like to address?
- What have you read or observed recently that piqued your curiosity?
- What local or school problem would you like to explore or help solve?
- Is there anything (lifestyles, political views, global events) that you find unusual or intriguing enough to investigate?

Once you have a topic, jot down all the questions you have about that topic. (Think about causes, consequences, processes, definitions, and values.) Choose the most specific question that will interest both you and your audience and that will help you address your assignment. Be sure the question cannot be easily answered with a *yes* or *no*.

8c   Testing research questions

You can test your research question to see whether it is effective by first making sure you and others are sincerely interested in answering this question. At the same time, double-check your assignment for length restrictions and decide whether your research question is specific enough to be addressed in the space available. Finally, because any assignment comes with deadlines, determine whether you have the time and resources available to answer the question by the due date.

TIPS FOR TESTING YOUR RESEARCH QUESTION

To test your research question, start a conversation about it by having a friend or classmate interview you about its potential. If no one is available, sharpen your ideas by *writing* your answers.

- Why is it important for you to answer this research question?
- Are there more than two ways of answering this question?
- Why is it important for your audience to know the answer to the question?
- Why does the answer to your question require research?
- What type of research might help you answer your question?
- Will you be able to carry out the necessary research in the amount of time and space allowed?

After you have a strong research question, you are ready to start gathering information and exploring sources. Your preliminary reading of appropriate sources will help you go from your research question to a tentative or working thesis statement (**8d**).

EXERCISE 8.1

Each of the following subjects would need to be narrowed down for a research paper. To experiment with framing a research question, compose two questions about each subject that could be answered in a ten-page paper.

1. college education
2. divorce
3. body image
4. social networking

8d   Creating a research plan

As you craft your research question, you may find it helpful to draft a plan for your research project as well.

   1. Create a research question.   *Due:* _____

It is easy to rush to answer your question, even before you have done any research. Try to keep an open mind until you have consulted some of your sources (**8a**, **8b**).

   2. Note the assignment's requirements.   *Due:* _____

Clarify your instructor's expectations. *What is the due date? What is the approximate length of the research project? What style manual should you use (MLA, APA, CMS, CSE)? What point of view is appropriate (first person, third person, a combination)? What is the medium of delivery? Are you expected to print out a document? Post a document online? Prepare an oral presentation? Incorporate visuals?* If you have not already received sufficient information about your assignment, ask your instructor these questions as soon as possible.

   3. Establish your audience and purpose.   *Due:* _____

Knowing who your readers are and what your purpose is will help you not only to decide what types of sources to use but also to establish an appropriate tone. Your instructor will be one of your readers. *Does your assignment expect you to consider other readers as well?*

   4. Decide which types of sources to use.   *Due:* _____

Assignments differ. *Will your research require the use of a wide range of sources—books, articles, and websites? Or does your assignment call for the use of historical archives?* If you are having trouble determining which sources to use, ask your instructor or a reference librarian for help.

5. Find, review, and evaluate sources.   *Due:* _____

Chapters **9** and **10** provide guidance in finding and evaluating sources. Be sure to give yourself plenty of time to locate your sources, read them, and take notes.

6. Develop a tentative thesis statement and an outline or description of the overall structure of your paper.
Due: _____

Once you have done sufficient research, you are ready to answer your question in the form of a thesis statement (**2b**). This statement will form the governing idea of your essay. Remember that thesis statements are related to your purpose. *Are you providing your audience with general information? Are you reporting on your analysis of information? Are you proposing a solution to a problem? Are you persuading your audience to change their opinion or take action?* The thesis statement generally appears in the first paragraph or two of a research project. The subsequent paragraphs serve as support for the thesis statement.

7. Write a first draft.   *Due:* _____

As you write, keep your thesis statement in mind, revising it if you need to. Be willing to do additional research if necessary.

8. Get the response of readers.   *Due:* _____

Allow time before you turn in your final draft to get feedback from other readers—students in your class or tutors at a writing center.

9. Revise.   *Due:* _____

Use reader feedback to revise your work (**4c**).

10. Edit, proofread, and polish (**4d**).   *Due:* _____

9 Finding Appropriate Sources

Whenever you do research, you can choose from a wide variety of sources—books, articles, online material, even your own fieldwork. Choosing appropriate sources depends on your assignment and research question. If you are unsure of what types of sources to use, ask a reference librarian or clarify the assignment with your instructor.

9a | Considering kinds of sources

As you consider which sources might be the most useful for your project, remember that there are significant differences among kinds of sources.

(1) Primary and secondary sources

Primary sources provide firsthand information. In the humanities, primary sources may include documents such as archived letters, historical records, and papers, as well as literary, autobiographical, and philosophical texts. Primary sources do not have to be in written form. Artwork, photographs, and audio and video recordings are also considered primary sources. In the social sciences, primary sources can be field observations, case histories, survey data, and interviews. In the natural sciences, primary sources are generally empirical and include field observations and experimental results. **Secondary sources** are commentaries on or descriptions of primary sources. They may offer summary or interpretation and appear as reviews, reports, scholarly biographies, and surveys of the work done on a specific topic.

(2) Scholarly and popular sources

Scholarly books and journals contain reports of original research written by experts for an academic audience. Professional or trade books and magazines feature articles written by staff writers or industry specialists. Popular books, magazines, and newspapers are generally written by staff writers, though scholars are frequently invited to contribute articles written for a lay audience.

(3) Current and older material

When writing about current issues, you will need to use up-to-date sources. However, to place an issue in a historical context, search for older sources and documents from the appropriate historical period.

(4) Biased or impartial sources

You will find the best support for your assertions by using sources that are impartial, that is, sources that treat all points of view fairly (chapter **10**). Nonetheless, including a clearly biased source can be useful to bring in other viewpoints or to demonstrate that certain ways of discussing an issue are faulty in some way (**5d**).

9b   Searching electronically

Whenever you are searching for sources—either electronic or print material—you will need to know how to use online search tools. Your library's website will likely have a search tool for its catalog of print sources and various search tools connected to the library's **databases**. The better you are at using these tools, the more efficient your research will be. If you are working in the library, a reference librarian will be able to help you learn to use these tools.

Whether you are using a popular **search engine** (such as Bing, Google, or Yahoo!), a **subject directory** designed for academic research (such as refseek* or The WWW Virtual Library), or a search tool on your library's website, you will be able to narrow your findings by conducting an **advanced search**.

Searches generally start with **keywords**, so choosing just the right word or phrase is important. If you start with a keyword search and find that you are not locating useful sources, you could first try a related term or a synonym, for example, using *wind energy* for *wind power*. You could also try using terms that are more specific or more general. If you were interested in sources of wind energy, a search for *wind farms* would be more specific than *wind energy* and more general than *wind turbines*. Most online search tools allow you to filter your results by searching for sources that match (1) the exact phrase, (2) some words but not others, (3) words related in form, or (4) alternative spellings of a word. When you know the name of an author or the title of a work, you will be able to search for the author or title directly.

TIPS FOR REFINING KEYWORD SEARCHES

The options for refining your search will vary depending on the database or search engine you choose, but most will include the following methods.

- Use **quotation marks** around terms to search for exact phrases. If you find that many search results are irrelevant when you do a general search, enclose a phrase in quotation marks to narrow results.

- Combine words or phrases using the connectors AND, OR, or NOT (sometimes called **Boolean operators**) to limit or widen a search. For example, you could try *Marion AND Ohio* for results that include both keywords, *Buckeye OR Ohio* for results that contain information about either keyword, or *Marion NOT Ohio* for results that exclude mention of Ohio.

(Continued on page 72)

TIPS FOR REFINING KEYWORD SEARCHES   *(Continued)*

- Use **truncation** to broaden a search so that results will include various forms of a word (for example, *manage, management, manager*). Use the root of the words you are searching for and place an asterisk after it (*manag**).

- Use **wildcards** (such as a question mark: *industriali?ation*) to broaden a search so that the results will include various spellings (for example, *industrialization* and *industrialisation*).

- Use **parentheses** around terms to further customize and group one term with keywords: *obesity AND (childhood OR preschoolers)*.

Most search tools have features that allow you to perform advanced searches and thus limit the results in a number of ways. The ProQuest database shown in fig. 9.1, for example, shows a few ways one user has limited a search by source type and date, among other options.

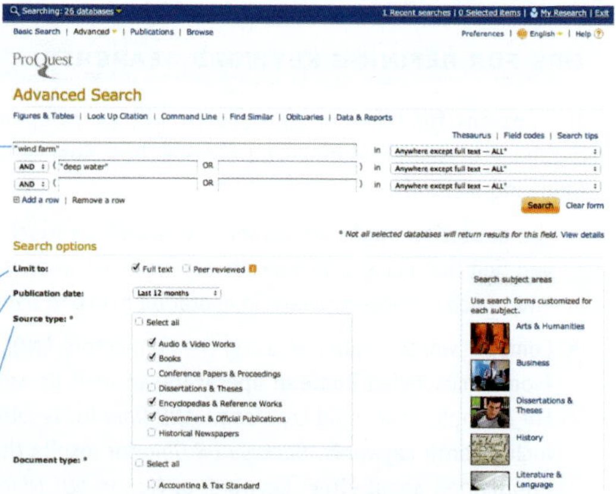

Keywords in quotation marks search for exact phrase

Limits results to recent full-text sources

Limits materials to those published in the last year

Specifies the type of materials

Figure 9.1   **Advanced search using keywords in a database.**
Source: ProQuest

9c Locating reference works

To begin a research project, you may find it useful to consult general or specialized reference works, including the encyclopedias, dictionaries, bibliographies, atlases, almanacs, and other resources available at your library. These works—many available online—will help you find background information about people, events, and concepts related to your topic. Especially helpful are specialized reference works—such as the *Encyclopedia of Emotion* or the *Dictionary of Environmental History*—which not only provide in-depth information on a topic but also offer extensive lists of other sources to consult. *Wikipedia* is a popular source for information, but it is sometimes considered unreliable because contributors are not always experts in a field and because facts are not always verified before they are published.

9d Locating articles

Articles in **periodicals** (publications that appear at regular intervals) offer information that is often more recent than that found in books. Periodicals include journals, magazines, and newspapers and can be published in print, online, or both. **Scholarly journals** contain reports of original research written by experts for an academic audience. **Professional** (or **trade**) **magazines** feature articles written by staff writers or industry specialists who address on-the-job concerns. **Popular magazines** and **newspapers**, generally written by staff writers, carry a combination of news stories that attempt to be objective and essays that reflect the opinions of editors or guest contributors.

To find articles, you may search the web, but such a general search will most likely yield unreliable sources as well as others that charge a fee for you to access an article. A better way to locate articles is to access your library's databases, which are collections of articles indexed according to author, title, date, keywords, and other features (9b). The databases you may access include general databases covering a wide range of subject areas and specialized databases and indexes that offer material specific to one subject or discipline. For older articles that are not online, you should consult a print index at your library.

GENERAL DATABASES

Academic Search Complete: Multidisciplinary database of journals and magazines, many full-text versions, via EBSCOhost

Expanded Academic ASAP: Database of journals and periodicals covering a wide variety of disciplines

Google Scholar: Search tool for articles, books, and other documents from academic sources and other sites, though it may be necessary to access the full text via your library

InfoTrac: Database of articles on a wide variety of subjects from journals and magazines

JSTOR: Database for digital library books, primary sources, and articles from journals in the arts, humanities, sciences, and social sciences

LexisNexis Academic: Database strong in coverage of legal as well as local, national, and world news sources

ProQuest: Large database of news and academic sources in areas ranging from arts, literature, and social sciences to business, technology, medicine, and natural sciences

SUBJECT-SPECIFIC DATABASES

ERIC: Database for information on education

MLA International Bibliography: Database of research in literature, language, and film

PsycINFO: Database for psychology research

ScienceDirect: Database for research in the physical, life, health, and social sciences

To search a database, you will usually begin with a keyword search for terms related to your research question. If your list of results is too large, use the tips for refining keyword searches (**9b**). A database search will usually yield an **abstract**, a short summary of an article. Scanning the abstract for relevance will help you decide whether to locate the complete text.

9e Locating books

Both print books and e-books that are published by reputable companies provide comprehensive and authoritative coverage of a topic. You can find books related to your research question by using your library's online catalog and conducting searches using a keyword, author, or title. Experiment with keywords, choosing a word or phrase you think might be found in the title of a book or in notes in the catalog's records. You can also try a subject search by entering words related to your topic; if the search does not yield any results, ask a reference librarian for a subject-heading guide. (A source's detailed record in your library catalog will feature subject headings that you may also use to expand your search.)

If you find an online catalog record for an e-book, you will be able to download, as a PDF, either a specific chapter or the entire book. If you find a record for a print book you would like to use, write down its **call number**, which indicates where the book is shelved. Some library catalogs will also allow you to send yourself a text message that includes the call number. Take time when you reach the shelves to scan for related books nearby that may offer additional information.

9f | Locating online sources

Material on the web varies greatly in its reliability. Although the facts provided on some websites have been carefully checked, facts on other websites have not undergone close examination.

Colleges, universities, and individual scholars may have reliable websites, blogs, or other information related to your topics. But quality can vary, so take time to evaluate any online source you are thinking of using (10c).

By sifting through your search results, you will be able to find a great deal of useful information, for example, current news events, maps, historical documents, and government reports, statistics, and legislative materials. Here is a list of types of websites to consider as you do your research:

- **Government sites.** Federal, state, and local governments provide an abundance of information. USA.gov directs you to sources on topics ranging from art to zoos.
- **News sites.** Newspapers, magazines, radio, and television stations sponsor websites that provide frequently updated news reports. Archived news stories are also sometimes available (though your library may offer easier access via a database).
- **Discussion lists and forums.** You may be able to find experts on topics by joining newsgroups, discussion groups, forums, or online mailing lists. To find such groups or access archived discussions, use a search engine or specialized service such as Google Groups.
- **Digital archives.** Archives are of particular interest if you need artifacts from the past—maps, speeches, drawings, documents, and recordings. The National Archives and the Library of Congress are good places to start.
- **Blogs and wikis.** As starting points, blogs and wikis can provide overviews of topics or issues as well as links to

primary sources. However, because they are not generally reviewed by experts, they are often not considered reliable academic sources. Avoid using information from these sources without your instructor's approval.

- **Images.** If your rhetorical situation calls for the use of images, the Internet offers you billions from which to choose. However, if an image you choose is copyrighted, you will need to contact the author, artist, or designer for permission to use it. You do not need to obtain permission to use images in the public domain (because they are not copyrighted) or those that are cleared for reuse. The SIRIS Image Gallery, which includes images from the Smithsonian archives, will allow you to use its images as long as there is no commercial gain involved.

9g Keeping track of your sources

As you start gathering sources, be sure to keep them organized. For online and other nonprint sources, it is a good idea to keep a separate record of the **access date** (the date on which you examined or retrieved the source) and the **publication date** (the date on which the source was published or last updated or modified). The publication date generally appears on the bottom of the website's home page.

- **Bookmarks.** Bookmark any sources you find on the web, using the most stable URL you can find, which in the case of online journals, magazines, and newspapers is a home page.
- **Database and library accounts.** Your library site may allow you to use your personal account to collect and organize sources using bookmarking tools. Some databases also offer this service, which will allow you to save and retrieve your search history.

- **Downloads.** If you decide to download PDFs or other materials, be sure to label them and place them in folders clearly labeled for your project.
- **Photocopies and printouts.** Keep printouts together by stapling them and placing them in clearly labeled file folders.
- **Reference management systems.** To organize your bibliographic entries, consider using a reference management system such as EndNote, RefWorks, or Zotero. Check to see which system your library supports.

9h   Doing field research

Interviews, observations, and surveys are the most common methods of **field research**, a study done in a natural setting, rather than in a laboratory. Any study you design may have to be approved by the institutional review board (IRB) at your college or university. The board's approval indicates that a study protects the privacy and welfare of participants.

(1) Interviews

Interviews can take place in person, over the phone, or via e-mail or videoconference.

1. **Arrange the interview.** E-mail or call to request an interview. Be sure to introduce yourself, briefly describe your project, and explain your reasons for requesting the interview. Try to accommodate the person you hope to interview by asking him or her to suggest an interview date. If you intend to record your interview, ask for permission.
2. **Prepare for the interview.** Consult sources on your topic, especially any written by the person you will be interviewing. Start preparing your list of questions

before the day of the interview, using a blend of open questions (*What are your views on _____?*) and focused questions (*How long have you worked as a/an _____?*)

3. **Conduct the interview.** Before the interview begins, remind the person that you are interviewing that you will be recording the conversation or taking notes. Although you will have prepared questions, do not feel that you must ask all your questions in the order you wrote them. Listen closely to responses and follow up with related questions, perhaps even ones you had not thought of beforehand. If responses are elaborate, you may find that you do not have to ask each of your questions.

4. **Reflect on the interview.** Review and expand your notes or transcribe the relevant parts of the recording. Write extensively about the interview, asking yourself what you found most important, most surprising, and most puzzling. Send your thanks via a written note or an e-mail message.

(2) Observations

Observations yield detailed information about human activity or animal behavior.

1. **Establish the goals of your observation.** With a clear purpose in mind, you will be able to focus your attention.

2. **Set up an appointment, if necessary.** In some settings, such as in a school or hospital, you will need to obtain permission for your observation.

3. **Take detailed notes.** A helpful method for note-taking during observations is to divide each page of your paper in half vertically. Keep your notes on the left side of the page and leave space on the right side of the page for later commentary.

4. **Analyze your observation.** Review your notes, looking for both patterns and behaviors or events that veer from the ordinary. On the right side of your notebook page, write down your comments; whenever possible, explain the patterns and deviations you have found.

(3) Surveys

Whereas an interview elicits information from one person whose name you know, a survey provides information from a number of anonymous people.

1. **Compile a list of questions.** To be effective, a survey questionnaire should be short and focused. If the list of questions is too long, people may not be willing to take the time to answer them all. If the questions are not focused on your research topic, you will find it difficult to integrate the results into your project.

2. **Decide who you would like to participate and how you will contact them.** Choose participants from an appropriate sector of the population. Make sure these participants are easy to reach. Some surveys are done in person or by phone. Others are sent to participants via regular mail or e-mail. Surveys conducted through e-mail often include a link to a web service such as Survey Monkey.

3. **Design the survey to introduce your purpose and review your distribution method.** Begin your survey questionnaire with an introduction stating the purpose of the questionnaire, how the results will be used, and how many questions it contains or approximately how long it should take to complete. In the introduction, assure participants that their answers will remain confidential. It is often helpful to ask a few friends to "test-drive" your questionnaire to see whether all the questions are clear.

4. **Analyze your results.** Once the questionnaires have been completed and returned, tally the results for all but the open questions. Read through the open

questions and look for patterns in the responses. Try to create categories for the responses that will help you tally the answers.

EXERCISE 9.1

Of all the types of sources discussed in this chapter, which will you use to address your research question? If you created a research plan (8d), return to that plan and set dates for deciding which types of sources to use.

10 Evaluating Print and Online Sources

After you find sources that seem to address your research question, you will need to judge their credibility.

10a Credibility of authors

Credible (or trustworthy) authors present facts accurately, support their opinions with compelling evidence, connect their ideas reasonably, and demonstrate respect for any opposing views. To evaluate the credibility of authors whose work you might like to use, consider their credentials, examine their values and beliefs, and note the response they receive from other readers. Credentials include academic or professional training, publications, and experience. The author's credentials may be found on the jacket or in the preface of a book, in a note in an article, or on a page in the journal or on the website devoted to providing background on contributors. Some search tools will allow you to see the influence of the author's work by including a link to other sources that cite articles or books written by the author.

> **CHECKLIST FOR ASSESSING AN AUTHOR'S CREDENTIALS**
>
> - Does the author's education or profession relate to the subject of the work?
> - With what institutions, organizations, or companies has the author been affiliated?
> - What awards has the author won?
> - What other works has the author produced?
> - Do other experts speak of the author as an authority or link to the author's work? Check Google Scholar, for example, for works by the author and then review the listed "cited by" information.

An author's values and beliefs underpin his or her research and publications. To determine what these values and beliefs are, consider the author's purpose and intended audience. For example, on the subject of malpractice suits, a lawyer may write an article to convince patients to sue health providers, a doctor may write an essay for other doctors to highlight the frivolous nature of malpractice claims, whereas a linguist might prepare a conference paper that reveals miscommunication to be at the core of malpractice suits. After you identify underlying values and beliefs, you can responsibly discuss information in your sources. Be sure to use with extreme caution the work of authors who benefit financially from performing studies that support a particular business or organization.

Published reviews can assist you in determining whether an author is credible. Though a work by any credible author may get some negative responses, use carefully the work of a writer whom more than one reviewer characterizes as biased, ill-informed, or injudicious with facts.

> ### CHECKLIST FOR DETERMINING AN AUTHOR'S BELIEFS AND VALUES
>
> - What is the author's educational and professional background?
> - With what types of organizations do the author and publisher affiliate themselves?
> - What is the author's stance? What is the stance of the organization publishing the author's work? How conservative, moderate, or liberal does the publisher appear to be?
> - What, if any, signs of bias on the part of the author or the publisher can you detect in the language used? In the title? In the advertising? Is the information presented factual? Objective?
> - To what types of websites do any links lead?
> - How can you use the source? As fact? Opinion? Example? Authoritative testimony? Material to be refuted?

10b Credibility of publishers

When doing research, consider not only the credibility of authors but also the credibility of the media through which their work is made available to you. The facts in some types of publications are checked more carefully than those in others.

When evaluating books and articles, you can usually assume that publishers associated with universities demand a high standard of scholarship, including review of the work by other scholars in the field. Work published in popular magazines and newspapers is generally reliable and may provide useful overviews of a topic, but such publications do not require scholarly review and may not include bibliographies or citation of sources for other researchers to consult. Because magazines and newspapers often report research results that were initially published elsewhere, try to find the original source to ensure the accuracy of their reports.

Credible publishers are also committed to objectivity. If you sense that the information in your source is unfair or one-sided, check to see whether the publisher has a record of producing books and articles whose bias may result in distortion of facts.

10c Online sources

If you are evaluating an online source that also appears in print, you can follow the guidelines for print-based sources. But if you are evaluating a web or other online source, you need to consider additional features of the medium. For help locating important information, see figs. 10.1 and 10.2, which show the top and bottom of the same web source.

Figure 10.1   Top of a web page from *Global Journalist*.

Source: Global Journalist

findings, it was "a terrible year" for personal online privacy against governments' cyberintelligence.

EFF researchers found that states around the world "are obtaining detailed logs of our entire lives online, and they are doing so under weaker legal standards than ever before. Several laws and proposals now afford many states warrantless snooping powers and nearly limitless data collection capabilities." The report contains examples to support the contention that digital privacy is under attack.

None of that bodes well for journalists.

BBC World Affairs producer Stuart Hughes believes certain protective techniques should be a standard practice for the media. "You wouldn't leave your notebook on a park bench or a train, so why would you leave your data wide open for all to see," Hughes wrote in a blog. He advises: "Be Paranoid."

Sherry Ricchiardi

Sherry Ricchiardi, Ph.D., is a writer for American Journalism Review, specializing in international issues. She is also a media development specialist, working with journalists in the Middle East and South Asia.

Home Stories Free Press Watch Opinions Radio Blogs About Us   Global Journalist is produced by the Missouri School of Journalism
Copyright © 2013

Figure 10.2   Bottom of a web page from *Global Journalist*.

1. Check the URL for information about the sponsoring organization. Colleges and universities are indicated by the suffix *.edu*, government departments and agencies by *.gov*, professional and nonprofit organizations by *.org*, and businesses by *.com*. As you access the various types of sites to evaluate their content, keep in mind that every site is shaped to achieve a specific purpose and to address a specific audience.

2. Locate the name of the sponsor. This information is generally found at the bottom of the page.

3. Determine the organization's or company's stance on your research question. You will be able to find out more information on an "About Us" or "Our Vision" page. Links may be found at the top of the page, at the bottom of the page, or both.

4. Examine the author's credentials. If the author's name is not given near the title, look at the bottom of the page. Information about the author's credentials can often also be found at the bottom of the page. Because this information is provided by the author, sponsor, or publisher, it is always a good idea to search elsewhere for additional information about the author (**10a**).

5. Identify the date of publication. Some articles place the publication date (or date of most recent update) near the title, but often it is at the bottom of the page. Determine whether the date is sufficiently current.

6. Check links and cited sources. By examining the sources the author uses, you will be able to gauge the reliability of the information provided. Consider unreliable any web source that does not provide a link or enough bibliographic details for you to track down the original source for information presented as factual.

CHECKLIST FOR EVALUATING ONLINE SOURCES

- Who is the author? Is this author credible? (10a)
- Who is the sponsor? A government agency? An institution of higher education? A business? An individual? Is the sponsor credible? (10b)
- To what extent has the source's information been reviewed by others?
- Is there a list of original sources available so that you can consult them to check facts?
- When was the source last updated? Is the information up to date? How current are the source's links? If it includes dead links, the source may not be recent enough to be useful.

10d   Recognizing fake news

Especially problematic in recent years is **fake news**—inauthentic news articles, broadcasts, or videos. Fake news stories may be created to entertain; unfortunately, they may also be intended to deceive. To avoid being duped, check whether information that seems exaggerated, sensational, or clearly biased can be found on other news sites that have a reputation for objectivity.

CHECKLIST FOR RECOGNIZING FAKE NEWS

- Is the information shocking, scandalous, or overdramatized? If so, check other websites considered reputable by an academic audience to make sure the information is accurate.

- Scan the publication for additional news stories. If you find any that seem questionable, verify the truth of all the publication's information against information from respected sources.

- Distinguish between fact-based investigative reports and opinion-based editorials. The purpose of reports is to inform, whereas the purpose of editorials is to persuade. Newspapers and many other news sources will carry both genres.

- When the results of polls are included, find out who conducted or sponsored the poll, how many people were surveyed, how participants were chosen, and how survey questions were phrased.

- Examine the URLs on websites. URLs that incorporate the name of a reputable source into the name of their own should be considered suspect (e.g., www.pbs-true-news.com).

- Be careful when using information spread through social media. Track down the original source of any suspicious news stories.

10e Reading closely and critically

Once you have determined that the sources you have collected might be useful, allow yourself time to read them closely. Not only will you educate yourself about your topic, but you will also be able to discuss the strengths and weaknesses of what you have read, and you will find it easier to write about it later. Approach each source with an open mind, but at the same time be prepared to question your sources. By reading critically, you will pay attention to both the claims an author makes and the support for those claims.

CHECKLIST FOR READING CLOSELY AND CRITICALLY

- What is the author's argument? (chapter 6)
- What is the purpose of the argument? Who is its audience?
- What specific claims does the author make? What evidence does the author use to support these claims?
- What are the author's assumptions? Do you share these assumptions?
- Does the author represent diverse points of view? Does the author respond to divergent points of view?
- After reading the article, do you find yourself agreeing with the author? Disagreeing with the author? Agreeing with some points and disagreeing with others?
- What questions would you like to ask the author?

EXERCISE 10.1

Find three different kinds of sources that contain material relevant to your research question or to a specific subject, such as fake news, saving energy, or disaster relief efforts. Explain the differences and similarities among the three sources you have chosen.

11 Using Sources Critically and Responsibly

For your research project, you will have to discuss what others have discovered, creating a conversation in which you play an essential role: you will decide how the different ideas in your sources connect to one another and to your own views. To make a smooth transition between the words you read and the words you write, you will need to develop a system for managing all the information you have found.

11a Taking and organizing notes

Managing information is critical for a research project in which you will have to attribute specific words and ideas to others while adding your own ideas. Most research projects start with note-taking. Choose the method that best meets the requirements of your project and your own working style:

- take notes in a notebook
- write notes on index cards
- type notes into computer files
- write notes directly on PDFs or on pages you have photocopied or printed out from an online source

Remember that your notes will be most useful to you when it comes time to begin your draft if they are comprehensive and accurate.

TIPS FOR TAKING AND ORGANIZING NOTES

- **Subject heading.** Use a short descriptive phrase to summarize the content of the note. This phrase will help you retrieve information later.

- **Type of note.** Indicate whether the note is a quotation (11d), a paraphrase (11e), a summary (11f), or your own thoughts. Place quotations between quotation marks (34). Indicate any changes to quotations with square brackets (11d, 35f) or ellipsis points (11d, 35g). If you are using a computer to take notes, you can change font color to indicate your own thoughts.

- **Bibliographic information.** Provide complete bibliographic information in a working bibliography (11b). Jot down the author's name and/or the title of the source. If the source has page numbers, indicate which pages your notes refer to.

- **Computer folders.** Create a master folder (or directory) for the project. Within that folder, create separate folders for your notes, drafts, and bibliography. In your notes folder, create a separate file for each source.

11b Creating a working bibliography

Effective research depends in part on meticulous record keeping. By creating a **working bibliography**, you will have a record of the sources you might use in your final project. A working bibliography contains all the information you might need in your final bibliography. For each work it should include title, authors' names, and publication date, along with other information needed to locate the source. Note that not all documentation styles require you to include the URLs for online sources in your final bibliography, but you will do well to record them for quick access later.

Creating a working bibliography can also help you evaluate the quality of your research. If you find that your most recent source is ten years old, for example, or that you have relied exclusively on information from magazines or websites, you may need to find some other sources.

Right from the start, entries should follow the bibliographic format you have been instructed to use. This book covers the most common formats: MLA (chapter **13**), APA (chapter **14**), CMS (chapter **15**), and CSE (chapter **16**).

If you are asked to prepare an **annotated bibliography** (also called an **annotated list of works cited**), provide a bibliographic entry for and a summary of each of your sources. You may also wish to include comments or personal responses on how information in the source is related to your research question or to the information in other sources. These comments will be helpful when you are drafting. Check with your instructor to find out whether your annotated bibliography should include both summaries and commentaries.

A working bibliography is equivalent to a rough draft. In final form, you will have to make sure that you have placed in conventional order each element of the bibliographic entry (author, title, date, and so on).

TIPS FOR CREATING AN ANNOTATED BIBLIOGRAPHY

- Find out which documentation style you should use: MLA, APA, CMS, or CSE.

- Provide a complete bibliographic entry for each of your sources in the required documentation style.

- Summarize the content of each source. Refer to the main point of the source (*What is it about?*). If relevant, describe the intended audience or the scope of the source (*What is the range of subtopics included? What historical period does the source cover?*).

- In writing your summaries, use your own words instead of inserting quotations. That way, when you consult your annotations, you will not inadvertently use quotations as your own words (**11f**).

- Comment on the sources by connecting the information you find to your research question and to the information you find in other sources.

The following sample annotated bibliography entry was written for a research project (following MLA style) on the question of whether it is better to write notes in longhand or type them into a computer.

Mueller, Pam A., and Daniel M. Oppenheimer. "The Pen Is Mightier Than the Keyboard: Advantages of Longhand over Laptop Note Taking." *Psychological Science*, vol. 25, no. 6, June 2016, pp. 1159-68.

Provides complete bibliograp[hic] informatio[n]

Summarizes the source

Connects information in this source to information found elsewhere

Additional comments focus on information related to the research question

In a study designed to see how taking notes in longhand or typing them into a computer affects learning, Pam A. Mueller, professor at Princeton University, and Daniel M. Oppenheimer, professor at the University of California, found that taking notes in longhand was more effective. Although a laptop permits students to take more notes, these students seem to be transcribing lectures rather than processing information deeply by summarizing or paraphrasing it. According to the authors, longhand note taking results in a better understanding of concepts introduced in a lecture.

Unlike Mueller and Oppenheimer's careful examination of how well students performed after taking notes, Richard Skolnik and Mia Puzo use only survey data to suggest that students using laptops are able to take more notes and organize them better. Mueller and Oppenheimer's results clearly show that the mere act of taking and organizing notes is not sufficient for thorough understanding of concepts to occur; however, they do not examine the use of a tablet with a stylus, which may combine the advantages of longhand and laptop note taking.

For some assignments, this entry would have to be condensed for the final draft of the annotated bibliography:

In a study designed to see how taking notes in longhand or typing them into a computer affects learning, Mueller and Oppenheimer found that although a laptop permits students to take more notes, students have a better understanding of concepts introduced in lecture when they take notes by hand.

11c Acknowledging your sources

You can integrate sources into your own writing in a number of ways: quoting exact words, paraphrasing sentences, and summarizing longer pieces of text or even entire texts. Whenever you use ideas from a source, you must give credit to that source. The way in which you introduce your source will depend on which documentation style you follow. Most style manuals offer two options: In MLA style, you may (1) put the author's name in parentheses at the end of the sentence or (2) introduce the author's name within a sentence. In either case, place a page number, if one is available, in parentheses (13a). The author's name refers the reader to the full bibliographic citation at the end of your essay.

Use the first method (author's name in parentheses) when you are using statistics or statements to support a major idea in your paragraph.

> Displaying body art, especially tattoos, is gaining in popularity (Grief, Hewitt, and Armstrong 371). However, little is known about the reasons college-age students obtain tattoos. Some students use body art to identify themselves with a specific group (Craig 37). Others see body art as self-expression (Armstrong 230), perhaps suggesting their adventurous nature (Duke 243). Still others use body art, especially tattoos, to remember a significant event (Reams 72). The purpose of this study is to explore whether these are typical reasons for students at this university to have tattoos and whether other reasons exist as well.

Cite the author's name in the text if you are going to discuss the source's statistics or ideas in more detail. It is common to first introduce the author's full name and include any important information about the author. For example, in an essay on the origins of literacy, the following statement becomes more credible if readers are given the added information about Catherine Snow's background.

➤ According to Catherine Snow, *professor of education at Harvard University,* college-level literacy is based on "the ability to read in ways adjusted to one's purpose" (12).

In subsequent references to the author, use just the last name. Other style guides such as APA require use of just the last names of authors for first and subsequent references.

➤ According to Snow (2012), college-level literacy is based on "the ability to read in ways adjusted to one's purpose" (p. 12).

Phrases such as *According to Catherine Snow* and *from the author's perspective* are called **attributive tags** (or signal phrases) because they indicate the source (both author and publication) from which the information was taken. In academic writing, most attributive tags consist of the name of an author (or a related noun or pronoun) and a verb such as *states*, *reports*, or *argues*.

ATTRIBUTIVE TAGS FOR QUOTING, PARAPHRASING, AND SUMMARIZING

Attributive tags indicate which source you are using and alert readers that the words or ideas that follow are from a source and are not your own.

- In "Cybersecurity Today" Chris Allen states that _____.
- According to Allen, _____.
- In Allen's view, _____.
- The writer points out that _____. She also stresses that _____.

The following is a list of verbs commonly found in attributive tags.

admit	conclude	find	reject
advise	deny	imply	reply
argue	disagree	indicate	state
believe	discuss	insist	suggest
claim	emphasize	note	think
concede	explain	observe	

Most often attributive tags begin a sentence, but they can also appear in the middle or at the end of a sentence.

➤ **According to Jim Cullen**, "The American Dream would have no drama or mystique if it were a self-evident falsehood or a scientifically demonstrable principle" (7).

➤ "The American Dream," **claims Jim Cullen**, "would have no drama or mystique if it were a self-evident falsehood or a scientifically demonstrable principle" (7).

➤ "The American Dream would have no drama or mystique if it were a self-evident falsehood or a scientifically demonstrable principle," **asserts Jim Cullen in his book** *The American Dream: A Short History of an Idea That Shaped a Nation* (7).

The placement of the attributive tag will depend on what part of the sentence you would like to emphasize and on how the sentence connects to surrounding sentences.

Attributive tags can include neutral, objective verbs (*Cullen stated*) or verbs that are more descriptive and subjective (*Cullen insists*). If your assignment allows the insertion of your opinion, you can use descriptive verbs or add an adverb to the verb in the attributive tag: *persuasively* argues, *inaccurately* represents. The appropriate verb tense for the attributive tag—simple present tense (*the author states*), the simple past tense (*the author stated*), or the present perfect (*the author has stated*)—will depend on the context of the sentence (**20b–c**) and on the guidelines for your discipline (chapters **13–16**).

If you include visuals or graphics as sources, you must introduce and label them as figures and assign them Arabic numbers (**7b**). You can then refer to them within the text in a parenthetical comment, as in this example (following APA style): "The Maori of New Zealand are also well-known for their hand-carved facial tattoos, known as *Moko* (see Figure 1)." Include a title or caption with the figure number.

Direct quotations draw attention to key passages. Include a direct quotation only if

- you want to retain the beauty or clarity of someone's words
- you need to reveal how the reasoning in a specific passage is flawed or insightful
- you plan to discuss the implications of the quoted material

Keep quotations as short as possible and make them an integral part of your text.

Place any quotation of another person's words in quotation marks. However, if you set off the material as an indented **block quotation**, leave the quotation marks out. The length of a passage determines whether it should be set off as a block quotation. According to MLA style, a quotation longer than four lines should be set off (chapter **13**). If you are following APA style, quotations are set off when they include forty or more words (chapter **14**). The general rule for CMS is to use block quotations for passages of one hundred words or more (chapter **15**). CSE does not specify a word or line limit.

If you need to clarify a quotation by changing it in any way, place square brackets around the added or changed words (**35f**).

➤ The critic notes that in this role, "he [Brad Pitt] successfully conveys a diverse range of emotion" (23).

If you want to omit part of a quotation, replace the deleted words with ellipsis points (**35g**).

➤ When asked about the future of the industry, Owens responded, "Overseas markets **. . .** are critical to the financial success of Hollywood films" (54).

When modifying a quotation, be sure not to alter its essential meaning.

Each quotation you use should also have an attributive tag to help readers understand why the quotation is important. A sentence that consists of only a quotation is called a **dropped quotation**. Notice how the attributive tag improves the dropped quotation below:

➤ *Joel Achenbach recognizes that compromises*
~~Compromises~~ must be made to promote safer sources of energy~~.~~ :
"To accommodate green energy, the grid needs not only more storage but more high-voltage power lines" (~~Achenbach~~ 137).

Readers want to know how a quotation is related to your point, so whenever possible, provide a sentence or two before or after the quotation explaining its relevance.

➤ Joel Achenbach recognizes that compromises must be made to promote safer sources of energy: "To accommodate green energy, the grid needs not only more storage but more high-voltage power lines" (137). If we are going to use green energy to avoid depending on types of energy that cause air pollution, we may have to tolerate visual pollution in the form of power lines strung between huge towers.

CHECKLIST FOR USING DIRECT QUOTATIONS

- Have you copied all the words and punctuation accurately?
- Have you attributed the quotation to a specific source?
- Have you used square brackets around anything you added or changed in a direct quotation? (35f)
- Have you used ellipsis points to indicate anything you omitted? (35g)
- Have you included an attributive tag with the quotation?
- Have you included a sentence or two before or after a quotation to indicate its relevance? Have you made it an integral part of the text?
- Have you used quotations sparingly? Rather than using too many quotations, consider paraphrasing or summarizing the information instead.

11e Paraphrasing

A **paraphrase** is a restatement of someone else's ideas in approximately the same number of words. Paraphrasing allows you to demonstrate that you have understood what you have read; it also enables you to help your audience understand it. Paraphrase when you want to

- clarify difficult material by using simpler language
- use another writer's idea but not his or her exact words
- create a consistent tone for your work
- interact with a point that your source has made

Your paraphrase should be entirely in your own words and should accurately convey the content of the original passage. As you compare the next source with the paraphrases that follow, note the similarities and differences in both sentence structure and word choice.

Source

Harari, Yuval Noah. *Sapiens: A Brief History of Humankind*. HarperCollins,

2015, p. 189.

Most past cultures have sooner or later fallen prey to the armies of some ruthless empire, which have consigned them to oblivion.

Inadequate paraphrase

Many past cultures have fallen victim to the armies of some cruel empire, which have relegated them to oblivion (Harari 189).

If you simply change a few words in a passage, you have not adequately restated it. You may be committing plagiarism (**12a–b**) if the wording of your version follows the original too closely, even if you provide a page reference for the source.

Adequate paraphrase

Yuval Noah Harari states that the majority of past cultures became extinct because they were overcome by empires using military force (189).

In the second paraphrase, both vocabulary and sentence structure differ from those in the original. This paraphrase also includes an attributive tag (*Yuval Noah Harari states*).

Any paraphrase must accurately maintain the sense of the original. If you unintentionally misrepresent the original because you did not understand it, you are being *inaccurate*. If you deliberately change the gist of what a source says, you are being *unethical*. Compare the following original statement with the paraphrases.

Source

Desmond, Matthew. *Evicted: Poverty and Profit in the American City*. Crown,

2016, p. 294.

America is supposed to be a place where you can better yourself, your family, and your community. But this is only possible if you have a stable home.

Inaccurate or unethical paraphrase

Americans are able to better themselves, their families, and their communities when they own their own homes (Desmond 294).

Accurate paraphrase

Matthew Desmond believes that the United States should be a country that offers its citizens the possibility of improving their own lives and the lives of their families and communities. For this improvement to occur, he considers stable homes as essential (294).

Although both paraphrases include a reference to an author and a page number, the first is misleading because it turns a belief into a statement of fact and because it introduces the idea of home ownership.

11f Summarizing

When you summarize, you condense the main point(s) of your source. Although a summary omits much of the detail used by the writer of the original source, it accurately reflects the essence of that work. In most cases, then, a **summary** reports a writer's main idea and the most important support given for it.

Whereas the length of a paraphrase (11e) is usually close to that of the original material, a summary is shorter than the material it reports. When you paraphrase, you restate an author's ideas to present or examine them in detail. When you summarize, you present the gist of the author's ideas without including background information and details. Summaries can include short quotations of key words or phrases, but you must always enclose another writer's exact words in quotation marks when you blend them with your own.

Source

Marshall, Joseph M., III. "Tasunke Witko (His Crazy Horse)." *Native Peoples,*
   Jan.-Feb. 2007, pp. 76-79.

The world knows him as Crazy Horse, which is not a precise translation of his name from Lakota to English. *Tasunke Witko* means "his crazy horse," or "his horse is crazy." This slight mistranslation of his name seems to reflect the fact that Crazy Horse the man is obscured by Crazy Horse the legendary warrior. He was both, but the fascination with the legendary warrior hides the reality of the man. And it was as the man, shaped by his family, community and culture—as well as the events in his life—that he became legend.

Summary

> The Lakota warrior English speakers refer to as "Crazy Horse"
> was actually called "his crazy horse." That mistranslation may dis-
> tort impressions of what Crazy Horse was like as a man.

This example reduces five sentences to two, retaining the key
idea but eliminating the source author's analysis and speculation. A writer who believes that the audience needs to understand the analysis might decide to paraphrase rather than
summarize the passage.

EXERCISE 11.1

Find a well-developed paragraph in one of your recent reading
assignments. Rewrite it in your own words, varying the sentence
structure of the original. Make your paraphrase approximately
the same length as the original. Next, write a one-sentence
summary of the same paragraph.

11g Analyzing and responding to sources

Though quotations, paraphrases, and summaries are key to
academic writing, thinking critically involves more than referring to someone else's work. Quotations, paraphrases, and
summaries call for responses. Your readers will want to know
what you think about an article, a book, or another source.
They will expect you to indicate its strengths and weaknesses
and to mention the impact it has had on your own ideas.

Your response to a source will be based on your analysis of
it. You can analyze a source according to its rhetorical situation
(**1a**), its use of rhetorical appeals (**5c**), or its reasoning (**6d(1)**).
You can also evaluate a source by using some common criteria:
timeliness, coverage, and reliability.

(1) Considering the currency of sources

Depending on the nature of your research, the currency of sources may be an important consideration. Using up-to-date sources is crucial when researching most topics. Historical research may also call for sources from a specific period in the past. When you consider the currency of a source, start by looking for the date of its publication. Then, examine any data reported. Even a source published in the same year that you are doing research may include data that are several years old and thus possibly irrelevant. In the following example, the writer questions the usefulness of an out-of-date statistic mentioned in a source:

> According to Jenkins, only 50 percent of all public schools have web pages (23); however, this statistic is taken from a report published in 1997. A more recent count would likely yield a much higher percentage.

(2) Noting the thoroughness of research

Coverage refers to the comprehensiveness of research. The more comprehensive a study is, the more convincing are its findings. Similarly, the more examples an author provides, the more compelling are his or her conclusions. Claims or opinions that are based on only one instance are often criticized for being merely anecdotal or otherwise unsubstantiated. The writer of the following response suggests that the author of the source in question may have based his conclusion on too little information:

> Johnson concludes that middle-school students are expected to complete an inordinate amount of homework given their age, but he bases his conclusion on research conducted in only three schools (90). To be more convincing, Johnson needs to conduct research in more schools, preferably located in different parts of the country.

(3) Checking the reliability of findings

Reliability is a requirement for reported data. Researchers are expected to report their findings accurately and honestly, not distort them to support their own beliefs or claim others' ideas as their own. To ensure the reliability of their work, researchers must also report all relevant information and refrain from excluding any that weakens their conclusions. When studies of the same phenomenon give rise to disputes, researchers should discuss conflicting results or interpretations. The writer of the following response focuses on the problematic nature of her source's methodology:

> Jamieson concludes from her experiment that a low-carbohydrate diet can be dangerous for athletes (73), but her methodology suffers from lack of detail. No one would be able to confirm her experimental findings without knowing exactly what and how much the athletes consumed.

Researchers use common phrases when responding to sources. The following list includes a few examples.

COMMON PHRASES FOR RESPONDING TO SOURCES

Responding, in agreement

- Recent research confirms that <u>Baron</u> is correct in asserting that _____.
- <u>Moore</u> aptly notes that _____.
- I agree with <u>Gyasi</u> that _____.

Responding, in disagreement

- Several of <u>Bender's</u> statements are contradictory. He asserts that _____, but he also states that _____.
- In stating that _____, <u>Porter</u> fails to account for _____.
- I disagree with <u>Lurie</u> on this point. I believe that _____.

Responding, in agreement and in disagreement

- Although I agree with <u>Blake</u> that _____ and that _____, I disagree with his conclusion that _____.
- In a way, the author is correct: _____. However, from a different perspective, _____.
- Though <u>Day</u> may be right that _____, I must point out that _____.

11h Synthesizing sources

While *thesis* is typically defined as a claim, an informed opinion, or a point of view, *synthesis* refers to combinations of claims, opinions, or points of view. When you synthesize sources, you combine them, looking for similarities, differences, strengths, weaknesses, and so on.

In the following excerpt, the writer reports two similar views on the topic of ecotourism.

> The claim that ecotourism can benefit local economies is supported by the observations of Ellen Bradley, tour leader in Cancun, Mexico, and Rachel Collins, county commissioner in Shasta County, California. Bradley insists that ecotourism is responsible for creating jobs and improved standards of living in Mexico (10). Likewise, Collins believes that ecotourism has provided work for people in her county who had formerly been employed by the timber industry (83).

Notice that the writer uses the transition *likewise* (3d(4)) to indicate a comparison. In the next excerpt, on the topic of voting fraud, the writer contrasts two different views, using the transition *although*.

> Although Ted Kruger believes voting fraud is not systematic (45), that does not mean there is no fraud at all. Kendra Berg points out that voter rolls are not updated often enough (18), which leaves the door open for cheaters.

In both examples, the writers not only summarize and respond to sources but synthesize them as well. You will find common phrases for synthesizing sources in the following.

COMMON PHRASES FOR SYNTHESIZING SOURCES

- The claim that _____ is supported by the observations of <u>Blair</u> and <u>Jones</u>. <u>Blair</u> insists that _____. Likewise, <u>Jones</u> believes that _____.

- <u>Perez</u> asserts that _____. <u>Mehan</u> supports this position by _____.

- Although <u>Miller</u> believes that _____, this interpretation is not held universally. For example, <u>Klein</u> notes that _____.

- <u>Kim</u> asserts that _____; however, she fails to explain _____. <u>Lee</u> points out that _____.

11i Critical thinking

At some point in your studies, you will undoubtedly come across the term *critical thinking*. Although there are a variety of models used to describe what it means to think critically, the one that is relevant to writing research projects was initially developed in 1956 by Benjamin Bloom and his colleagues. Known as the *Bloom Taxonomy*, this model has evolved over the years, but six main skills remain at its core: remembering, understanding, applying, analyzing, evaluating, and creating.

When you summarize sources, you demonstrate your ability to remember and understand. When you respond to sources, you apply your understanding of a topic and/or evaluate the work of others. When you analyze and synthesize sources, you evaluate the ideas of others and then tie them together, along with your own thoughts. In so doing, you create something new.

KNOWLEDGE TRANSFER

Course connections: Definitions

To make their arguments clear, writers in various disciplines begin by establishing definitions for key terms, especially when various definitions exist for these terms or when existing definitions are vague. Find three definitions for one of these terms: *American Dream, democracy, critical thinking, rhetoric,* or a term from one of your other courses. Write a two- or three-page paper analyzing and synthesizing these definitions. Conclude by choosing the best definition or by composing your own.

Workplace connections: Mission Statement

Many organizations, companies, and schools write mission statements to guide their work. Find three or four mission statements from similar types of workplaces. Develop a set of criteria for evaluating these mission statements; use these criteria to decide which statement is the strongest or to compose a statement for a hypothetical organization, company, or school.

Community connections: Interviews

As a member of the student government, you have been asked to respond to a claim that students who live in college-owned dormitories and apartments perform better academically than students who do not. Interview two students who live on campus and two students who live off campus. Ask each student what the advantages and disadvantages are of living on or off campus. In a four- or five-page paper, analyze and synthesize their responses; if possible, propose steps that could improve college life for more students.

12 Crediting Others and Avoiding Plagiarism

When you do research, your work depends on the research that was done before you, and the research that you are working on has the potential to influence future research. An essential part of this scholarly tradition is the acknowledgment of previous work—not just scientific research but artistic, political, philosophical, religious, and other work as well. In fact, acknowledging the contributions of others is so highly valued that copyright and patent laws exist to protect intellectual property. Before you start drafting your project, be sure you understand what to acknowledge, how to acknowledge it, and how to avoid **plagiarism**—the presentation of someone else's ideas as your own.

12a Determining what to acknowledge

Although you will need to acknowledge the great majority of your sources, it is not necessary to credit information that is **common knowledge**—well-known facts, noncontroversial information, or information that is available in a variety of sources. For example, writing *The* Titanic *hit an iceberg and sank on its maiden voyage* is not problematic: this event has been the subject of many books and movies, so the general outline of the event is considered common knowledge. However, if you are preparing a research project about the *Titanic* and wish to include new information about its sinking, such as the role of the tides, you will be providing information or ideas that must be documented. By carefully recording your own thoughts as you take notes, you should have little difficulty distinguishing between what you knew to begin with and what you have learned through research.

Here are two questions you can ask yourself to decide whether information is considered common knowledge:

- Can the information be found in a number of sources? Check several to find out. These sources should not refer to other sources.
- Is the information commonly known among other students taking the course?

If you have any doubts about whether information is common knowledge, err on the side of caution and acknowledge your source. Taking even part of someone else's work and presenting it as your own can result in charges of plagiarism.

Plagiarism is illegal, and penalties range from receiving a failing grade on an essay or in a course to being expelled from school. Never compromise your integrity or risk your future by submitting someone else's work as your own.

CAUTION

Although it is fairly easy to copy material from a source or even to purchase a paper online, it is just as easy for a teacher or employer to locate that same material and determine that it has been plagiarized. Your instructors routinely use search engines such as Google or special services such as Turnitin when they see abrupt changes in writing or shifts within an essay that lead them to suspect that a student has submitted work that was plagiarized, downloaded, or written by others. Take extra care to avoid such deceptive, deliberate plagiarism.

Rules for **fair use**—the section of U.S. copyright law that permits material to be used without permission—covers most of the writing you will do in your courses. You are required to cite and document your source material, but you do not have to seek written permission from authors. If, however, you decide to post your research online, you will have to seek permission for images or extensive portions of text. In such situations, ask your instructor for guidance.

MATERIALS THAT SHOULD BE ACKNOWLEDGED

- Written works, both published and unpublished
- Opinions and judgments that are not your own
- Statistics and other facts that are not widely known
- Images and graphics, such as works of art, drawings, charts, graphs, tables, photographs, maps, and advertisements
- Personal communications, such as interviews, letters, and e-mail messages
- Electronic communications, including television and radio broadcasts, motion pictures and videos, sound recordings, websites, blogs, wikis, and online discussion groups

12b Citing quoted or paraphrased material

To draw responsibly on the words and ideas of others, consider the following examples (in MLA style).

Source

> We propose that while social network use does make people feel better about themselves, these increased feelings of self-worth can have a detrimental effect on behavior.

Wilcox, Keith, and Andrew T. Stephen. "Are Close Friends the Enemy? Online Social Networks, Self-Esteem, and Self Control," *Journal of Consumer Research*, vol. 4, no. 1, June 2013, pp. 90-103. (page 90)

Quotation with documentation

> Keith Wilcox and Andrew T. Stephen, both professors of business, claim that "while social network use does make people feel better about themselves, these increased feelings of self-worth can have a detrimental effect on behavior" (90).

Quotation marks show where the copied words begin and end; the number in parentheses indicates the exact page on which those words appear (**11d**). The authors' names are identified in the sentence, although their names could have been omitted at the beginning of the sentence and noted within the parenthetical reference instead:

> Although users of social networks may experience an increase in self-esteem, "these increased feelings of self-worth can have a detrimental effect on behavior" (Wilcox and Stephen 90).

Paraphrase with documentation

> Keith Wilcox and Andrew T. Stephen, both professors of business, claim that using social networks may increase self-esteem but that such increased positive feelings can adversely affect behavior (90).

This example, in MLA style, includes both authors' names and a parenthetical citation, which marks the end of the paraphrase and provides the page number where the information can be found. Remember that your paraphrases must be both accurate and ethical (**11e**).

Patchwriting. Be sure to review any paraphrase closely to make sure that both the words and the ordering of words differ significantly from those of the source material. Just as you cannot falsely represent someone else's ideas as your own, you cannot pass off someone else's writing style as your own. Patchwriting refers to paraphrases that are too close to the wording of the source. If you have trouble thinking of new ways to express the original information, move away from your desk for an hour or more. When you return, write down what you remember without looking at the source. You may find it easier to use your own words and style without the original material in front of you. If you are still having trouble, spend some time rereading your source so that you thoroughly understand it.

12c Understanding citation and documentation

Citation and documentation go hand in hand. When you mention someone else's work by quoting, paraphrasing, or summarizing it, you are *citing* that work. Documentation refers to the information you include in parentheses, footnotes, or bibliographies that allows readers to find the material you used.

Systems for documentation vary according to discipline. Each system provides two main sets of guidelines. First are guidelines for citing each instance of quotation, paraphrase, or summary of a source *in* the text. These are generally referred to as *in-text citations* or *in-text documentation guidelines*. They are usually shortened forms, including just the author's name and page number, for example.

Second is a system of documentation that requires complete bibliographic information about sources. In most cases, the bibliographic information is included in a list at the end of a work. This book covers four documentation systems: MLA (chapter 13), APA (chapter 14), CMS (chapter 15), and CSE (chapter 16).

EXERCISE 12.1

After reading the source material, decide which of the quotations and paraphrases that follow it are written correctly and which are problematic. Be prepared to explain your answers, using the information from this chapter and the previous chapter.

Source

Finegan, Edward. *Language: Its Structure and Use*. Wadsworth, 2012, p. 403.

Language is a central factor in a person's identity. Asking people to change their customary language patterns is not like asking them to
(continued on page 112)

(continued)

wear different styles or colors of sweaters. It is asking them to assume a new identity and to espouse the values associated with that identity, that is the identity of speakers of a different dialect. One reason nonstandard varieties successfully resist the urgings of education is that vernacular language varieties are deeply entwined with the social identities and values of their speakers.

1. Asking people to use another language is akin to asking them to acquire new identities.
2. Edward Finegan believes that asking people to use another language is akin to asking them to acquire new identities (403).
3. According to Edward Finegan, speakers of any nonstandard variety of English are uneducated (403).
4. Edward Finegan states that language is a central part of a person's identity (403).
5. Language choices, social identities, and values are intertwined (Finegan 403).
6. "One reason nonstandard varieties successfully resist the urgings of education is that vernacular language varieties are deeply entwined with the social identities and values of their speakers" (Finegan 403).

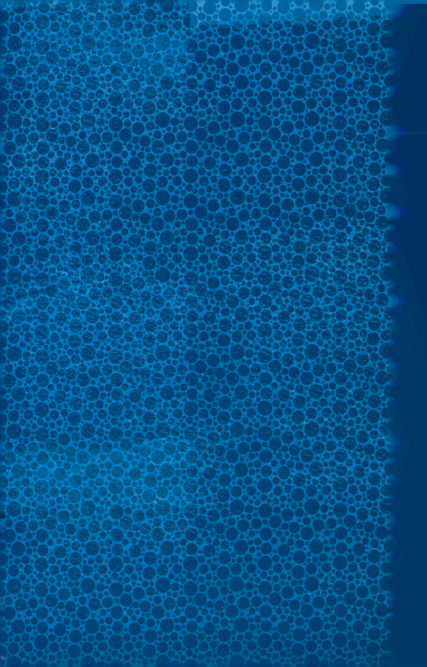

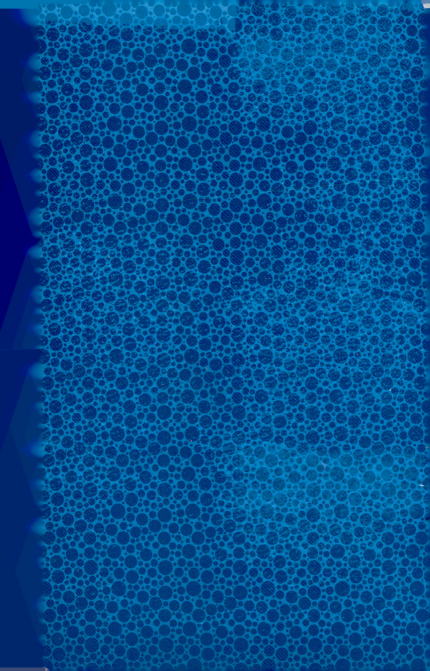

D

DOCUMENTATION

Visit the MindTap® for this book for additional information and resources.

MLA

13 MLA Documentation

If you are following the style recommended by the Modern Language Association (MLA), you will acknowledge your sources within the text of your paper by referring just to authors and page numbers, known as *In-Text Citations*, and include a Works Cited page at the end of your paper. The guidelines and examples below are based on the *MLA Handbook*, 8th ed. and *The MLA Style Center* website (style.mla.org).

13a MLA-style in-text citations

(1) Citing material from other sources

The citations you use within the text of a research project refer your readers to the list of works cited at the end of the paper, tell them where to find the borrowed material in the original source, and indicate the boundaries between your ideas and those you have borrowed. In the following example, the in-text (parenthetical) citation guides the reader to page 38 of the book by Carter in the works-cited list.

In-text (or parenthetical) citation

Whereas the last execution in Canada took place in 1962, in 2011 there were 598 murders in Canada and 14,610 in the United States (Carter 38).

Works-cited entry

Carter, Jimmy. *A Call to Action: Women, Religion, Violence, and Power*. Simon and Schuster, 2014.

MLA guidelines suggest reserving numbered notes for supplementary comments—for example, when you wish to explain a point further or provide background or tangential information. Superscript numbers are inserted in the appropriate places in the text (generally after a period), and the notes are gathered at the end of the paper on a separate page titled Notes placed before the Works Cited page. Each note begins with an indent.

In-text note number

Many proponents of the death penalty argue that it deters murder and violent crimes.[1]

Notes entry

1. Researchers Roy D. Adler and Michael Summers argue that "each execution carried out is correlated with about 74 fewer murders the following year" (A13).

Many notes will supply specific information that would otherwise interrupt the flow of the paper. Note 1 supplies additional information as well as an additional citation. MLA style does not provide specific guidance for formatting notes; however, your instructor may have formatting preferences.

The MLA provides detailed guidance for creating in-text citations, which usually provide two pieces of information about borrowed material: (1) information that directs the reader to the relevant source on the works-cited list and (2) information that directs the reader to a specific page or section within that source. The author's last name and a page number suffice. To create an in-text citation, place both the author's last name and the page number in parentheses or introduce the material being cited by giving the author's name in the sentence and supply only the page number in parentheses. Any sentence punctuation, such as a period, appears outside of the parentheses.

One of the arguments against the death penalty is that the United States remains the only NATO or North American country that "still executes citizens" (Carter 37).

OR

Former President Jimmy Carter, an anti-death-penalty activist, writes that he and Rosalyn regularly "intercede with U.S. governors . . . who may be able to commute the ultimate punishment to life imprisonment" (37).

When referring to information from a range of pages, separate the first and last pages with a hyphen: (34-42). If the page numbers have the same hundreds or thousands digit, do not repeat it when listing the final page in the range: (234-42) or (1350-55) but (290-301) or (1395-1402).

The following examples are representative of the types of in-text citations you might be expected to use.

Directory of In-Text Citations According to MLA Guidelines

1. Work by one to two authors

Although the state of New York publishes a booklet of driving rules, Katha Pollit has found no books on "the art of driving" (217).

No books exist on "the art of driving" (Pollit 217).

Other researchers, such as Steven Reiss and James Wiltz, rely on tools like surveys to explain why reality television is popular (734-36).

Survey results can help us understand why reality television is popular (Reiss and Wiltz 734-36).

The authors' last names can be placed in the text or within parentheses with the page number. The parenthetical citation should appear as close as possible to the information documented—usually at the end of the sentence or after any quotation marks.

2. Work by three or more authors

When parenthetically citing a source by three or more authors, provide just the first author's last name followed by the abbreviation *et al.* (Latin for "and others"): (Stafford et al. 67). The abbreviation *et al.* should not be underlined or italicized in citations.

3. Work by an unknown author

The Tehuelche people left their handprints on the walls of a cave, now called Cave of the Hands ("Hands of Time" 124).

If the author is unknown, use the title of the work in place of the author's name. If the title is long, shorten it by excluding initial articles like *a*, *an*, and *the* (*The Double Vision* becomes *Double Vision*) and by beginning with the first word used in the corresponding works-cited entry ("Wandering" for "Wandering with Cameras in the Himalaya"). If you use the title in the text, however, you do not have to place it in the parenthetical reference.

MLA

4. An entire work

Throughout *How Proust Can Change Your Life*, Alain de Botton uses literary examples to explore the reasons people decide to travel.

Notice that no page numbers are necessary when an entire work is cited.

5. A multivolume work

President Truman asked that all soldiers be treated equally (Merrill 11: 741).

When you cite from more than one volume of a multivolume work, include the volume number and page number(s). The volume and page numbers are separated by a colon.

6. Two or more works by the same author(s)

Online shopping has breached our privacy: "The growth of market psychology to 'cluster' consumers by region, gender, race, education, and age, as well as the use of computer technology, means that our movements and individual tastes are always being tracked as unerringly as though by a bloodhound" (Williams, *Open* 57).

Patricia Williams argues that peace without justice constitutes an illusion (*On Intellectual Activism* 91).

To distinguish one work from another, include a title. If the title is long (such as *Open House: Of Family, Friends, Food, Piano Lessons, and the Search for a Room of My Own*), shorten it, beginning with the first word used in the corresponding works-cited entry (*Open*). Notice that the first example includes the author's last name, the first word of the book title, and the page number. A comma separates the author's last name from the book title.

7. Two or more works by different authors with the same last name

If the military were to use solely conventional weapons, the draft would likely be reinstated (E. Scarry 241).

To distinguish one author from another, use their initials. If the initials are the same, spell out their first names.

8. Work by a corporate or government author

While fifty years ago we wanted to improve the national diet to eliminate dietary diseases like pellagra or rickets, today our dietary concerns focus on chronic life-threatening conditions like heart disease and diabetes (American Heart Association xiv).

When the corporation or government agency is listed as the author in the works-cited entry, provide the name of the corporate or government author and a page reference (as in the preceding example). If a government author includes several administrative units, include them all in the in-text citation (United States Dept of Education 45). In this case, abbreviate *Department* to *Dept.*

Sometimes, the works-cited entry may list a work by a government or corporate publication with the title of the work listed first, followed by the name of the government agency or corporation that serves as the publisher.

If the work-cited entry begins with a title, treat the in-text citation as you would for an unknown author and cite the title (and edition, if necessary) in the in-text citation. (See Item 4, Book by a corporate author on page 132.)

9. Indirect source

According to Sir George Dasent, a reader "must be satisfied with the soup that is set before him, and not desire to see the bones of the ox out of which it has been boiled" (qtd. in Shippey 289).

Use the abbreviation *qtd.* to indicate that you found the quotation in another source.

10. Work in an anthology or book collection

"Good cooking," claims Jane Kramer, "is much easier to master than good writing" (153).

Either in the text or within parentheses with the page number, use the name of the author of the particular section (chapter, essay, or article) you are citing, not the editor of the entire book, unless they are the same.

11. Poem

The final sentence in Philip Levine's "Homecoming" is framed by conditional clauses: "If we're quiet / . . . if the place had a spirit" (38–43).

Do not use page numbers. Instead, provide line numbers.

12. Drama

After some hesitation, the messenger tells Macbeth what he saw: "As I did stand my watch upon the hill / I looked toward Birnam and anon methought / The wood began to move" (*Mac.* 5.5.35-37).

Instead of page numbers, indicate act, scene, and line numbers.

13. Bible

The image of seeds covering the sidewalk reminded her of the parable in which a seed falls on stony ground (Matt. 13.18-23).

Identify the book of the Bible (using the conventional abbreviation if the name of the book is more than four letters long) and, instead of page numbers, provide chapter and verse(s). Note that books of the Bible are not italicized.

14. Two or more works in one parenthetical citation

Usage issues are discussed in both academic and popular periodicals (Bex and Watts 5; Lippi–Green 53).

Use a semicolon to separate citations.

15. Material from the Internet

Alston describes three types of rubrics that teachers can use to evaluate student writing (pars. 2-15).

Evolution is one possible cause of tensions between science and religion in "our cultural terror of curiosity" (McGowan).

If an online publication numbers pages, paragraphs, sections, chapters, or screens, provide those numbers in the citation. Precede paragraph numbers with *par.* or *pars.*, screen numbers with *screen* or *screens*, or section numbers with *sec.* or *secs.* If the source does not number any of these divisions, refer to the entire work in your text by citing the author, either in the text of your sentence (as in the example above) or in a parenthetical citation (McGowan).

(2) Guidelines for in-text citations and quotations

PLACEMENT OF IN-TEXT CITATIONS

When you acknowledge your use of a source by placing the author's name and a relevant page number in parentheses, insert this parenthetical citation directly after the information you used, generally at the end of a sentence but *before* the final punctuation mark.

Oceans store almost half the carbon dioxide released by humans into the atmosphere (Wall 28).

However, you may need to place a parenthetical citation earlier in a sentence to indicate that only the first part of the sentence contains borrowed material. Place the citation after the clause containing the material but before a punctuation mark (a comma, semicolon, or colon).

Oceans store almost half the carbon dioxide released by humans into the atmosphere (Wall 28), a fact that provides hope for scientists studying global warming but alarms scientists studying organisms living in the oceans.

If you cite the same source more than once in a paragraph with no intervening citations of another source, you can place one parenthetical citation at the end of the last sentence in which the source is used: (Wall 28, 32).

LENGTHY QUOTATIONS

When a quotation is more than four lines long, set it off from the surrounding text by indenting it one-half inch from the left margin (the depth of a standard paragraph indent), keeping it double-spaced. The right-hand margin is not indented, nor does the passage appear in quotation marks.

In *Between the World and Me*, Ta-Nehisi Coates writes about his childhood admiration of Malcolm X:

> I loved Malcolm because Malcolm never lied, unlike the schools and their façade of morality, unlike the streets and their bravado, unlike the world of the dreamers. I loved him because he made it plain, never mystical or esoteric, because his science was not rooted in the actions of spooks and mystery gods but in the work of the physical world. Malcolm was the first political pragmatist I knew, the first honest man I'd ever heard. (36)

For these reasons, Malcolm X served as an inspiration for Coates to make a name for himself in the world.

Note that the period precedes the parenthetical citation at the end of an indented (block) quotation. Note, too, how the writer introduces and then comments upon the block quotation from Coates, explaining the significance of the block quotation in the writer's larger essay.

PUNCTUATION WITHIN CITATIONS AND QUOTATIONS

Punctuation marks clarify meaning in quotations and citations. The following list summarizes their common uses.

- A colon separates volume numbers from page numbers in a parenthetical citation.

  (Raine 2: 247)

- A comma separates the author's name from the title when it is necessary to list both in a parenthetical citation.

  (Pipher, *Writing to Change the World*)

  A comma also indicates that page or line numbers are not sequential.

  (44, 47)

- Ellipsis points indicate an omission within a quotation.

  According to Krutch, "They lived in an age of increasing complexity and great hope; we in an age of . . . growing despair" (Krutch 2).

- A hyphen indicates a continuous sequence of pages or lines.

  (44-47)

- A period separates acts, scenes, and lines of dramatic works.

  (3.1.56)

- A question mark placed inside the final quotation marks indicates that the quotation itself is a question. Notice that the period after the parenthetical citation marks the end of a sentence.

  Peter Elbow asks, "What could be more wonderful than the pleasure of creating or appreciating forms that are different, amazing, outlandish, useless—the opposite of ordinary, everyday, pragmatic?" (542).

  When placed outside the final quotation marks, a question mark indicates that the quotation has been incorporated into a question posed by the writer of the research paper.

  What does Kabat-Zinn mean when he advises people to practice mindfulness "as if their lives depended on it" (305)?

- Square brackets enclose words that have been added to the quotation as clarification and are not part of the original material.

  "From Boyle's perspective, the "novel [*Beloved*] establishes Morrison as the most important writer of our time" (17).

13b MLA guidelines for documenting works cited

All the works you cite should be listed at the end of your paper, beginning on a separate page with the heading *Works Cited* (not in italics). And every works-cited entry you list should have a corresponding in-text citation. For sample lists of works cited, see pages 51, 164-165.

TIPS FOR PREPARING A LIST OF WORKS CITED

- Center the heading *Works Cited* (not italicized) one inch from the top of the page.

- Arrange the lists of works alphabetically by the author's last name.

- Double-space the entire works-cited list—between lines of an entry and between entries.

- The first line of each entry begins flush with the left margin, and subsequent lines are indented one-half inch.

- If your list includes entries with URLs, omit the *http://* and *https://* prefixes but include *www.* (not italicized) when part of the address. If the URLs are long enough to run onto a second line, break them before or after a punctuation mark (like a slash or hyphen); however, if you have to break a URL at a period, then the line break comes *before* the period, not after it.

- For entries including a publisher's name, omit articles and corporate terms (Co., Inc.). To cite something from a university press, include abbreviations as in *U of Missouri P*. Otherwise, spell out publishers' names, including words like *Books* and *Press*.

The guidelines in the *MLA Handbook,* 8th ed., have been simplified to focus on nine core elements for your works-cited entries, whatever the medium—print or online. Provide only those elements that apply to the source you are citing.

The core elements include the (1) author(s), (2) title of source, (3) container—the source within which an article or posting is found, such as a newspaper, journal, or website, (4) other contributors—such as a translator or an editor, when there is one, (5) version—such as the King James Version of the Bible or edition number of a book published in multiple editions, (6) number—for example, the issue number in a series, (7) publisher, (8) date of publication, and (9) location—page numbers and/or the source's URL (preferably a stable or permalink URL address, if available) or DOI (digital object identifier). A DOI is a unique code of numbers and letters assigned to many scholarly articles (doi: 10.1023/a:1015789513985) and is a permanent link, so it will not change once it is assigned.

When citing a work, begin with the author, followed by a period, and then the title of the source (e.g., book, article, or online posting), also followed by a period.

1. **Author(s).** Alphabetize your works-cited list by author's last name. Use a comma to separate the last name from the first, and place a period at the end of this unit of information (Welty, Eudora.). Other configurations for author entries, and how to alphabetize them, are included later in this chapter.

2. **Title of Source.** The title of the source is italicized if it is a book, website, television series, movie, music album, or work of art (a play, painting) (*The World Is Flat*.). If there is a subtitle, use a colon to separate the subtitle from the title and italicize every part of the title and subtitle, including any colon (*Visual Explanations: Images and Quantities, Evidence and Narrative*). If the source is an article, include the title in quotation marks: "Sounding Cajun: The Rhetorical Use of Dialect in Speech and Writing."

   The elements that follow the title of the source should appear in the following order (though few source listings will include all nine elements). Each of these elements is followed by a comma.

MLA

3. **Container,** If the work you are citing is part of a larger whole (an article in a magazine, a song in an album, a specific posting on a social media site, etc.), then include the title of the container in which the source appears. Italicize the full container name—including *A*, *An*, and *The*—for magazines (*The Quarterly*), journals (*Cultural Critique*), newspapers (*The New York Times*). Also italicize websites (*Google Books*), social networking sites (*Twitter*), and databases (*ProQuest*). See Online Sources for more on how to include websites, posts on online networks, and databases.

4. **Other Contributors,** When there are other contributors, spell out the relationship of the other contributor to the main source (*edited by, translated by*). You will not always have other contributors in your works-cited entry.

5. **Version,** You will also not always have a version (or edition) for your works-cited entry, but if you are citing a particular edition of a book, you will indicate what version you are citing (for example, *3rd ed.* or *unabridged version*) (not in italics) to indicate the version of the source you are citing.

6. **Number,** All journal entries must contain volume and issue numbers except those journals with issue numbers only. MLA requires you to abbreviate "volume" as *vol.* (not italicized). The issue "number" is abbreviated *no.* (not italicized). Include a period after *vol.* and *no.* and separate with a comma (*vol. 10, no. 3*). A number is also included for a numbered series, such as a season and episode in a television series (*season 4, episode 3*) or a book that is part of a series or is a volume in a multi-volume work. You will not always have a relevant number for your works-cited entry.

7. **Publisher,** Use a publisher's full name (*Random House* or *Alfred A. Knopf*), not the parent organization (Random House Penguin Group). Also use the abbreviation

UP for University Press (*Yale UP* for Yale University Press). Do not include business information in the name of the publisher (*Company, Co., Corporation, Corp., Inc.,* or *Ltd.*).

Magazines, journals, and newspapers do not include the publisher's name. Websites do not include the publisher's name when it is the same as the name of the website.

Include the city where the publisher is located only when doing so adds essential clarification. For example, when the city of publication is not included in the name of a newspaper, it can be inserted in brackets within the citation: (*The Weekly Gazette* [Colorado Springs]).

8. **Date of Publication,** The publication date that you provide depends on the type of publication you are citing. The copyright date is included for a book (found on the title page or the page following the title page, called the *copyright page*). For an article in a monthly magazine, include the publication month and year (*Dec. 2015*). Abbreviate and add a period to the names of all months except May, June, and July. For a weekly or daily publication, indicate the day, the month, and the year (*17 Mar. 2016*). If you are citing an online work, include the date that it was posted or was last updated (whichever is more recent).

9. **Location.** If you are citing a selection within a book or an article within a magazine or an online source, you will need to provide the location of your source. MLA requires that the page numbers be preceded by *p.* or *pp.* (not in italics) or that the online location be included. An online location is indicated with a URL (Internet address—use stable or permalink addresses when they have been assigned) or a DOI (digital object identifier). Note that when page numbers are included, larger page numbers should include ranges with two digits, pp. 52-55, pp. 102-09 (include the "0"). Include more digits when needed for clarity, pp. 395-401,

MLA

pp. 1608-774. For some types of works (lectures, live peformances, works of art), the location informaton is the name of a city or venue.

CORE ELEMENTS

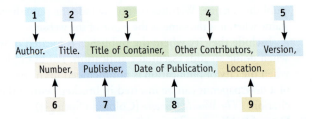

For more details on various types of sources, use the following directory to find relevant sections. For an example of a works-cited list, see the paper at the end of this chapter.

Directory of Works-Cited Entries According to MLA Guidelines

BOOKS

1. Book by one author

You, Xiaoye. *Writing in the Devil's Tongue: A History of English Composition in China*. Southern Illinois UP, 2009.

2. Book by two authors

Gies, Joseph, and Frances Gies. *Life in a Medieval City*. Harper & Row Publishers, 1981.

When two authors are listed, only the first author's name is inverted. List the authors' names in the order in which they appear on the title page, not in alphabetical order. Include full names for both authors, even if they have the same last name.

CITATION MAP 13.1: BOOK, MLA STYLE

TITLE PAGE

ESSENTIAL

CINEMA

Title of source (book)

An Introduction to Film Analysis ← Subtitle of book

Author → JON LEWIS
OREGON STATE UNIVERSITY

Publication date
(copyright year)

WADSWORTH
CENGAGE Learning

COPYRIGHT PAGE

WADSWORTH
CENGAGE Learning

Essential Cinema: An Introduction to Film Analysis
Jon Lewis

Publisher: Michael Rosenberg
Senior Development Editor: Leslie Taggart
Development Editor: Cynthia Ward
Assistant Editor: Erin Bosco
Editorial Assistant: Rebecca Donahue
Media Editor: Jessica Badiner
Senior Content Project Manager: Michael Lepera
Senior Market Development Manager: Kara Kindstrom
Senior Marketing Communication Manager: Linda Yip
Marketing Coordinator: Brittany Blais
Executive Brand Manager: Ben Rivera
Senior Art Director: Marissa Falco
Senior Rights Acquisition Specialist: Mandy Groszko
Manufacturing Planner: Doug Bertke
Production Service/Compositor: Lachina Publishing Services
Text Designer: Ke Design
Cover Designer: Roycroft Design

Publisher
(list division
only)

WADSWORTH
CENGAGE Learning

Australia • Brazil • Japan • Korea • Mexico • Singapore • Spain • United Kingdom

© 2014 Wadsworth, Cengage Learning

ALL RIGHTS RESERVED. No part of this work covered by the copyright herein may be reproduced, transmitted, stored, or used in any form or by any means graphic, electronic, or mechanical, including but not limited to photocopying, recording, scanning, digitizing, taping, Web distribution, information networks, or information storage and retrieval systems, except as permitted under Section 107 or 108 of the 1976 United States Copyright Act, without the prior written permission of the publisher.

For product information and technology assistance, contact us at
Cengage Learning Customer & Sales Support, 1-800-354-9706
For permission to use material from this text or product,
submit all requests online at **cengage.com/permissions.**
Further permissions questions can be emailed to
permissionrequest@cengage.com.

Library of Congress Control Number: 2012950823
ISBN-13: 978-1-4390-8368-0
ISBN-10: 1-4390-8368-1

Wadsworth
20 Channel Center Street
Boston, MA 02210
USA

City of
publication

Cengage Learning is a leading provider of customized learning solutions with office locations around the globe, including Singapore, the United Kingdom, Australia, Mexico, Brazil, and Japan. Locate your local office at:

WORKS-CITED ENTRY FOR A BOOK

Author   Title

Lewis, Jon. *Essential Cinema: An Introduction to Film Analysis.*
Wadsworth, 2014.

Publisher   Publication date
(copyright year)

3. Book by three or more authors

Belenky, Mary, et al. *Women's Ways of Knowing: The Development of Self,*
        Voice, and Mind. Basic Books, 1986.

For three or more authors, provide the first author's name inverted, followed by the abbreviation *et al.* (not italicized). The first author is the first name as it appears on the title page.

4. Book by a corporate author

American Heart Association. *The New American Heart Association Cookbook.*
        6th ed., Clarkson Potter, 2001.

Omit any article (*a*, *an*, or *the*) that begins the name of a corporate author and alphabetize the entry in the works-cited list according to the first major word of the corporate author's name. If the corporate author is the same as the publisher, begin with the title of the book and list the corporation as the publisher.

5. Book by an anonymous author

Primary Colors: A Novel of Politics. Warner Books, 1996.

Alphabetize the entry according to the first major word in the title of the work.

6. Book with an author and an editor

Dickens, Charles. *Pickwick Papers*. Edited by Malcolm Andrews, Everyman's
        Library, 1998.

Begin the entry with the author's name. Place the editor's name after the title of the book, preceding the name with *Edited by* (not italicized).

7. Book with an editor instead of an author

Baxter, Leslie A., and Dawn O. Braithwaite, editors. *Engaging Theories in*
        Interpersonal Communication: Multiple Perspectives. SAGE Publications, 2008.

Begin the entry with the name(s) of the editor(s) followed by *editor(s)* (not in italics).

8. Second or subsequent edition

Cameron, Rondo, and Larry Neal. *A Concise Economic History of the World:*

From Paleolithic Times to the Present. 4th ed., Oxford UP, 2003.

After the title, include the version of the book you are citing when that information helps clarify the source you have cited. If the version you are citing is a second or subsequent edition, place the number of the edition in its ordinal form, followed by ed. for "edition." Note that the letters *th* following the number appear in regular type, not as a superscript.

9. Introduction, preface, foreword, or afterword to a book

Peri, Yoram. Afterword. *The Rabin Memoirs*, by Yitzhak Rabin, U of California

P, 1996, pp. 422-32.

Begin the entry with the name of the author of the introduction, preface, foreword, or afterword, followed by the name of the part being cited (e.g., *Afterword*). If the part being cited has a title, include the title in quotation marks between the author's name and the name of the part being cited. Provide the title of the book (see Container, earlier in this chapter), followed by a comma and *by* with the name of the author of the book (see Other Contributors, earlier in this chapter). Complete the entry with the page number(s) of the part being cited after the publication information.

10. Anthology or book collection

Ramazani, Jahan, and Richard Ellman, editors. *The Norton Anthology of*

Modern and Contemporary Poetry. 3rd ed., W. W. Norton, 2003.

The entry begins with the anthology's editor(s), with the first (or only) editor's name inverted, followed by a comma and *editor* or *editors* (not in italics).

11. Single work from an anthology or book collection

Muños, Gabriel Trujillo. "Once Upon a Time on the Border." *How I Learned*

English, edited by Tom Miller, National Geographic Society, 2007,

pp. 141-48.

Begin the entry with the name of the author of the work you are citing, not the name of the anthology's editor. The title of the work appears in quotation marks between the author's name and the title of the anthology. The editor's name is preceded by *edited by* (not in italics). After the publisher and date of publication, conclude with the numbers of the pages on which the work appears.

12. Two or more works from the same anthology or book collection

Miller, Tom, editor. *How I Learned English*. National Geographic Society, 2007.

Montero, Mayra. "How I Learned English . . . or Did I?" Miller, pp. 221-25.

Padilla, Ignacio. "El Dobbing and My English." Miller, pp. 237-41.

When citing more than one work from the same anthology, include an entry for the entire anthology as well as entries for the individual works. In entries for individual works, list the names of the author(s) and the editor(s) and the title of the work, but not the title of the anthology. Then list the last name of the general editor and specify the page or range of pages on which the work appears.

13. Two or more works by the same author

Rodriguez, Richard. *Brown: The Last Discovery of America*.
    Penguin Books, 2002.

- - -. *Hunger of Memory: The Education of Richard Rodriguez*.
    Bantam Books, 1982.

If you have used more than one work by the same author (or team of authors), alphabetize the entries according to title. For the first entry, provide the author's name; for any subsequent entries, substitute three hyphens (---).

14. Two or more works by the same first author

Bailey, Guy, and Natalie Maynor. "The Divergence Controversy." *American
    Speech*, vol. 64, no. 1, Spring 1989, pp. 12-39.

Bailey, Guy, and Jan Tillery. "Southern American English." *American Language
    Review*, vol. 4, no. 4, 2000, pp. 27-29.

If two or more entries have the same first author, alphabetize the entries according to the second author's last name.

15. Book with a title within the title

Koon, Helene Wickham. *Twentieth-Century Interpretations of* Death of a Salesman:

   A Collection of Critical Essays. Prentice Hall, 1983.

When an italicized title includes the title of another work that would normally be italicized, do not italicize the embedded title. If the embedded title actually requires quotation marks (rather than italics), it should be italicized as well as enclosed in quotation marks.

16. Translated book

Rilke, Rainer Maria. *Duino Elegies*. Translated by David Young,

   W. W. Norton, 1978.

The translator's name appears after the book title, preceded by *Translated by* (not in italics). However, if the material cited in your paper refers primarily to the translator's comments rather than to the translated text, the entry should appear as follows:

Young, David, translator. *Duino Elegies*. By Rainer Maria Rilke,

   W. W. Norton, 1978.

17. Multivolume work

Sewall, Richard B. *The Life of Emily Dickinson*. Farrar, Straus, and Giroux,

   1974. 2 vols.

Provide only the specific volume number (e.g., *Vol. 1*, not in italics) after the title if you cite material from one volume. Include the total number of volumes (e.g., *2 vols.*, not in italics) if you cite material from more than one volume.

18. Book in a series

Restle, David, and Dietmar Zaefferer, editors. *Sounds and Systems*. De Gruyter,

   2002. Trends in Linguistics, 141.

Provide the name of the series and the number of the book in the series (if any), separated by a comma.

19. Encyclopedia entry

"Heckelphone." *The Encyclopedia Americana*, vol. 14, Grolier, 2001, p. 205.

Begin with the title of the entry unless an author's name is provided. Provide the title of the encyclopedia, the edition number (if any), the volume number (if a multi-volume set), the publisher's name, the year of publication, and the page number for the entry.

20. Dictionary entry

"Foolscap." Definition. 3. *Merriam-Webster's Collegiate Dictionary*, 11th ed.,

Merriam-Webster, 2003, p. 442.

A dictionary entry is documented similarly to an encyclopedia entry. If the definition is one of several listed for the word, provide the definition number or letter, preceded by *Definition* (not italicized).

ARTICLES

ARTICLE IN A JOURNAL

You can generally find the name of the journal, the volume and issue numbers, the season or month, as well as year of publication on the cover of the journal. Sometimes this information is also included in the journal's page headers or footers. MLA does not make a distinction between journals that are numbered continuously (for example, vol. 1 ends on page 208, and vol. 2 starts on page 209) and those numbered separately (that is, each volume starts on page 1). To find the title of the article, the author's name, and the page numbers, you will need to locate the article within the journal. See Online Sources for information on citing articles from online sources.

ARTICLE IN A MAGAZINE

To find the name of the magazine and the date of publication, look on the cover of the magazine. Sometimes this information is also included in the magazine's page headers or footers. To find the title of the article, the author's name, and the page

CITATION MAP 13.2: ARTICLE IN A JOURNAL, MLA STYLE

To cite an article from a journal, include the following elements.

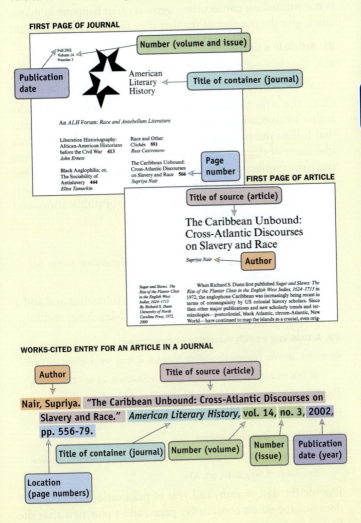

FIRST PAGE OF JOURNAL

Number (volume and issue)

Publication date

Title of container (journal)

American Literary History

Fall 2002
Volume 14
Number 3

An *ALH* Forum: *Race and Antebellum Literature*

Liberation Historiography: African-American Historians before the Civil War 413
John Ernest

Black Anglophilia; or, The Sociability of Antislavery 444
Elisa Tamarkin

Race and Other Clichés 551
Russ Castronovo

The Caribbean Unbound: Cross-Atlantic Discourses on Slavery and Race 566
Supriya Nair

Page number

FIRST PAGE OF ARTICLE

Title of source (article)

The Caribbean Unbound: Cross-Atlantic Discourses on Slavery and Race

Supriya Nair ← Author

Sugar and Slaves: The Rise of the Planter Class in the English West Indies, 1624–1713
By Richard S. Dunn
University of North Carolina Press, 1972, 2000

When Richard S. Dunn first published *Sugar and Slaves: The Rise of the Planter Class in the English West Indies, 1624–1713* in 1972, the anglophone Caribbean was increasingly being recast in terms of consanguinity by US colonial history scholars. Since then other major publications and new scholarly trends and terminologies—postcolonial, black Atlantic, circum-Atlantic, New World—have continued to map the islands as a crucial, even orig-

WORKS-CITED ENTRY FOR AN ARTICLE IN A JOURNAL

Author   Title of source (article)

Nair, Supriya. "The Caribbean Unbound: Cross-Atlantic Discourses on Slavery and Race." *American Literary History*, vol. 14, no. 3, 2002, pp. 556-79.

Title of container (journal)   Number (volume)   Number (issue)   Publication date (year)

Location (page numbers)

numbers, you will have to look at the article itself. If the article is not printed on consecutive pages, as often happens in magazines, give the number of the first page followed by a plus sign.

21. Article in a journal

Burt, Susan Meredith. "Solicitudes in American English." *International Journal of Applied Linguistics*, vol. 13, no. 1, June 2003, pp. 78-95.

Place the title of the article in quotation marks after the author's name, with a period after each element. The elements that follow the title are separated by commas. The container (the name of the journal) follows in italics. Provide the volume and issue numbers, the month or season (if applicable) and the year of publication, and the range of pages. The elements that follow the title (container, number, date of publication, and location) are separated by commas.

22. Article in a monthly magazine

Moran, Thomas E. "Just for Kicks Soccer Program." *Exceptional Parent*, Feb. 2004, pp. 36-37.

Include the publication month and year. Abbreviate and add a period to the names of all months except May, June, and July.

23. Article in a weekly magazine or newspaper

Gonzalehz, Jennifer. "Community-College Professor, Visiting Yale, Explores the Ethics of Treating Animals." *The Chronicle of Higher Education*, 23 Apr. 2010, p. A4.

Provide the day, month, and year of publication after the title of the publication.

24. Article in a daily newspaper

Lewin, Tamara. "Teenage Insults, Scrawled on Web, Not on Walls." *The New York Times*, 6 May 2010, pp. A1+.

Provide the day, month, and year of publication. If the article does not appear on consecutive pages, add a plus sign after the first page number.

25. Unsigned article

"Beware the Herd." *Newsweek*, 8 Mar. 2004, p. 61.

Alphabetize the entry according to the first major word in the title, ignoring any article (*a, an,* or *the*).

26. Editorial in a newspaper or magazine

Marcus, Ruth. "In Arizona, Election Reform's Surprising Consequences."

Editorial. *The Washington Post*, 5 May 2010, p. A21.

After the title of the editorial, place the word *Editorial* (not in italics) followed by a period. Then include the name of the newspaper or magazine, the date of publication, and the location.

27. Letter to the editor

Willens, Peggy A. Letter to the Editor. *The New York Times*, 1 May 2010, p. A30.

Following the author's name, include the published title of the letter if there is one. Then insert the description Letter (not italicized) followed by a period. If the letter is not titled, then use the description *Letter to the Editor* (not in italics) as in the preceding example. Conclude with the name of the periodical, the date of publication, and the page number.

28. Book or film review

Morgenstern, Joe. "See Spot Sing and Dance: Dog Cartoon 'Teacher's Pet' Has

Enough Bite for Adults." Review of *Teacher's Pet*, directed by Timothy

Björklund. *The Wall Street Journal*, 16 Jan. 2004, pp. W1+.

Place the reviewer's name first, followed by the title of the review (if any) in quotation marks. Next, provide the title of the work reviewed, preceded by *Review of* (not in italics). Then mention other contributors important to the review with an indication of their contribution (not in italics): *directed by* precedes a director's name; *performance by* precedes an actor's name.

MLA

ONLINE SOURCES

When citing online sources, use the list of core elements to guide you just as you would for print. There are a few variations that are specific to online sources. The location for an online source is indicated with a web address—the DOI (digital object identifier) or a stable permalink of the URL when possible. In addition, online sources frequently have more than one container—for instance, an article might be found in a journal (container 1), which is accessed as part of an online collection (container 2) within a database (container 3). When there is a second and occasionally third container, the name of the second and third containers are placed at the end of the entry and followed by the web address.

Author.

Treat authors as you would for print with the exception that Internet handles and pseudonyms are acceptable author names for online sources. An author's name is followed by a period.

Title of Source.

Titles are punctuated as they are in print, followed by a period. When there is no title for a tweet, use the full post included in quotation marks as a title. When citing an e-mail message, use the subject line as the title and enclose the subject line in quotation marks.

Container (Container 1),

Italicize online container names, just as you would for print, followed by a comma. Journals, magazines, and newspapers, as well as online collections of works, and websites where articles are posted are all containers. Standardize the name of a website if the punctuation is unusual.

Online sources commonly have more than one container. Often a second and sometimes third container simply hosts the first container—rather than contributes to the content of the source. Include the name of the host site (in italics) to help others locate the source. It is placed at the end of the entry, prior to the web address. Host sites include *YouTube* for videos or *ProQuest* for online subscription services.

Publisher,
The publisher who sponsors a website is usually at the bottom of the home page (for example, the *Oxford English Dictionary's* website www.oed.com is published by Oxford University Press). Look at the "About" page to find the publisher who sponsors a website if it is not otherwise clear. A publisher contributes to the content of the site. *Blogspot*, for example, might host a blog, but it is not the publisher (see Container 2). The publisher's name is not included when the name of the website would simply be repeated as that of the publisher.

Date of Publication,
Include the date that the source was posted online or was last updated or modified, whichever is more recent. If you are accessing a source online that is also available in print (such as a newspaper or journal article), be sure to use the online publication date in your citation. If the source includes a time stamp (10:00 a.m.), add the time after the date (day, month, year) and separate the date and time with a comma. If the date of publication is the last entry before Container 2, conclude with a period as you would with print.

Location (page numbers or web address).
Sometimes page numbers from the print source are available as part of the database that has been accessed. Include them and follow them with a period if this is the last entry before Container 2. If there is no second container, add a comma and the web address.

MLA

Container (Container 2),
When the first container is located within a second or third container, include all the container names. Subsequent containers include databases of works (*African Journals Online [AJOL]*), social media networks (*Twitter*), or online library subscriptions (*JSTOR*); these container names are italicized and come after the date of publication (and after the page numbers when page numbers are available).

Additional information for the second or third container, such as other contributors, version, number, publisher, and date of publication, is included when it is available, separated by commas.

Location (web address).
Conclude with a web location. MLA prefers a stable or permalink for the URL or a DOI, which is also a permanent link, if either of these is available. Check with your instructor to learn whether different or additional information is required.

It is important to include only information that helps others locate your source online and avoid extraneous information that might be confusing. Only include the date of access if the URL is likely to be removed or updated.

Date of Access.
Because online sources can be easily changed or moved, you may sometimes need to include a date of access in a citation. If a source has no date or publication, is constantly changing, or is frequently updated, include a date of access at the end of the citation.

Online sources vary significantly; therefore, as you prepare your works-cited list, you will need to follow the models shown here closely.

CITATION MAP 13.3: ARTICLE IN A DATABASE, MLA STYLE

Include the following elements when citing an article in a database.

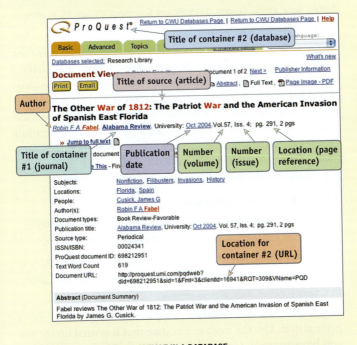

WORKS-CITED ENTRY FOR AN ARTICLE IN A DATABASE

Author — Title of source (article) — Title of journal — Numbers (volume and issue)

Fabel, Robin F. A. "The Other War of 1812: The Patriot War and the American Invasion of Spanish East Florida." *Alabama Review,* vol. 57, no. 4, 2004, pp. 291-92. *ProQuest, proquest.umi.com/pqdweb? did=698212951&sid=1&Fmt=3&clientid=16941&RQT=309&V Name=PQD.*

Publication date (year) — Location for container #1 (page numbers) — Title of container #2 (database) — Location for container #2 (URL)

29. Online book

Austen, Jane. *Emma*. London, 1815. *Project Gutenberg*, 21 Jan. 2010, www
.gutenberg.org/ebooks.158.

Begin with the information you always provide for an entry for a book (author, title, and publication information, if available). In this instance, because the original work is older and was published before 1900, the city of publication (London) is included rather than the name of a publisher. The name of the website (italicized) where the book is located, the date of publication or release on the site, and the web address conclude the entry. Note that MLA guidelines require concluding each entry with a period, even if the web address does not end in a period.

30. Article in an online publication

Dayen, David. "Snapshot of a Broken System: How a Profitable Company
Justifies Laying Off 1400 Workers and Moves Their Jobs to Mexico."
Salon, 22 Mar. 2016, www.salon.com/2016/03/22/snapshot_of_a_
broken_system_how_a_profitable_company_justifies_laying_off_1400_
people_moved_their_jobs_to_mexico/.

Begin with the information you provide for an entry for a print article. Use the most recent date that is posted on the site you have accessed. Conclude with the location.

31. Article in a print publication accessed online

Cloud, John. "The YouTube Gurus." *Time*, 16 Dec. 2006, content.time.com/
time/magazine/article/0,9171,1570795,00.

Begin with the information you provide for a print citation, adapting the date of publication to the date it was posted online (even if it differs from the date on the print publication). Conclude with the online location.

32. Article from a database (or library subscription service)

Fenn, Donna. "Generation Why Not." *Inc.*, July–Aug. 2014, pp. 46-54. *General
OneFile*, go.galegroup.com/ps/i.do?p=GPS&sw=w&u=nysl_me_wls&v=2.1&id=
GALE%7CA374333194&it=r&asid=f99fa4ca6483d426761d360883bcbecb.

CITATION MAP 13.4: WORK FROM A WEBSITE, MLA STYLE

Include the following elements when citing a document you find on the web.

Location (URL)

Title of container (site) and Publisher (sponsor)

Title of source (short work/page)

Publication date (last update)

Title of source (short work/page)

Title of container (site) and Publisher (sponor)

"Climate Change Impacts. "United States Environmental Protection Agency, 23 Feb. 2016, www3.epa.gov/climatechange/impacts/.

Publication date (last update)

Location (URL)

Provide the complete print information for the article. A period precedes the listing of subsequent containers.

33. Website

Amon Carter Museum of American Art. 2017, www.cartermuseum.org.

Provide the title of the site (italicized) followed by a period. Include the version number (if provided), the name of the publisher if different from the name of the website, and the date of publication or latest update. Conclude with the online location.

34. Article posted on a website

Gumm, Brian. "Blowing Smoke: Chemical Companies Say, 'Trust Us,' But Environmental and Workplace Safety Violations Belie Their Rhetoric." *Center for Effective Government*, 22 Oct. 2015, www.foreffectivegov.org/files/regs/blowing-smoke.pdf.

If the section has an author, list his or her name (inverted) first. Place the title of the article you are citing in quotation marks before the title of the website (in italics). If the name of the website is the same as that of the publisher, list only the website.

35. Television program accessed online

"AKA Ladies Night." *Jessica Jones*, season 1, episode 1, Marvel Studios, 2015. *Netflix*, www.netflix.com/watch/80002312. Accessed 23 Feb. 2017.

Begin with the title of the episode in quotation marks followed by a period. Include the title of the program in italics, the season number, and the episode number. Next, depending on which is more relevant for your research, include either the production company and the year the episode was broadcast (as in the preceding example) or the distribution company and the date the episode aired. Then list the online provider in italics, the web address, and the date of access (because content available on sites such as *Netflix, Amazon Video*, and *Hulu* often move or become unavailable). See also Items 43, 44, 45, and 46 for film and television series.

36. Video posted online

"Jim Holt: 'Why Does the Universe Exist?'" *YouTube*, uploaded by TED,

2 Sept. 2014, www.youtube/zORUUqJd81M.

Provide the author of the video, title of the video, the name of the source or container site (in italics), the date the video was posted online, and the online location, using the most direct URL available. In the case of a video that was posted by someone other than the author (as in the preceding example), insert the "uploaded by" information after the title of the hosting site.

37. Facebook post or comment

Cengage Learning. "Check out this timeline of milestones in #LGBTQ

history from the Gale Archives of Sexuality and Gender >>

#PrideMonth." Facebook, 21 June 2017, www.facebook.com/

CengageLearningCorporate/posts/1576411919060374.

38. Twitter post

@jkrums. "There's a plane in the Hudson. I'm on the ferry going to pick up

the people. Crazy." *Twitter*, 15 Jan. 2009, 12:36 p.m., twitter.com/

jkrums/statuses/1121915133.

39. Blog entry

Moroz, Sarah. "A Bygone Era of Big City Life." *Lens: Photography, Video and

Visual Journalism, The New York Times*, 19 June 2017, nyti.ms/2sQrRsL.

40. E-mail message

Kivett, George. "Re: Hydrogen Fuel Cell Technology." Received by Theodore

Ellis, 28 Jan. 2010.

Give the name of the author of the message, the title (taken from the subject line of the message and enclosed in quotation marks), and followed by a period, the recipient of the message, and the date the message was sent.

41. Wiki entry

"The Winds of Winter." *Game of Thrones Wiki*, Wikia, 8 June 2016,
gameofthrones.wikia.com/wiki/The_Winds_of_Winter. Accessed 27 Jan.
2017.

OTHER SOURCES

42. Personal interview

Ross, Laura. Personal interview. 26 June 2017.

43. Film

Bus Stop. Twentieth Century Fox, 1956.

Monroe, Marilyn, performer. *Bus Stop*, directed by Joshua Logan, Twentieth
Century Fox, 1956.

If you are discussing a film in a general way, provide the title of
the film in italics, the name of the company that distributed the
film, and the year the film was released (see the first example above).
If your focus is on the work of a specific contributor to the film,
then start your citation with the name of the contributor (last name
first), include a description of the contributor's role (e.g., director,
performer), followed by the film title and the names of other key
contributors if appropriate (see the second example above).

44. Television series

Downton Abbey. Created by Julian Fellowes, MASTERPIECE, 2010–2015.

Robbins, Anna Mary Scott, costume designer. *Downton Abbey*. Seasons 5–6,
MASTERPIECE, 2014-2015.

If you are discussing a television series in a general way, provide the title of the series in italics, the name of the company
that produced the series, and the years that the series was aired.
Television series, like films, have many contributors. Your citation can also include a key creator or contributor (as in the
examples above).

If your research focuses on the work of a specific contributor to the series, then start your citation with the name of the contributor (last name first), include a description of the contributor's role (e.g., director, performer) followed by a comma and an indication of the nature of the contribution (*performer, director, screenplay writer*, not in italics). See the second example above.

45. Radio program or television episode

"Back Where It All Began." *A Prairie Home Companion*, narrated by Garrison
    Keillor, National Public Radio, 2014.

"Confessions." *Breaking Bad*, created by Vince Gilligan, performance by Bryan
    Cranston, season 5, episode 11, AMC, 5 Aug. 2013.

As with a film or television series, if your focus is the contribution of a specific individual, place the individual's name and the contribution before the title. Otherwise, begin with the title of the segment (in quotation marks), the title of the program (in italics), other contributors when they are important to the focus of your research (such as the name of an author, performer, director, or narrator), and the season and episode numbers.

Depending on your research purposes, you might include the production company and the year the episode was broadcast. Or you might include the distribution company or network where the episode aired and the full date that the episode aired (as in the second example above). For example, if your focus includes the historical context of the episode, you may want to cite the exact date that it was aired.

46. Video streamed through app

The Crown. Netflix app, Left Bank Pictures/Sony Pictures Television Production
    UK, 2016.

47. Podcast streaming

Marc Maron, host. "Sofia Coppola." *WTF with Marc Maron*, episode 822,

22 June 2017, www.wtfpod.com/podcast/episode-822-sofia-coppola.

Downloaded, via app

Whitehurst, Annie Sage, performer. "Napoleon." *Limetown*, written by Dan

Moyer, episode 3, Two-Up Productions, 12 Oct. 2015. *Podcasts*, iTunes.

48. Sound recording

The White Stripes. "Seven Nation Army." *Elephant*, V2 Records, 2003.

Begin with the name of the performer, composer, or conductor, depending on which you prefer to emphasize. When referring to an individual song, provide its name in quotation marks after the name of the performer, composer, or conductor. Then provide the title of the album, the manufacturer's name, and the date of the recording. Note that the above entry should be alphabetized as though it begins with *w*, not *t*.

49. Play performance

Roulette. By Paul Weitz, directed by Tripp Cullmann, 9 Feb. 2004, John

Houseman Theater, New York.

Indicate the key contributors and their contributions (*directed by, performed by*) and the date of the performance followed by a comma. Then list the location of the performance (the theater and the city). Do not include the city if it is in the name of the venue.

50. Lecture or presentation

Joseph, Peniel. "The 1960's, Black History, and the Role of the NC A&T Four."

Gibbs Lecture, 5 Apr. 2010, North Carolina A&T State U, Greensboro.

Ryken, Leland. Class lecture. English 216, 4 Feb. 2010, Wheaton College, Illinois.

Provide the name of the speaker followed by a period. Then list the title of the lecture (if any) in quotation marks. If the lecture or presentation is untitled, provide a description after the name of the speaker. The sponsoring organization (if applicable) follows and then the date of the lecture or presentation. The location follows, including the city. The city need not be included if it is part of the name of the location.

51. Work of art

Lange, Dorothea. *Migrant Mother*. 1936, Prints and Photographs Division,

Library of Congress, Washington.

Provide the artist's name (inverted and followed by a period) and the title of the work (italicized and followed by a period). The date the work was created follows and then the name and location of the institution that houses the work. If the work of art has no title, include a brief description instead.

52. Video game

Fallout 4. Bethesda Softworks, 10 Nov. 2015, www.fallout4.com.

53. Graphic novel, comic book, cartoon, or comic strip

Martin, George R.R. *The Hedge Knight II: The Sworn Sword*. Pencils and inks

by Mike S. Miller, Jet City Comix, 2014.

Cheney, Tom. "Back Page by Tom Cheney." *The New Yorker*, 12 Jan. 2004, p. 88.

For a graphic novel or comic book, begin with the name of the author, then the italicized title. Following the title can be other contributors and a description of their contribution. Comic books are often published as part of a larger series. Include the title of the comic book (in italics) followed by a period. Then include the name of the series (in italics) when there is one, the issue number, the publisher, and the date of publication. For a cartoon or comic strip, begin with the name of the artist. Follow with the title of the cartoon or comic strip in quotation marks.

Include the italicized name of the publication where the cartoon or comic strip appeared followed by the date of publication and the page number.

54. Text message

Gray, Loretta. Message to the author, 30 June 2017.

55. Advertisement

McCormick Pure Vanilla Extract. *Cooking Light,* Mar. 2004, p. 177.

Adding descriptions of unusual or unexpected sources clarifies them for readers. Identify the item being advertised before the usual publication information.

56. Map or chart

Scottsdale and Vicinity. Rand McNally, 2000.

Treat the map or chart as you would an anonymous book before including the usual publication information.

57. Pamphlet or bulletin

Ten Ways to Be a Better Dad. National Fatherhood Institute, 2000.

An entry for a pamphlet is similar to one for a book. If an author is identified, list the author's name first.

58. Government publication

United States, Department of Agriculture, Center for Nutrition Policy and
    Promotion. *Stay Fit on Campus: 10 Tips for College Students to Stay Active*.
    Government Publishing Office, 2013, purl.fdlp.gov/GPO/gpo65065.

If no author is provided, list the name of the government (e.g., *United States, Montana,* or *New York City*) followed by a comma and the name of the agency issuing the publication. Then list any part of the agency that is specifically responsible for the publication. The title of the publication follows. Conclude with the usual publication data. If you have accessed the publication online, add the web location after the date of publication.

59. Historical document

Eisenhower, Dwight D. Farewell Address. 1961. *Our Documents: 100 Milestone Documents from the National Archives*, foreword by Michael Beschloss, Oxford UP, 2003, pp. 217-19.

60. Legal source
PRINT

Chavez v. Martinez. 538 US 760. Supreme Court of the United States. 2003. *United States Reports*, Government Printing Office, 2004.

ONLINE

Tennessee v. Lane. 541 US 509. Supreme Court of the United States. 2004. *Supreme Court Collection*, Legal Information Institute, Cornell U Law School, 28 Jan. 2014, www.law.cornell.edu/supct/html/02-1667 .ZS.html.

61. Public law
PRINT

No Child Left Behind Act of 2001. Pub. L. 107-10. 115 Stat. 1425-2094. 8 Jan. 2002.

ONLINE

Individuals with Disabilities Education Act. Pub. L. 105-17. 104 Stat. 587-698. Library of Congress, 4 June 1997, thomas.loc.gov/cgi-bin/query/z? j108:I06264:j108IGNACE.html.

MLA

The MLA recommends omitting a title page (unless your instructor requires one) and instead providing the identification on the first page of the paper. One inch from the top, on the left-hand side of the page, list your name, the name of the instructor, the name of the course, and the date—all double-spaced. Below these lines, center the title of the paper, which is in plain type (no italics, quotation marks, underlining, or boldface). Of course, if the title of your paper includes the title of a short or long work, you will use quotation marks or italics respectively and exclusively on that title. On the right-hand side of each page, one-half inch from the top, use your last name and the page number as a header. Double-space the text throughout the paper (including the Works Cited), and use one-inch margins on the sides and bottom. Indent every paragraph (including the first one) one-half inch.

Coles 1

Greg Coles

Dr. Cheryl Glenn

ENGL 101

21 April 2016

Slang Rebels

What is slang? Although the word *slang* is used often,
research by Bethany K. Dumas and Jonathan Lighter suggests
that people have very different opinions about which words and
phrases should be classified as slang (10). Robert L. Moore calls
slang a "notoriously slippery concept" (61). Summarizing several
definitions of slang, he states, "These definitions all have one
trait in common: they define slang in terms of an extensive list of
traits" (62). Among these traits are the idea that slang is usually
spoken instead of written (Hummon 77) and the idea that slang is
a response to or rebellion against social norms (Green 103; Moore
61). By combining these two ideas, I argue in this essay that slang
is a rebellion against the literate mindset—that is, against the
way that writing tries to make us think. Part of the reason slang
so easily takes hold of language (Mattiello 7) is that it fulfills our
desire to develop language in conversation with human beings

The running head includes the author's last name and page number.

Doublespace header and entire paper

Center the title.

Build a credible argument by analyzing and synthesizing definitions.

Two citations from different sources are separated with a semi-colon.

Coles 2

The thesis is clearly stated.

instead of following the rules of correctness and incorrectness that usually define written communication.

Each paragraph begins with an indent of one-half inch (or five spaces).

Most of today's readers would probably consider words like *gleek* (to squirt water between the teeth), *gurgitator* (a competitive eater), and *paleoconservative* (a very conservative person with outdated beliefs) to be made-up words. However, writes Mark Peters, "If 'a real word' is one with multiple citations by different authors over a substantial period of time, then they're all real as rain" (110). Though these words do not appear in most dictionaries, they fulfill the requirements of official words. Perhaps in fifty years they will be so much a part of our language that scientists and anthropologists will use them in formal papers.

The strong topic sentences shape the argument.

Hermann is clearly the source of the quotation, hence only a page number in the citation.

It is the nature of language to be constantly changing, observes Jean Aitchison (18). This effect is particularly noticeable in the area of slang. Slang words come quickly in and out of usage (Aitchison 21). Yet although slang itself might be called "ephemeral" (Mattiello 9) and "short-lived" (Senström 3), its effects on language can be permanent. Most slang disappears with time, but some slang terms transition into general usage and become part of the "established" language (Aitchison 19). Keith R. Herrmann provides a number of examples of now-established English words that began as military slang. Three such examples are the words *boycott*, *lynch*, and *shrapnel*, all of which were originally the last names of military officers (319).

Coles 3

Fig. 1. While the term *boycott* was originally a slang term named after Captain C. C. Boycott, the word is now common and is recognized by dictionaries as part of standardized English usage.

Pacific Press/Getty Images

> When a work has no author, use a shortened form of the work's title in your citation.

> The block quotation is introduced with a descriptive transitional sentence.

> The author's use of library research findings enhances his ethos and the logos.

> The citation for the block quotation usually includes author's last name and page number (except in the case of online sources). The final period appears at the end of the quotation.

Though these words are no longer considered slang by most people and are not classified as such by dictionaries (*Oxford; American*), they all came into being as slang terms. By the same logic, it is possible that *gleek, gurgitator,* and *paleoconservative* could lose their labels as slang and become a part of Standard English, no matter how strange or phony they may sound to people today. In a recent *New York Times* essay, Kory Stamper uses the flexibility of language to defend the validity of slang, writing,

> English is fluid and enduring: not a mountain, but
> an ocean. A word may drift down through time from
> one current of English (say, the language of World
> War II soldiers) to another (the slang of computer
> programmers). Slang words are quicksilver flashes of cool
> in the great stream. (A19)

MLA

Coles 4

There are two arguments most commonly used to condemn slang, and both rely on a print-literate, writing-based mindset. The first is that slang is uneducated and improper. Dumas and Lighter, summarizing the broad spectrum of views on slang, quote scholars who call slang an "epidemic disease" of language, "the advertisement of mental poverty," "at once a sign and a cause of mental atrophy" (6-7). Those who use slang are called "coarse," "ignorant," or "less educated" (6, 9). By attacking the education of slang users, these scholars reveal their own bias in favor of print literacy instead of spoken language. Education has long been defined in terms of reading and writing (Bellous). The very idea of scholarship, after all, implies the existence of writing. In cultures that do not write their language, there is no such thing as study (Ong 8-9). To be educated means something entirely different for literate people than it does in cultures that use only spoken words. Education in a non-writing culture involves the passing down of wisdom from one generation to the next through apprenticed, experiential learning; listening; repetition; and assimilation. It has nothing to do with internalizing linguistic rules—and without these rules, there is no reason to look down on slang as "rule breaking."

The second argument against slang states that slang is inferior to "standard" language. John C. Hodges calls slang "the sluggard's way of avoiding the search for the exact, meaningful word" (qtd. in Dumas and Lighter 5). Novelist Tom Robbins writes, "Slang . . .

This source is quoting from another source. Always try to cite from the original source.

Coles 5

devalues experience by standardizing and fuzzing it" (qtd. in Leahy 305). Both of these statements regard slang words as too vague to communicate well. Though they may give a general impression of what is meant, they do not speak precisely. If a thing is called awesome, for instance, we know only that the speaker thinks it good. If it is called delicious, we know that it *tastes* good. Formal language demands accuracy. Slang fails to meet the same standards.

Besides being vague, slang can also be ambiguous. "A major general trend among young people at the current time," writes Aitchison, "is the use of 'bad' words to mean 'good, excellent'" (21). Among the words she lists that may mean "good" are "wicked," "bad," "deadly," "filthy," and "savage." Because these words, in a slang context, mean the opposite of their dictionary definitions, they could easily lead to ambiguous communication. "Your shirt is filthy" might mean the shirt is great, or it might mean the wearer should consider a change of clothes. "This cake is deadly" could be a compliment for the cook or a caution for the people about to eat it. The easiest way to avoid this kind of confusion is to use only dictionary definitions. Slang, its detractors say, is too ambiguous to be useful in communication.

These complaints, once again, only make sense within the context of written literacy. In writing, the statement "This cake is deadly" is definitely ambiguous. In speech, however, its meaning could be made clear by the use of nonverbal cues. Accompanied

This strong topic sentence also serves as a transition between topics.

The author's demonstration of library research findings enhances his ethos and the logos.

MLA

Coles 6

by a smile from the speaker, the statement means that the cake is excellent; a look of horror on the speaker's face or a dead body nearby would suggest a more literal interpretation of the speaker's words. In spoken language, the meanings of words are communicated by context, "which is not, as in a dictionary, simply other words, but includes also gestures, vocal inflections, facial expression, and the entire human existential setting in which the real, spoken word always occurs" (Ong 47). A similar answer may be given in response to complaints of slang's vagueness. A physical context of extreme beauty would make the precise meaning of *awesome* clear.

Even in cases where context or nonverbal clues do not clarify ambiguity, spoken language can resolve this ambiguity by leaving room for listeners to ask clarifying questions whenever necessary. If the new arrival at the party still has not figured out whether the "deadly" cake is delicious or poisonous, she need only ask. Spoken language leaves room for creative or ambiguous speech, because words that are spoken do not always need to be understood on the first try. Writing, on the other hand, doesn't leave space for question asking. Walter Ong, reporting Plato's objections to the development of writing, observes,

> a written text is basically unresponsive. If you ask a person to explain his or her statement, you can get an explanation; if you ask a text, you get back nothing except the same, often stupid, words which called for your question in the first place (78).

MLA

Again, the author uses a topic sentence as a transitional sentence.

Writing doesn't get a second chance to be understood.

The need for complete clarity in writing may help explain why people tend to oppose the use of slang in writing more than in speech. Leslie N. Carraway, cautioning against the use of slang in scientific writing, does not argue that slang is altogether unhelpful, just that it is "more appropriate to familiar conversation than to formal speech or science writing" (365). Anna Leahy's objections to slang, specifically regarding its vagueness and inaccuracy, are also set specifically within the written context (305). On the other hand, slang's defenders typically treat it within the context of speech. Elisa Mattiello calls slang "the state-of-the-art vocabulary which people use in familiar relaxed conversations . . . in which educated formal registers would be situationally inappropriate and unconventional language is instead privileged" (35-36). From her perspective, slang and formal language are each appropriate in some contexts and inappropriate in others. For slang, she believes, the appropriate context is spoken conversation. Joseph P. Mazer and Stephen K. Hunt, who study slang in teacher-student communication, also praise slang as a useful tool for spoken communication while ignoring it in writing.

If slang were defended only in terms of speech and condemned only in terms of writing, there would be no need for disagreement. Thus, some of the current disagreement regarding slang could be avoided by specifying what form of slang is under

Instead of citing a specific page from this source, the writer has summarized the entire argument of the source.

discussion. If opinions like "Slang is good" and "Slang is bad" are modified to state that "Spoken slang is appropriate" and "Written slang is inappropriate," people who have previously disagreed may find unexpected common ground. Conflict still arises, though, when people who typically think about language in terms of writing try to make the rules of literacy apply to spoken language, or when people who primarily view language as a speaking tool try to carry the freedom of their speech into writing.

One of the typically recognized functions of slang is to "oppose established authority" (Moore 61). This raises the question of precisely which established authority is being opposed. Slang cannot be used as a weapon in opposition to just any authority. It does not, for the most part, oppose governmental authority because most governments have not legislated the use of slang. Nor could slang be used to oppose an authority that approved of slang. Slang, in itself, is not oppositional. It can oppose an authority only if that authority disapproves of slang. Because slang views language in terms of speech and violates the "rules" of writing, slang opposes authorities who try to enforce a rule-based mindset of written literacy. Most often, these authorities are parental and academic.

Slang is most often associated with adolescents and young adults (Moore 63), who are already stereotyped as rebellious apart from their linguistic preferences; therefore, it is easy to assume that slang is just one more weapon in the arsenal of youths intent on rebellion. However, this is not necessarily the case. Certainly people of this age have a tendency to rebel against authority, and it seems equally certain that slang is a part of this rebellion. Still, a distinction should be made between slang as a part of rebellion and slang as mere rebellion with no other rationale. Just because slang fights authority does not mean that it exists for the sole purpose of fighting authority. It is possible that adolescents and young adults who use slang are reacting, at least in part, against the literate mindset being forced onto them. Statements like "Why does it matter how I say it as long as you know what I'm saying?" reveal an innate understanding of language as a spoken, conversational tool defined by social interaction.

Walt Whitman calls slang "an attempt of common humanity to escape from bald literalism, and express itself illimitably" (573). It is no coincidence that the words *literalism* and *literacy* are so similar in sound: both are derived from the Latin *lit(t)era*, meaning "letter" (*Shorter Oxford*). Slang is an escape from the limits of written letters and the rules that come with them. It is, as William C. Gore writes, "a sign of life in language," a sign that "the structure of language is not liable to stiffen so as to become an inadequate means for the communication of new ideas" (197). In the conflict between spoken language and written language, slang terms are the fighting words of our spoken inheritance.

The author works to indentify with the interests of his audience, establishing an authentic emotional connection (pathos).

MLA

Coles 10

Works Cited

Aitchison, Jean. "Whassup? Slang and Swearing among School Children." *Education Review*, vol. 19, no. 2, Autumn 2006, pp. 18-24.

The American Heritage Dictionary of the English Language. 5th ed., Houghton Mifflin Harcourt, 2016.

Bellous, Joyce. "Spiritual and Ethical Orality in Children: Educating an Oral Self." *International Journal of Children's Spirituality*, vol. 5, no. 1, 2000, doi:10.1080/713670893.

Carraway, Leslie N. "Improve Scientific Writing and Avoid Perishing." *American Midland Naturalist*, vol. 155, no. 2, Apr. 2006, pp. 361-70.

Dumas, Bethany K., and Jonathan Lighter. "Is Slang a Word for Linguists?" *American Speech*, vol. 53, no. 1, Spring 1978, pp. 5-17.

Gore, William C. "Notes on Slang." *Modern Language Notes*, vol. 11, no. 7, 1896, pp. 193-98.

Green, Jonathon. "Slang by Dates." *Critical Quarterly*, vol. 48, no. 1, Spring 2006, pp. 99-104.

Herrmann, Keith R. "The War of Words." *War, Literature & the Arts: An International Journal of the Humanities*, vol. 18, nos. 1-2, 2006, pp. 319-23.

Hummon, David M. "College Slang Revisited: Language, Culture, and Undergraduate Life." *The Journal of Higher Education*, vol. 65, no. 1, Jan.-Feb. 1994, pp. 75-98.

MLA

The works-cited list begins on a new page, with the heading centered.

Every entry on the list begins flush with the left margin and has subsequent lines indented one-half inch (a hanging indent). Entries are listed in alphabetical order.

This entry documents an article from a professional journal.

Coles 11

Leahy, Anna. "Grammar Matters: A Creative Writer's Argument."
     Pedagogy, vol. 5, no. 2, Spring 2005, pp. 304-07.

Mattiello, Elisa. "The Pervasiveness of Slang in Standard and Non-
     Standard English." *Mots Palabras Words,* June 2005, pp. 7-41,
     www.ledonline.it/mpw/allegati/mpw0506Mattiello.pdf.

Mazer, Joseph P., and Stephen K. Hunt. "'Cool' Communication
     in the Classroom: A Preliminary Examination of Student
     Perceptions of Instructor Use of Positive Slang." *Qualitative
     Research Reports in Communication*, vol. 9, no. 1, 2008,
     pp. 20-28.

Moore, Robert L. "We're Cool, Mom and Dad Are Swell: Basic Slang
     and Generational Shifts in Values." *American Speech*, vol. 79,
     no. 1, Spring 2004, pp. 59-86.

Ong, Walter J. *Orality and Literacy*. Routledge, 2002.

Peters, Mark. *Bull Shit*. Three Rivers Press, 2015.

Senström, Anna-Brita. "From Slang to Slanguage: A Description Based
     on Teenage Talk." *I Love English Language*, aggslanguage
     .wordpress.com/slang-to-slanguage. Accessed 27 Feb. 2017.

Shorter Oxford English Dictionary. 6th ed., Oxford UP, 2007. 2 vols.

Stamper, Kory. "Slang for the Ages." *The New York Times*, 3 Oct.
     2014, nyti.ms/2kuGtqc.

Whitman, Walt. "Slang in America." *The Collected Writings of Walt
     Whitman: Prose Works 1892*, edited by Floyd Stovall, vol. 2,
     New York UP, 1964, pp. 572-76.

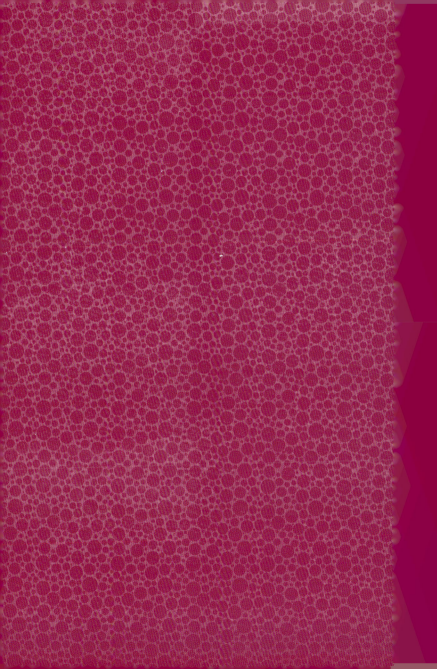

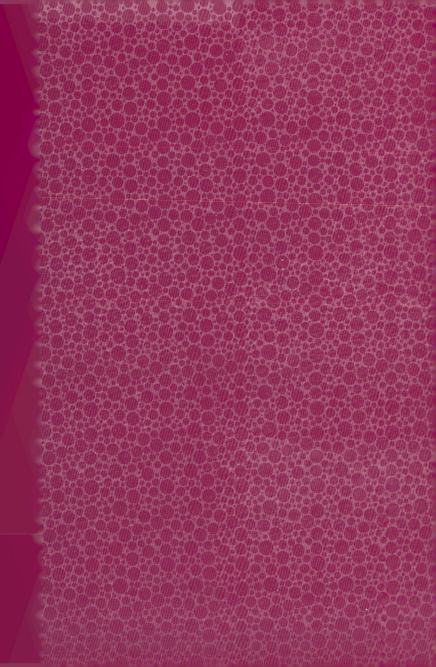

14 APA Documentation

The American Psychological Association (APA) publishes a style guide entitled *Publication Manual of the American Psychological Association* (currently, the sixth edition). Its documentation system (called an *author-date system*) is used in psychology and many other disciplines, including education, economics, and sociology.

14a APA-style in-text citations

APA-style in-text citations usually include just the last name(s) of the author(s) of the work and the year of publication. If you do not know the author's name, use a shortened version of the source's title instead.

Be sure to specify the page number(s) for any quotations you use in your paper. The abbreviation *p.* (for "page") or *pp.* (for "pages") should precede the number(s). If visible paragraph numbers are provided instead of page numbers, use the abbreviation *para.* For documents that have neither page nor paragraph numbers, include the name of the section or an abbreviated heading. Then determine the number of the paragraph and include that number.

The following examples are representative of the types of in-text citations you can expect to use.

> **Directory to APA-Style Parenthetical Citations**

1. Work by one author

Arguing that microbes are invaluable to our existence, Young (2016) describes them as "not takers of life but its guardian" (p. 11).

OR

Microbes are invaluable to our existence: They are "not takers of life but its guardian" (Young, 2016, p. 11).

Use commas to separate the author's name from the date and the date from the page number. Include page numbers only when quoting from the source.

2. Work by two authors

According to Goodie and Fortune (2013), "impaired control . . . is a gambler's belief that he or she cannot control his or her own problematic gambling behaviors" (p. 2).

OR

Many compulsive gamblers believe they have no control over their behaviors (Goodie & Fortune, 2013).

When the authors' names are in parentheses, use an ampersand (&) to separate them.

3. Work by more than two authors

Interference between conversation and driving occurs because both are "complex, multimodal, attention-demanding tasks" (Bergen, Medeiros-Ward, Wheeler, Drews, & Strayer, 2013, Introduction section, para. 2).

For works with three to five authors, cite all the authors the first time the work is referred to, but in subsequent references give only the last name of the first author followed by *et al.* (meaning "and others").

The research of Bergen et al. (2013) confirms previous studies "demonstrating that language use, even without a handheld device, interferes with successful control of a vehicle" (Discussion section, para. 2).

For works with six or more authors, provide only the last name of the first author followed by *et al.* in both the first and subsequent citations.

4. Anonymous work

Use a shortened version of the title to identify an anonymous work.

The rate of tobacco use among teens dropped over 17% in 20 years ("Teen Substance Use," 2016).

This citation refers to an article identified in the bibliography as "Teen substance use shows promising decline."

If the word *Anonymous* is used in the source itself to designate the author, it appears in place of an author's name.

The documents could damage the governor's reputation (Anonymous, 2017).

5. Two or more works by different authors in the same parenthetical citation

The coherence effect has been observed in decision-making tasks (Carpenter, Yates, Preston, & Chen, 2016; DeKay, Miller, Schley, & Erford, 2014).

Arrange the citations in alphabetical order, using a semicolon to separate them.

6. Two or more works by the same author in the same parenthetical citation

Corpus-based techniques are used in studies of language usage based on gender (Baker, 2010, 2014).

According to Pinker (2016a, 2016b), rates of violent crime in the United States are lower than they were in the late 20th century.

Order the publication dates of works by the same author from earliest to most recent; however, if the works have the same publication date, distinguish the dates with lowercase letters (a, b, c, and so on) assigned according to the order in which the entries for the works are listed in your bibliography. The letters should be included in bibliographic entries as well.

7. Personal communication

State educational outcomes are often interpreted differently by teachers in the same school (J. K. Jurgensen, personal communication, May 4, 2017).

Letters, memos, e-mail messages, interviews, and telephone conversations are cited in the text only, not in the reference list.

8. Indirect source

Cook (2016) points out Eleanor Roosevelt's conviction that "our future is linked with the welfare of the world as a whole" (pp. 569-570).

Eleanor Roosevelt (as cited in Cook, 2016) believed that "our future is linked with the welfare of the world as a whole" (pp. 569-570).

In the reference list, include a bibliographic entry for the source read, not for the original source. Use an indirect source only when you are unable to obtain the original.

9. Block quotation

In examining the nature of grit, Duckworth (2016) observed the performance of West Point cadets, whose typical day of initial training is highly structured:

> The day begins at 5:00 a.m. By 5:30, cadets are in formation, standing
> at attention, honoring the raising of the United States flag. Then
> follows a hard workout—running or calisthenics—followed by a non-
> stop rotation of marching in formation, classroom instruction, weapons
> training, and athletics. Lights out, to a melancholy bugle song called
> "Taps," occurs at 10:00 p.m. (pp. 4-5)

Indent quotations of forty words or more. Do not use quotation marks to set off block quotations; however, you will need
to use double quotation marks to set off quotations within
a block quotation. Place the page citation at the end of the
quoted material, outside the end punctuation.

14b APA-style reference list

All of the works you cite should be listed at the end of your
paper, beginning on a separate page with the heading References. The following tips will help you prepare your list.

TIPS FOR PREPARING A REFERENCE LIST

- Center the heading References one inch from the top of the page.

- Include entries for only those sources you explicitly cite in your
  paper but not for personal communications or original works cited
  in indirect sources.

- Arrange the list of works alphabetically by the author's last
  name or by the last name of the first author. For a work without
  an author, alphabetize the entry according to the first important
  word in the title.

- If you use more than one work by the same author(s), arrange
  the entries according to the date of publication, placing the entry
  with the earliest date first. (See Entry 6.) If two or more works by
  the same author(s) have the same publication date, the entries

(Continued on page 172)

(Continued)

are arranged so that the titles of the works are in alphabetical order, according to the first important word in each title; lower-case letters are then added to the date (2017a, 2017b) to distinguish the works. (See Entry 7.)

- When an author's name appears both in a single-author entry and as the first name in a multiple-author entry, place the single-author entry first.

- Type the first line of each entry flush with the left margin and indent subsequent lines one-half inch or five spaces (a hanging indent).

- Double-space between lines of each entry and between entries.

APA

Directory to APA Entries for the Reference List

APA

AUTHORS IN REFERENCE ENTRIES

Citations begin with the authors' last names, followed by initials for first and middle names. Consult this section when deciding how to list different numbers of authors.

1. One author

Read, A. (2013, May). Rural sustainability: Factors and resources for

communities to consider. *Public Management 95*(4), 14-17. Retrieved

from http://icma.org/en/press/pm_magazine/about_pm

2. Two to seven authors

Zenz, G., Tahmasebi, N., & Risse, T. (2013). Towards mobile language

evolution exploitation. *Multimedia Tools and Applications 66*(1),

147–159. doi:l0.1007/s11042-011-0973-0

Invert the last names and initials of all authors. Use a comma after each last name and after each set of initials except the last. Use an ampersand (in addition to the comma) before the last author's name.

3. Eight or more authors

Kawakami, K., Phills, C. E., Greenwald, A. G., Simard, D., Pontiero, J., Brnjas, A., . . . Dovidio, J. F. (2012). In perfect harmony: Synchronizing the self to activated social categories. *Journal of Personality and Social Psychology, 102*(3), 562–575.

List the first six names followed by a comma and three ellipsis points and then the last author's name.

4. No author listed

Atlas of the world (19th ed.). (2012). New York, NY: Oxford University Press.

Start the entry with the title.

5. Corporate author

American Psychiatric Association. (2013). *Diagnostic and statistical manual of mental disorders* (5th ed.). Washington, DC: Author.

When the author and the publisher are the same, use the word *Author* as the publisher at the end of the entry.

6. Two or more works by the same author

The work published first is listed first.

Lewis, M. (2010). *The big short: Inside the doomsday machine*. New York, NY: W. W. Norton.

Lewis, M. (2017). *The undoing project: A friendship that changed our minds*. New York, NY: W. W. Norton.

7. Two or more works by the same author published in the same year

If works appear in the same year, list them alphabetically by title and add letters (*a*, *b*, and so on) to the year. These letters should match those used in the in-text citations.

Wheelen, C. (2013a). *The centrist manifesto*. New York, NY: W. W. Norton.

Wheelen, C. (2013b). *Naked statistics: Stripping the dread from the data*. New York, NY: W. W. Norton.

ARTICLES (PRINT)

8. Article in a journal paginated by volume

Bean, S., & Groth-Marnat, G. (2016). Video gamers and personality: A five-

factor model to understand game playing style. *Psychology of Popular*

Media Culture, 5, 27–38. doi:10.1037/ppm0000025

Capitalize only the first word of the title and subtitle (if there is one) and any proper nouns. Italicize the title of the journal; capitalize all major words, as well as any other words consisting of four or more letters. Also italicize the volume number. Some journals include a DOI (digital object identifier) on the first page of an article, in both print and electronic versions. Include the DOI at the end of the entry. When each issue in a volume does not begin with page 1, only the volume number is given.

9. Article in a journal paginated by issue

Hall-Lew, L., & Stephens, N. (2013). Country talk. *Journal of English*

Linguistics, 40(3), 256-280.

When each issue includes page 1, provide the issue number (placed in parentheses) directly after the volume number (italicized).

10. Abstract of a journal article

Huang, H. D., & Hung, S. A. (2013). Comparing the effects of test anxiety

on independent and integrated speaking test performance [Abstract].

TESOL Quarterly, 47(2), 244-269.

11. Article in a monthly, biweekly, or weekly magazine

Finkel, M. (2013, June). First Australians. *National Geographic, 223*(6), 66–83.

For monthly publications, provide both the year and the month. For magazines published weekly or biweekly, add the day of the issue: (2013, May 8).

CITATION MAP 14.1: ARTICLE IN A JOURNAL, APA STYLE

To cite an article from a journal paginated by volume, include the following elements. Issue numbers are included only for articles from journals paginated by issue.

FIRST PAGE OF ARTICLE

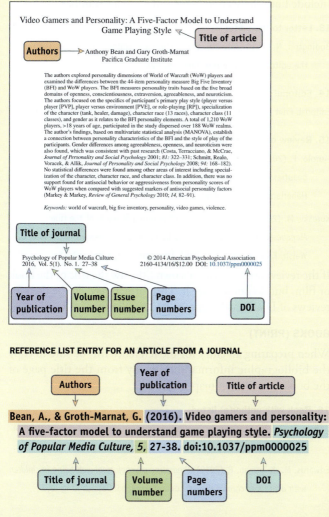

Title of article

Video Gamers and Personality: A Five-Factor Model to Understand Game Playing Style

Authors

Anthony Bean and Gary Groth-Marnat
Pacifica Graduate Institute

The authors explored personality dimensions of World of Warcraft (WoW) players and examined the differences between the 44-item personality measure Big Five Inventory (BFI) and WoW players. The BFI measures personality traits based on the five broad domains of openness, conscientiousness, extraversion, agreeableness, and neuroticism. The authors focused on the specifics of participant's primary play style (player versus player [PVP], player versus environment [PVE], or role-playing [RP]), specialization of the character (tank, healer, damage), character race (13 races), character class (11 classes), and gender as it relates to the BFI personality elements. A total of 1,210 WoW players, >18 years of age, participated in the study dispersed over 188 WoW realms. The author's findings, based on multivariate statistical analysis (MANOVA), establish a connection between personality characteristics of the BFI and the style of play of the participants. Gender differences among agreeableness, openness, and neuroticism were also found, which was consistent with past research (Costa, Terracciano, & McCrae, *Journal of Personality and Social Psychology* 2001; *81*: 322–331; Schmitt, Realo, Voracek, & Allik, *Journal of Personality and Social Psychology* 2008; *94*: 168–182). No statistical differences were found among other areas of interest including specialization of the character, character race, and character class. In addition, there was no support found for antisocial behavior or aggressiveness from personality scores of WoW players when compared with suggested markers of antisocial personality factors (Markey & Markey, *Review of General Psychology* 2010; *14*, 82–91).

Keywords: world of warcraft, big five inventory, personality, video games, violence.

Title of journal

Psychology of Popular Media Culture
2016, Vol. 5(1). No. 1. 27–38

© 2014 American Psychological Association
2160-4134/16/$12.00 DOI: 10.1037/ppm0000025

| **Year of publication** | **Volume number** | **Issue number** | **Page numbers** | **DOI** |

REFERENCE LIST ENTRY FOR AN ARTICLE FROM A JOURNAL

| **Authors** | **Year of publication** | **Title of article** |

Bean, A., & Groth-Marnat, G. (2016). Video gamers and personality: A five-factor model to understand game playing style. *Psychology of Popular Media Culture, 5*, 27-38. doi:10.1037/ppm0000025

| **Title of journal** | **Volume number** | **Page numbers** | **DOI** |

12. Article in a newspaper

Das, A. (2014, October 24). Benefit puts the wind in his sails. *The Wall Street Journal*, pp. C1-C2.

Include both the section letter and the page number.

13. Letter to the editor

Budington, N. (2010, July 20). Social class and college admissions [Letter to the editor]. *The New York Times*, p. A26.

14. Editorial

Editorial: Print is dead! Or is it? [Editorial]. (2012). *New Oxford Review, 79*(10), 4-7.

15. Review of book or film

Murolo, P. (2016). The difficulty of solidarity [Review of the book *Striking beauties: Women apparel workers in the US South, 1930–2000,* by M. Haberland]. *Women's Review of Books, 33*(6), 16-17.

Koresky, M. (2016). The world is full of weeping [Review of the film *Manchester by the sea,* produced by Damon, M., Steward, K., Moore, C., Walsh, K. J., & Beck, L., 2016]. *Film Comment, 52*(6), 48-52.

If the review does not have its own title, use the title of the book or film, but do not italicize it. This format may also be used for reviews of DVDs, video games, and similar types of media.

BOOKS (PRINT)

When preparing an entry for the reference list, be sure to copy the bibliographic information directly from the title page of the book (see citation map 14.2).

16. Book with author(s) listed

Gehart, D. R. (2016). *Case documentation in counseling and psychotherapy: A theory-informed, competency-based approach*. Stamford, CT: Cengage.

Edwards, M., & Titman, P. (2010). *Promoting psychological well-being in children with acute and chronic illness*. London, England: Jessica Kingsley.

CITATION MAP 14.2: BOOK, APA STYLE

Include the following elements when citing a book.

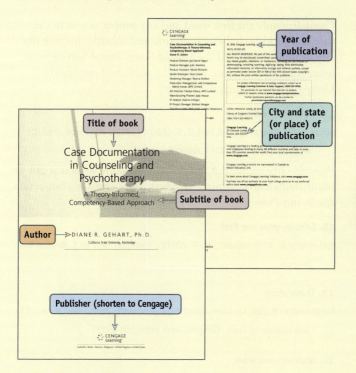

Title of book

Case Documentation in Counseling and Psychotherapy

A Theory-Informed, Competency-Based Approach ← **Subtitle of book**

Author ▸ DIANE R. GEHART, Ph.D.
California State University, Northridge

Year of publication

City and state (or place) of publication

Publisher (shorten to Cengage)

REFERENCE LIST ENTRY FOR A BOOK

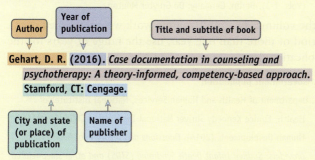

Author | **Year of publication** | **Title and subtitle of book**

Gehart, D. R. (2016). *Case documentation in counseling and psychotherapy: A theory-informed, competency-based approach.* Stamford, CT: Cengage.

City and state (or place) of publication | **Name of publisher**

Capitalize only the first word and any proper nouns in the title and subtitle. Italicize both title and subtitle. Include the city of publication and the United States Postal Service two-letter state abbreviation. For books published outside the United States, include the country.

17. Book with editor(s)

Reich, J. W., Zautra, A. J., & Hall, J. S. (Eds.). (2012). *Handbook of adult resilience*. New York, NY: Guilford Press.

Provide only enough of the publisher's name so that it can be identified clearly. Omit *Publishers, Inc.*, and *Co.*, but retain *Books* and *Press*.

18. Edition after the first

Radvansky, G. A., & Ashcraft, M. H. (2013). *Cognition* (6th ed.). Boston, MA: Pearson.

19. Translation

Gombrowicz, W. (2014). *Trans-Atlantyk* (D. Borchardt, Trans.) New Haven, CT: Yale University Press. (Original work published 1953)

20. Multivolume work

Li, Y., & Wei, L. (2013-2015). *Language policies and practices in China* (Vols. 1-3). Berlin, Germany: De Gruyter Mouton.

If the volumes in a multivolume work were published over a period of more than one year, use the range of years for the publication date.

21. Government publication

U.S. Department of Health and Human Services, National Institutes of Health, Eunice Kennedy Shriver National Institute of Child Health and Human Development. (2014). *Questions and answers for health care providers: Sudden Infant Death Syndrome (SIDS) and other sleep-related causes of infant death* (NIH Publication No. 14-7202). Washington, DC: Government Printing Office.

22. Chapter or article from an edited book

Canavan, G. (2016). Don't point that gun at my mum: Geriatric zombies. In

L. Servitje & S. Vint (Eds.), *The walking med: Zombies and the medical*

image (pp. 17-38). State College: The Pennsylvania State University Press.

If the publisher is a university press whose name mentions a state, do not include the state abbreviation.

23. Selection from a reference work

Evans, K. M. (2014). Advertising. In *Encyclopedia of business and finance* (3rd

ed., Vol. 1, pp. 16-20). Farmington Hills, MI: Gale.

24. Republished book

Plath, S. (2015). *The bell jar*. London, England: Faber & Faber. (Original work

published in 1966)

25. Book with a title within its title

Sørbø, M. N. (2014). *Irony and idyll: Jane Austen's* Pride and prejudice *and*

Mansfield Park *on screen*. Amsterdam, The Netherlands: Rodopi.

A title within a book title is not italicized. Capitalize only the first word of the title and subtitle (if there is one) and any proper nouns.

ONLINE SOURCES

The APA guidelines for online sources are similar to those for print sources. Many scholarly journals use a digital object identifier (DOI) to simplify searching for an article. The DOI is listed on the first page of the article, which usually contains the abstract. Citation map 14.3 shows the location of a DOI and other pertinent bibliographic information on the first page of an online journal. If available, insert the DOI (without a period following it) at the end of the entry.

To cite an article without a DOI, use the URL for the periodical's home page. If the URL has to continue on a new line, break it before a punctuation mark or other special character. Do not add a period after the URL.

If you find that some bibliographic information is missing, follow these guidelines:

- Missing author → Begin with the title.
- Missing title → Place a description of the document in square brackets (e.g., [Audio file]).
- Missing author and title → Begin with a description of the document in square brackets.
- Missing date → Use *n.d.* (not italicized) for *no date*. If the date can be estimated, use *ca.* and the approximate date.

26. Article from a database

Schantz, A. D., & Bruk-Lee, V. (2016). Workplace social stressors, drug-

alcohol-tobacco use, and coping strategies. *Journal of Workplace*

Behavioral Health, *31*, 222-241. doi:10.1080/15555240.2016.1213638

This article comes from a journal paginated by volume. If the article you have selected is from a journal paginated by issue (each issue has page 1), include the issue number as well (see Entry 9). The following entry is for a magazine article.

Specter, M. (2017, January 2). Rewriting the code of life. *The New Yorker*,

92(43), 34-43. Retrieved from http://www.newyorker.com

27. Article from an online journal

Buhrmester, M. D., Blanton, H., & Swann, W. B., Jr. (2011). Implicit self-esteem:

Nature, measurement, and a new way forward. *Journal of Personality and*

Social Psychology, *100*(2), 365-385. doi:10.1037/a0021341

Stewart, J. (2014). Violence and nonviolence in Buddhist animal ethics.

Journal of Buddhist Ethics, 21, 623-655. Retrieved from http://blogs

.dickinson.edu/buddhistethics/

28. Article from an online magazine

Engber, D. (2016, December 21). The irony effect: How the scientist who

founded the science of mistakes ended up mistaken. *Slate*. Retrieved

from http://www.slate.com

CITATION MAP 14.3: ARTICLE IN A DATABASE, APA STYLE

Include the following elements when citing an article in a database. If there is no digital object identifier (DOI), use the URL for the journal's home page instead of the URL of the article.

DATABASE RECORD FOR AN ARTICLE

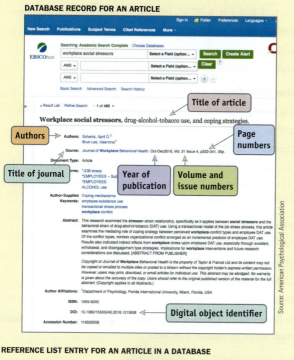

REFERENCE LIST ENTRY FOR AN ARTICLE IN A DATABASE

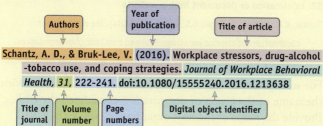

Authors	Year of publication	Title of article

Schantz, A. D., & Bruk-Lee, V. (2016). Workplace stressors, drug-alcohol-tobacco use, and coping strategies. *Journal of Workplace Behavioral Health, 31,* 222-241. doi:10.1080/15555240.2016.1213638

Title of journal	Volume number	Page numbers	Digital object identifier

APA

APA

29. Article from an online newspaper

Shellenbarger, S. (2010, July 21). Kids quit the team for more family time. *The Wall Street Journal.* Retrieved from http://online.wsj.com/home-page

30. Online book or electronic version of print book

Burgher, K. E., & Snyder, M. B. (2014). *Volunteering*. Retrieved from http://www .bookboon.com

Lewis, M. (2017). *The undoing project: A friendship that changed our minds*. [Kindle Paperwhite version]. Retrieved from http://www.amazon.com

31. Online book chapter

Attardo, S. (2015). Humor and laughter. In Tannen, D., Hamilton, H. E., & Schiffrin, D. (Eds.), *The handbook of discourse analysis* (pp. 168-188). http:dx.doi.org/10.1002/9781118584194

If the book has a DOI, place that number after http://dx.doi .org/. If there is no DOI, use the URL of the home page of the online resource.

32. Lecture notes or PowerPoint presentation posted online

Schneider, G. E. (2014). *Lecture 26: Forebrain Evolution* [Lecture notes]. Retrieved from https://ocw.mit.edu/courses/brain-and-cognitive -sciences/9-14-brain-structure-and-its-origins-spring-2014 /lecture-notes/

To cite PowerPoint slides, place *PowerPoint presentation* instead of *Lecture notes* in square brackets.

33. Information or document from a website

Thomas, K.A., DeScioli, P., Haque, O.S., & Pinker, S. (2014). The psychology of coordination and common knowledge. Retrieved from http://stevenpinker.com /files/pinker/files/the_psychology_of_coordination_and_common_knowledge.pdf

For some material from the web, you will need to begin with the name of the group or organization considered the author. Provide the name of the host organization before the URL.

CITATION MAP 14.4: ONLINE REPORT, APA STYLE

Include the following elements when citing an online report.

TITLE PAGE OF A WORK FROM A WEBSITE

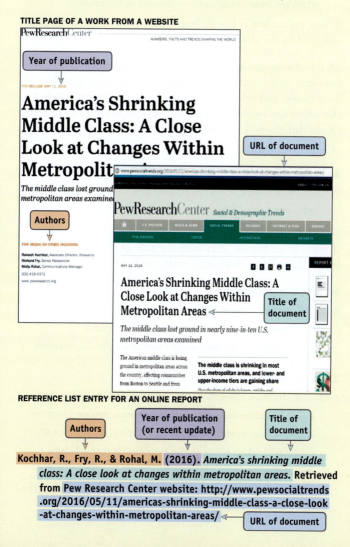

REFERENCE LIST ENTRY FOR AN ONLINE REPORT

Kochhar, R., Fry, R., & Rohal, M. (2016). *America's shrinking middle class: A close look at changes within metropolitan areas.* Retrieved from Pew Research Center website: http://www.pewsocialtrends.org/2016/05/11/americas-shrinking-middle-class-a-close-look-at-changes-within-metropolitan-areas/

Science Education Resource Center. (2016). *Engagement triggers and tasks for
    interactive segments.* Retrieved from Carleton College website:
    http://serc.carleton.edu/sp/library/interactive/triggers.html

When no author is listed, begin with title of the document,
followed by the date.

34. E-mail messages and other personal communication
Personal communications such as e-mail messages, letters,
interviews, and telephone conversations are not included in
the reference list but should be cited in the text as follows:
(S. L. Johnson, personal communication, September 3,
2017).

35. Online encyclopedia
Burton, B. K., & Dunn, C. P. (2016). Ethics of care. In *Encyclopedia
    Britannica.* Retrieved from https://www.britannica.com/topic
    /ethics-of-care

If there is no author, start with the title of the entry, followed
by the date. For a Wikipedia entry, see Entry 46.

36. Article in a newsletter
Brady, B. Essential strategies for teaching large classes. (2013, August).
    TESOL Connections. Retrieved from http://www.tesol.org
    /read-and-publish/newsletters-other-publications/tesol-connections

37. Online report
Kochhar, R., Fry, R., & Rohal, M. (2016). *America's shrinking middle class:
    A close look at changes within metropolitan areas.* Retrieved from Pew
    Research Center website: http://www.pewsocialtrends.org/2016/05/11
    /americas-shrinking-middle-class-a-close-look-at-changes-within
    -metropolitan-areas/

If the report has a number, mention the number in parentheses after the title: *Title* (Report No. XX).

38. Online government document

Zelazo, P. D., Blair, C. B., & Willoughby, M. T. (2016). *Executive function:*
   Implications for education (NCER 2017–2000). Washington, DC: National
   Center for Education Research, Institute of Education Sciences, U.S.
   Department of Education. Retrieved from Institute of Education Sciences
   website: https://ies.ed.gov/ncer/pubs/20172000/pdf/20172000.pdf

Note that the first letter of a title or a subtitle is capitalized.

39. Online audio and video

Minow, N. (1961, May 9). *Television and the public interest* [Audio file].
   Retrieved from http://www.americanrhetoric.com/top100speechesall.html

For podcasts, place the main contributor at the beginning of
the entry; place in parentheses the contributor's role (producer,
director, writer, host, presenter). Place between square brackets
the medium (audio podcast or video podcast).

Crespi, S. (Presenter). (2017, March 9). *Human pheromones lightly debunked,*
   ignoring cyberattacks, and designer chromosomes [Audio podcast]. Retrieved
   from http://www.sciencemag.org/podcast/podcast-human-pheromones
   -lightly-debunked-ignoring-cyberattacks-and-designer-chromosomes

For videos, pay special attention to the URL. A TED talk
viewed on the TED website will differ from a TED talk viewed
on YouTube.

Autor, D. (2016, September). *David Autor: Why are there still so many jobs?*
   [Video file]. Retrieved from https://www.ted.com/talks/david_autor_
   why_are _there_still_so_many_jobs

Autor, D. (2016, September). *David Autor: Why are there still so many jobs?* [Video
   file]. Retrieved from https://www.youtube.com/watch?v=KbEwNQNJWK4

40. Dissertation from a database

Aakre, J. M. (2010). Attributional style in schizophrenia: Associations with
   suspiciousness and depressed mood (Doctoral dissertation). Retrieved
   from http://www.ohiolink.edu

41. Interview published online

Bell, G. (2012). Why people really love technology: An interview with

    Genevieve Bell [Interview by A. C. Madrigal]. Retrieved from

    http://www.theatlantic.com/

An interview you conducted personally is considered a personal communication. See entry 34.

42. Map or chart

Central Intelligence Agency (Cartographer). (2011). China physiography

    [Map]. Retrieved from https://www.cia.gov/Library/publications

    /cia-maps-publications/

43. Speech or address

The White House, Office of the Press Secretary. (2013, April 23).

    Remarks by the president at teacher of the year event. Retrieved from

    http://www.whitehouse.gov/the-press-office/2013/04/23

    /remarks-president-teacher-year-event

44. Mobile application (app) reference entry

Resilience. (2016). In The American Heritage Dictionary of the English

    Language (5th ed.) [Mobile application software]. Retrieved from

    https://itunes.apple.com/us/app/american-heritage-english

    /id1118313580?mt=8

SOCIAL MEDIA

45. Blog posts and comments

Myers, P. Z. (2015, January 6). The genetic load problem [Web log post].

    Retrieved from http://scienceblogs.com/pharyngula/2015/01/06

    /the-genetic-load-problem/

If you are quoting a comment instead of the original post, place in square brackets *Web log comment* (not in italics).

46. Wiki entry

Déjà vu. (2016, December 18). In *Wikipedia*. Retrieved from http://en
.wikipedia.org/wiki/Deja_vu

47. Facebook page, individual or group author

Murray, P. [Patty]. (2016, November 13). The path forward [Facebook page].
Retrieved February 10, 2017, from https://www.facebook.com/notes
/patty-murray/the-path-forward/10154742426514640

Hawaii Emergency Management Agency. (2016, December 21). Protect Hawai'i
from mosquito-borne diseases [Facebook page]. Retrieved January 2,
2017, from https://www.facebook.com/HawaiiEMA/

48. Tweet, individual author and group author

Holthaus, E. [EricHolthaus]. (2017, January 1). Now that it's over, we can
say for sure: 2016 was the warmest year we've ever measured on Earth
[Tweet]. Retrieved from https://twitter.com/EricHolthaus
/status/815638631775731712

Mayo Clinic. [MayoMedEd]. (2017, January 3). A recent @MayoClinic study
finds that post-op complication measurements differ. mayocl.in/2j4FLDg
[Tweet]. Retrieved from https://twitter.com/mayomeded?lang=en

49. Social media video

Gladwell, M. [Malcolm]. (2016, July 11). Revisionist history: The big man
can't shoot [Video file]. Retrieved from https://www.facebook.com
/MalcolmGladwellBooks/videos/vb.480164368705460
/1061972320524659/?type=2&theater

OTHER SOURCES

50. Film, video, or DVD

Seidler, D. (Writer), & Hooper, T. (Director). (2011). *The king's speech* [Motion
picture]. England: Momentum Pictures.

51. Television series episode

Weiner, M. (Writer), & Hornbacher, S. (Director). (2013). The doorway
    [Television series episode]. In M. Weiner (Executive producer), *Mad
    men*. New York, NY: AMC.

If referring to the series as a whole, write *Television series* (not in italics) in the square brackets.

52. Advertisement

RosettaStone [Advertisement]. (2010, July). *National Geographic, 218*(1), 27.

53. Work of art

Lin, M. (2014). *Cloudline: Mt. Rose at 8,500 ft.* [Sculpture]. Reno, NV: Nevada
    Museum of Art.

Nu, W., & Aung, T. W. (2012). *Four pieces (of white)* [Painting]. New York, NY:
    Guggenheim Museum.

54. Photograph

[Photograph of Louise Bieriot]. (1909). Bain Collection. Library of Congress,
    Washington, DC.

If you are using a photograph you have taken yourself, you do not need to include an entry on your references page.

55. Video game

Pokémon Moon [Video game]. Bellevue, WA: The Pokémon Company International.

14c Sample APA-style paper

The APA recognizes that a paper may have to be modified so that it adheres to an instructor's requirements. The following boxes offer tips for preparing a title page, an abstract page, and the body of a typical student paper. For tips on preparing a reference list, see 14b.

TIPS FOR PREPARING THE TITLE PAGE OF AN APA-STYLE PAPER

- The title page includes both the full title of the paper and a shortened version of it. The shortened version, along with a page number, is placed in the header. On the left side of the header, include the words "Running head:" (note the colon) and a version of your title that consists of no more than fifty characters. Use all uppercase letters for this title. On the right side of the header, insert the page number. The title page is page 1 of your paper.

- Place the full title in the upper half of the page with your name below it. You may include your affiliation or a course name or number if your instructor requests one. Double-space these lines.

TIPS FOR PREPARING THE ABSTRACT AND THE BODY OF AN APA-STYLE PAPER

- The header for the remaining parts of the paper (including the abstract page, which is page 2) is similar to the header on the title page. It should have the shortened title on the left and the page number on the right. The body of the paper begins on page 3.

- Center the word *Abstract* (not in italics) one inch from the top of the page.

- Unless your instructor provides a word limit, be sure that your abstract is no more than 250 words. For advice on summarizing, see **11f**.

- Double-space throughout the body of the abstract. Do not indent the first line of the abstract.

- Provide the title again on page 3. Center it one inch from the top of the page.

- Use one-inch margins on both the left and right sides of all pages.

- Double-space throughout the body of the paper, indenting each paragraph one-half inch or five to seven spaces.

(Continued on page 192)

APA

(Continued)

- Use headings to set off sections and subsections. The APA specifies five levels of headings, but most papers that students write require only the first two or three levels:

Level 1 headings are centered and boldfaced, with each major word capitalized:

Methodology for Data Analysis

Level 2 headings are flush with the left margin and boldfaced, with each major word capitalized:

Materials and Procedures

Level 3 headings are boldfaced and indented. They begin with a capital letter and end with a period.

    Sampling procedures.

Level 4 headings are boldfaced, italicized, and indented. They begin with a capital letter and end with a period.

    Use of a random generator.

Level 5 headings are italicized and indented. They begin with a capital letter and end with a period.

    Problems with general data points.

Running head: SOCIAL STATUS OF AN ART   1

The running head should consist of no more than 50 characters.

The Social Status of an Art:

Historical and Current Trends in Tattooing

Rachel L. Pinter and Sarah M. Cronin

Central Washington University

Use one-inch margi on both sides of th page.

APA

If required by the instructor, the course name and number replace the institutional affiliation.

SOCIAL STATUS OF AN ART   1 inch   2

1/2 inch

Abstract

Current research demonstrates that the social practice of tattooing

has changed greatly over the years. Not only have the images

chosen for tattoos and the demographic of people getting tattoos

changed, but the ideology behind tattooing itself has evolved.

This paper first briefly describes the cross-cultural history of the

practice. It then examines current social trends in the United

States and related ideological issues.

Center the heading.

An abstract is generally not longer than 250 words.

APA

The Social Status of an Art: Historical and

Current Trends in Tattooing

Tattoos, defined as marks made by inserting pigment into the skin, have existed throughout history in countless cultures. Currently, tattoos are considered popular art forms. They can be seen on men and women from all walks of life in the United States, ranging from a trainer at the local gym to a character on a television show or even a sociology professor. Due to an increase in the popularity of tattooing, studies of tattooing behavior have proliferated as researchers attempt to identify trends. This paper seeks to explore both the history of tattooing and its current practice in the United States.

Artifacts such as 7,000-year-old engravings attest to the long history of tattooing (Krcmarik, 2003). Tattoos have been identified on a number of Egyptian and Nubian mummies (Krcmarik, 2003), as well as on Ötzi, the 5,300-year-old Iceman mummy found in the Alps (Owen, 2013). However, unlike the tattoos displayed today, early tattoos may have had purposes other than adornment. Ötzi's tattoos, for example, are thought to mark acupuncture points (Owen, 2013).

The practice of tattooing is not only old but widespread as well. In Asia, tattooing has existed for thousands of years in Chinese, Japanese, Middle Eastern, and Indian cultures (Krcmarik, 2003). In the British Isles, the pre-Roman Picts living in present-day Scotland practiced tattooing, but the type of tattooing recognized today did not flourish until the 19th century (Perzanowski, 2013). Many of the sailors traveling with Captain James Cook returned to England with tales of exotic tattooing practices and sometimes with actual tattoos.

Center the title and subtitle.

Use one-inch margins on both sides of the page.

The writers' thesis statement forecasts the content of the essay.

The writers provide historical and cultural information about tattooing.

SOCIAL STATUS OF AN ART   4

The Samoans in the South Pacific, whom Cook and his crew would have seen, are famous for their centuries-old tattooing practice, known as *tatau*—the word from which *tattoo* is said to have originated. The Maori of New Zealand are also well known for their hand-carved facial tattoos, known as *Moko* (see Figure 1).

In the western hemisphere, tattooing has been noted in the written accounts of European explorers and colonists who encountered tattooed members of indigenous tribes such as the Mayans in Central America and the Natchez who lived in present-day Mississippi (Perzanowski, 2013). Tattooing became popular in the United States during the 1900s, with a dramatic rise in the 1960s (Krcmarik, 2003).

Clearly, the history of tattooing spans generations and cultures. The practice has gained and lost popularity, often as a result of rather extreme changes in the ideologies supporting or discouraging it. This roller-coaster pattern of acceptance is well

Tim Graham/Getty Images

Figure 1. **A Maori man with a facial tattoo.** From Tim Graham (Photographer). (n.d.). Traditional Tattoos on Face of Maori Warrior [Photograph]. Retrieved from http://www.gettyimages.com/detail/photo/maori-warrior-uk-high-res-stock-photography/sb10066698pt-002

SOCIAL STATUS OF AN ART   5

demonstrated in the United States. Since the 19th century, the

wearing of tattoos has allowed for subculture identification by

such persons as sailors, bikers, circus "freak" performers, and

prison inmates (DeMello, 1995). As a collective group behavior

indicating deviant subculture membership, tattooing flourished

during this time but remained plagued by negative stereotypes

and associations. In the last 15 years, however, the practice has

represented a more individualistic yet mainstream means of body

adornment. As Figure 2 illustrates, it is not unusual to see a white-

collar worker sporting a tattoo.

The writers discuss changing perspectives on the appropriateness of tattoos.

Eric Anthony Johnson/Photolibrary/Getty Images

Figure 2. **Tattoos are becoming more common among middle-class professionals.** From Eric Anthony Johnson (Photographer). (n.d.). Father with Tattooed Arm Holding Baby Daughter [Photograph]. Retrieved from http://www.gettyimages.com/detail/photo/ father-with-tattooed-arm-holding-baby-high-res-stock-photogra phy/128263816

Tattooing is now common among both teenagers and older adults, men and women, urbanites and suburbanites, the college-educated and the uneducated, and the rich as well as the poor (Kosut, 2006). Today, according to The Harris Poll (2012), 21% of adults in the United States have one or more tattoos. Table 1 indicates the wide range of Americans wearing tattoos in 2003, 2008, and 2012.

Citation of a work by one author

APA

Table 1
Percentages of American adults with one or more tattoos

Category	Year		
	2003	**2008**	**2012**
All adults	16	14	21
Region			
East	14	12	21
Midwest	14	10	21
South	15	13	18
West	20	20	26
Age range			
18–24	13	9	22
25–29	36	32	30
30–39	28	25	38
40–49	14	12	27
50–64	10	8	11
65+	7	9	5
Sex			
Male	16	15	19
Female	15	13	23

Note. Adapted from "One in Five U.S. Adults Now Has a Tattoo," by S. Braverman, 2012, *Harris Interactive*.

The trend toward acceptance of tattoos may be a result of how American society views the people who wear them. Earlier, tattoos were depicted in mainstream print and visual media as worn by people with low socioeconomic or marginal status; now, they are considered to be an artful expression among celebrities as well as educated middle- and upper-class individuals (Kosut, 2006). This shift in the symbolic status of tattoos—to a form of self-expression among the social elite rather than deviant expression among the lower classes—has allowed tattoos to be obtained in greater numbers, owing in great part to the importance placed on self-expression in the United States. Even in the workplace, where employees had often been forbidden to display tattoos, employers now "take advantage of the open-mindedness and innovation that younger [tattooed] employees bring into the workplace" (Org, 2003, p. D1).

As the popularity and acceptability of tattoos has increased, tattooing has become part of the greater consumer culture and has thus undergone the process of commercialization that frequently occurs in the United States (Perzanowski, 2013). Tattoos are now acquired as status symbols, and their prevalence helps to sell tattoo maintenance products, clothing, and skateboards (Kosut, 2006). This introduction into the consumer culture allows tattoos to gain even more popularity; they are now intertwined with mainstream culture.

Two citations of articles, both written by four authors, are separated by a semicolon.

Statistics on the frequency of tattooing among specific age groups generally show increases (Armstrong, Owen, Roberts, & Koch, 2002; Mayers, Judelson, Moriarty, & Rundell, 2002), although one study (Corso, 2008) showed a slight decrease. The Harris Poll has been tracking the popularity of tattoos since 2003. Between 2003 and 2012, popularity among adults increased by 5%. The

The writers list statistics to support a claim.

most likely to have tattoos are between the ages of 30 and 39, and the least likely to have tattoos are those 65 and older. Women are currently 4% more likely to have tattoos than men, though before 2012 men were more likely to have tattoos.

Significantly, the increase in acquisition of tattoos has resulted in trends concerning the images and locations of tattoos, which appear to be divided along lines of gender. Many of the tattoo images commonly found on men include, but are not limited to, death themes, various wildlife, military insignia, tribal armbands, and family crests or last names. During the 1980s, cartoon images such as Bugs Bunny and the Tasmanian Devil were also popular for males. Males choose various locations for tattoos, but the most popular male sites are the upper body, especially the chest and arms, according to tattoo artist Mike Powell (personal

SOCIAL STATUS OF AN ART   9

communication, March 20, 2015). Conversely, females often obtain

tattoos that symbolize traditional femininity. A noticeable trend for

females in the 1980s was the rose tattoo, which was often located

on the breast or ankle. Stars, hearts, butterflies, and other flowers

now rival the rose in popularity. The ankle continues to be a

popular location for females today. Other popular spots for tattoos

include the hip, foot (see Figure 3), and back. Regardless of their

site, tattoos on women are now larger than they used to be (M.

Powell, personal communication, July 12, 2015).

ColorBlind Images/Blend Images/Corbis

Figure 3. **Many females who get a tattoo choose to have it on the foot.** From ColorBlind Images (Photographer). (n.d.). Tattoo on a Young Woman's Foot [Photograph]. Retrieved from https://secure.corbisimages.com /stock-photo/royalty-free/42-15416265/tattoo -on-a-young-womans-foot

The art of tattooing has existed in many culturally

determined forms throughout human history, and its current

manifestations are as varied as the cultures themselves. However,

based on the current literature, the social behavior of tattooing

is still quite common in the United States. In fact, Kosut (2006)

argues, "New generations of American children are growing up in

The writers include a photograph to support a point.

The last paragraph is the conclusion.

a cultural landscape that is more tattoo-friendly and tattoo flooded than any other time in history" (p. 1037). Because today's children see tattoos and tattoo-related products everywhere, usually in neutral or positive situations, they will likely be more accepting of tattoos than earlier generations were. Certainly, the tattooing trend shows no signs of decreasing significantly.

The last paragraph is the conclusion.

APA

References

Armstrong, M. L., Owen, D. C., Roberts, A. E., & Koch, J. R. (2002). College students and tattoos: Influence of image, identity, and family. *Journal of Psychosocial Nursing, 40*(10), 20-29.

Braverman, S. (2012, February 23). *One in five U.S. adults now has a tattoo*. Retrieved from http://www.harrisinteractive.com /NewsRoom/HarrisPolls/tabid/447/mid/1508/articleId/970 /ctl/ReadCustom%20Default/Default.aspx

Corso, R. A. (2008, February 12). *Three in ten Americans with a tattoo say having one makes them feel sexier*. Retrieved from http://www.harrisinteractive.com/Insights/HarrisVault.aspx

DeMello, M. (1995). Not just for bikers anymore: Popular representations of American tattooing. *Journal of Popular Culture, 29*(3), 37-53. Retrieved from http://www.wiley.com /WileyCDA/WileyTitle /productCd-JPCU.html

Kosut, M. (2006). An ironic fad: The commodification and consumption of tattoos. *Journal of Popular Culture, 39*(6), 1035–1049. Retrieved from http://www.wiley.com/WileyCDA /WileyTitle/productCd-JPCU.html

Krcmarik, K. L. (2003). *History of tattooing*. Retrieved from Michigan State University website: http://www.msu .edu/~krcmari1 /individual/history.html

Center the heading.

Alphabetize the entries according to the author's (or first author's) last name.

APA

Indent second and subsequent lines of each entry one-half inch or five spaces.

No period follows a URL at the end of an entry.

SOCIAL STATUS OF AN ART 12

Mayers, L. B., Judelson, D. A., Moriarity, B. W., & Rundell, K. W.

(2002). Prevalence of body art (body piercing and tattooing)

in university undergraduates and incidence of medical

complications. *Mayo Clinic Proceedings, 77*, 20-34.

Org, M. (2003, August 28). The tattooed executive. *The Wall Street

Journal.* Retrieved from http://online.wsj.com/public/us

Owen, J. (2013, October 16). 5 surprising facts about Ötzi the

Iceman. Retrieved from http://news.nationalgeographic

.com/news/2013/10/131016-otzi-ice-man-mummy-five-facts

Perzanowski, A. (2013). Tattoos & IP norms. *Minnesota Law Review,

98*(2), 511-591. Retrieved from http://www

.minnesotalawreview.org

An entry for an article from a database without a digital object identifier (DOI) includes the URL for the journal's home page.

15 CMS Documentation

The Chicago Manual of Style (CMS), now in its seventeenth edition and published by the University of Chicago Press (2017), provides guidelines for writers, editors, and publishers in history and other subject areas in the arts and humanities. The CMS documentation system uses either footnotes or endnotes and, for most assignments, a bibliography. Each of these citations demonstrates that you have conducted relevant research, credited your sources, and provided the details necessary for your reader to locate your source.

15a CMS note and bibliographic forms

According to CMS style, in-text citations take the form of sequential superscript numbers that refer to **footnotes** (notes at the bottom of each page) or **endnotes** (notes at the end of the text). The information in these notes may be condensed if a bibliography lists all the sources used in the text. The condensed, or short, form for a note includes only the author's last name, the title (which may be shortened if longer than four words), and the relevant page number(s): Eggers, *Court Reporters*, 312-15.

When a text has no bibliography, the full note form is used for the first citation of each source. For either footnotes or endnotes, place a superscript number in the text wherever documentation of a source is necessary. The number should be as close as possible to whatever it refers to, following most punctuation that appears at the end of the direct quotation or paraphrase but preceding a dash.

TIPS FOR PREPARING FOOTNOTES

- Most word-processing programs will footnote your work automatically. In your software, review the toolbars and menus to locate the tool to allow you to insert a footnote. A superscript number will appear in the cursor's position. A box will also appear at the bottom of your page in which you can insert the requisite information.

- Each note begins with a full-size number (or superscript) followed by a period and a space.

- Indent only the first line of a note five spaces (or a half-inch).

- Single-space lines within a footnote and between footnotes.

- When the source cited in an entry is the same as the source in the preceding entry, the source's title should be excluded. Repeat page numbers even if the same pages are cited. For example:

  3. Robinson, *Gilead*, 22–23.

  4. Robinson, 22–23.

  5. Robinson, 57.

- No bibliography is necessary when the footnotes provide complete bibliographic information for all sources.

TIPS FOR PREPARING ENDNOTES

- Place endnotes on a separate page, following the last page of your text and preceding the bibliography (if one is included).

- Center the word *Notes* (not italicized) at the top of the page.

- When the source cited in an entry is the same as the source in the preceding entry, the source's title should be excluded. Repeat page numbers even if the same pages are cited. For example:

  3. Robinson, *Gilead*, 22–23.

  4. Robinson, 22–23.

  5. Robinson, 57.

- Indent the first line of a note five spaces.

- Single-space within an endnote and between endnotes.

- No bibliography is necessary when the endnotes provide complete bibliographic information for all sources used in the paper.

TIPS FOR PREPARING A BIBLIOGRAPHY

- Start the bibliography on a separate page, following the last page of the body of the text if footnotes are used or following the last page of endnotes.

- Center the word *Bibliography* (not italicized) at the top of your page.

- Alphabetize entries in the bibliography according to the author's last name.

- If a source has more than one author, alphabetize by the last name of the first author.

- For a work without an author, alphabetize the entry according to the first important word in the title.

- To indicate that a source has the same author(s) as in the preceding entry, begin an entry with six hyphens or a 3-em dash (———) instead of the name(s) of the author(s). (If you do not know how to create this mark, search for *em dash*, using the Help function of your word processor.)

- Indent the second and subsequent lines of an entry five spaces (that is, use a hanging indent).

- Double-space within and between entries.

CMS

Directory to CMS Note and Bibliographic Forms

CMS

The following list contains entries for the full note form and the bibliographic form. The short note form is provided only for the first example.

BOOKS

1. Book with one author

Full note form

> 1. Ta-Nehisi Coates, *Between the World and Me* (New York: Spiegel and Grau, 2015), 64-65.

Provide the author's full name, in normal order, followed by a comma. Italicize the titles of books, magazines, journals, and films. Capitalize all major words. The city of publication, publisher, and date of publication are all within parentheses. Omit the words *Inc.*, *Publishing*, *Publishers*, and *Co.*, but retain the words *Press* and *Books*. You may shorten *University* to *Univ.* as long as you do so consistently.

Short note form

> 1. Coates, *Between the World and Me*, 64-65.

If the title is longer than four words, it is sometimes shortened.

Bibliographic form

Coates, Ta-Nehisi. *Between the World and Me*. New York: Spiegel and Grau, 2015.

Provide the author's full name, last name first, followed by a comma and the first name and a period. Provide either the full name of the publisher or an abbreviated version, followed by the year of publication. The style chosen must be used consistently throughout the notes and the bibliography. End the entry with a period.

2. Book with two authors

Full note form

> 2. Alice H. Eagly and Linda L. Carli, *Through the Labyrinth: The Truth about How Women Become Leaders* (Boston: Harvard Business School Press, 2007), 28.

Use the word *and* between the authors' names.

Bibliographic form

Eagly, Alice H., and Linda L. Carli. *Through the Labyrinth: The Truth about How Women Become Leaders*. Boston: Harvard Business School Press, 2007.

CITATION MAP 15.1: BOOK, CMS STYLE

Include the following elements when citing a book.

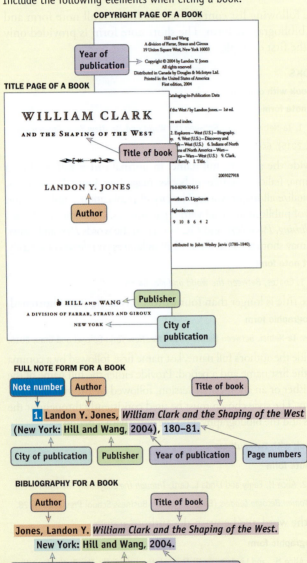

COPYRIGHT PAGE OF A BOOK

Year of publication

TITLE PAGE OF A BOOK

WILLIAM CLARK

AND THE SHAPING OF THE WEST

Title of book

LANDON Y. JONES

Author

HILL AND WANG
A DIVISION OF FARRAR, STRAUS AND GIROUX
NEW YORK

Publisher

City of publication

FULL NOTE FORM FOR A BOOK

Note number | Author | Title of book

1. Landon Y. Jones, *William Clark and the Shaping of the West* (New York: Hill and Wang, 2004), 180–81.

City of publication | Publisher | Year of publication | Page numbers

BIBLIOGRAPHY FOR A BOOK

Author | Title of book

Jones, Landon Y. *William Clark and the Shaping of the West.* New York: Hill and Wang, 2004.

City of publication | Publisher | Year of publication

Invert the first author's name and follow it with a comma, the word *and* (not italicized), and the second author's name in normal order. The second and subsequent lines of an entry are indented five spaces by using the hanging indent in your word processing program.

3. Book with three authors

Full note form

3. Karen A. Foss, Sonja K. Foss, and Cindy L. Griffin, *Feminist Rhetorical Theories* (Thousand Oaks, CA: SAGE, 1999).

Bibliographic form

Foss, Karen A., Sonja K. Foss, and Cindy L. Griffin. *Feminist Rhetorical Theories*. Thousand Oaks, CA: SAGE, 1999.

Only the first author's name is inverted. If the city of publication is not widely known, include a two-letter state abbreviation.

4. Book with more than three authors

Full note form

4. Mike Palmquist et al., *Transitions: Teaching Writing in Computer-Supported and Traditional Classrooms* (Greenwich, CT: Ablex, 1998), 153.

In a note, use the first person's name followed by the phrase *et al.* (not italicized), which means *and others*. Include all authors' names in the bibliographic form.

Bibliographic form

Palmquist, Mike, Kate Kiefer, James Hartvigsen, and Barbara Goodlew. *Transitions: Teaching Writing in Computer-Supported and Traditional Classrooms*. Greenwich, CT: Ablex, 1998.

5. Multiple works by the same author

In the bibliography, list the works alphabetically by title. After the first work, type six hyphens or a 3-em dash in place of the author's name for subsequent entries.

Bibliographic form

Diaz, Junot. *The Brief Wondrous Life of Oscar Wao*. New York: Riverhead
Books, 2007.

———. *This Is How You Lose Her*. New York: Riverhead Books, 2012.

6. Author not named or unknown

Full note form

6. *Beowulf: A New Verse Translation*, trans. Seamus Heaney (New York:
Farrar, Strauss, and Giroux, 2000), 24.

Bibliography form

Beowulf: A New Verse Translation. Translated by Seamus Heaney. New York:
Farrar, Strauss, and Giroux, 2000.

7. Book with an editor

Full note form

7. Hanna Schissler, ed., *The Miracle Years* (Princeton, NJ: Princeton
University Press, 2001).

Place the abbreviation *ed.* (not italicized) after the editor's
name. If there is more than one editor, use *eds.*

Bibliographic form

Schissler, Hanna, ed. *The Miracle Years*. Princeton, NJ: Princeton University
Press, 2001.

8. Book with an author and an editor

Full note form

8. Ayn Rand, *The Art of Fiction*, ed. Tore Boeckmann (New York: Plume, 2000).

Use the abbreviation *ed.* for "edited by." Do not use *eds.* in this
position, even if there is more than one editor.

Bibliographic form

Rand, Ayn. *The Art of Fiction*. Edited by Tore Boeckmann. New York: Plume, 2000.

Write out the words *Edited by*.

9. Translated book

Full note form

> 9. Orhan Pamuk, *Silent House*, trans. Robert Finn (New York: Knopf, 2012).

Use the abbreviation *trans.* for "translated by."

Bibliographic form

Pamuk, Orhan. *Silent House*. Translated by Robert Finn. New York: Knopf, 2012.

Write out the words *Translated by* in the bibliography.

10. Entry in a reference work

Full note form

> 10. Robert Cox and Christina R. Foust, "Social Movement Rhetoric," in *The SAGE Handbook of Rhetorical Studies*, ed. Andrea A. Lunsford, Kirt H. Wilson, and Rosa A. Eberly (Thousand Oaks, CA: SAGE, 2009), 613.

Bibliographic form

Cox, Robert, and Christina R. Foust. "Social Movement Rhetoric." In *The SAGE Handbook of Rhetorical Studies*. Edited by Andrea A. Lunsford, Kirt H. Wilson, and Rosa A. Eberly, 605-27. Thousand Oaks, CA: SAGE, 2009.

After the editors' names, write the inclusive page numbers on which the entry appears within the reference work.

11. Sacred text

Full note form

> 11. John 3:16 (New Revised Standard Version).

> 11. Qur'an 7:1–7.

CMS does not include sacred or religious texts in the bibliography.

12. Source quoted in another source

Full note form

> 12. Toni Morrison, *Playing in the Dark* (New York: Vintage, 1992), 26, quoted in Jonathan Goldberg, *Willa Cather and Others* (Durham, NC: Duke University Press, 2001), 37.

Bibliographic form

Goldberg, Jonathan. *Willa Cather and Others*. Durham, NC: Duke University Press, 2001.

In the note, cite both the original work and the secondary source in which it is quoted. In the bibliography, cite only the secondary source.

13. Edition after the first

Full note form

13. Edward O. Wilson, *On Human Nature*, 14th ed. (Cambridge: Harvard University Press, 2001).

Bibliographic form

Wilson, Edward O. *On Human Nature*. 14th ed. Cambridge: Harvard University Press, 2001.

14. One volume in a multivolume work

Full note form

14. Thomas Cleary, *Classics of Buddhism and Zen*, vol. 3 (Boston: Shambhala, 2001), 116.

Bibliographic form

Cleary, Thomas. *Classics of Buddhism and Zen*. Vol. 3. Boston: Shambhala, 2001.

15. Government document

Full note form

15. US Bureau of the Census, *Statistical Abstract of the United States*, 120th ed. (Washington, DC, 2001), 16.

Bibliographic form

US Bureau of the Census. *Statistical Abstract of the United States*. 120th ed. Washington, DC, 2001.

16. Selection from an anthology

Full note form

16. Elizabeth Spencer, "The Everlasting Light," in *The Cry of an Occasion*, ed. Richard Bausch (Baton Rouge: Louisiana State University Press, 2001), 171-82.

If you are citing information from a specific page or pages of a book or an article, place the page number(s) at the end of the note. If the page numbers have the same hundreds or thousands digit, do not repeat it when listing the final page in the range: 234–42 and 1350–55 but 290–301 and 1395–402.

Bibliographic form

Spencer, Elizabeth. "The Everlasting Light." In *The Cry of an Occasion*. Edited

by Richard Bausch, 171-82. Baton Rouge: Louisiana State University

Press, 2001.

Use quotation marks to enclose the titles of selections from anthologies. The title is followed by a comma in the note form or by a period in the bibliographic form.

When only one selection from an anthology is used, inclusive page numbers precede the publication data in the bibliographic entry.

17. Published letter

Full note form

17. Lincoln to George McClellan, Washington, DC, 13 October, 1862, in

This Fiery Trial: The Speeches and Writings of Abraham Lincoln, ed. William E.

Gienapp (New York: Oxford University Press, 2002), 178.

Bibliographic form

Lincoln, Abraham. *This Fiery Trial: The Speeches and Writings of Abraham Lincoln*.

Edited by William E. Gienapp. New York: Oxford University Press, 2002.

In your bibliography, cite only the collection in which the letter appears, not the specific letter.

ARTICLES

18. Article in a journal

Full note form

18. Andreas Schedler, "The Menu of Manipulation," *Journal of Democracy*

13, no. 2 (2002): 48.

When initials are used in the original publication for an author's first and middle names, use them; otherwise use complete names. Use no punctuation between journal title and volume number and a comma between volume and issue number. Include the page number of the specific citation.

Bibliographic form

Schedler, Andreas. "The Menu of Manipulation." *Journal of Democracy* 13, no.

2 (2002): 36-50.

In the bibliographic form, include the page span of the article.

19. Article in a magazine

Full note form

19. John O'Sullivan, "The Overskeptics," *National Review*, June 17, 2002, 23.

Bibliographic form

O'Sullivan, John. "The Overskeptics." *National Review*, June 17, 2002, 22-26.

For a magazine published monthly, include only the month and the year with no comma inserted between them. In a note, mention only the cited page. In the bibliography, include the full page range of the article.

20. Review or book review

Full note form

20. Franny Howes, review of *Out of Athens: The New Ancient Greeks*, by Page duBois, *Rhetoric Society Quarterly* 42, no. 1 (2012), 88.

Bibliographic form

Howes, Franny. Review of *Out of Athens: The New Ancient Greeks*, by Page

duBois. *Rhetoric Society Quarterly* 42, no. 1 (2012): 88-90.

21. Newspaper article

Full note form

21. Rick Bragg, "An Oyster and a Way of Life, Both at Risk," *New York Times*, June 15, 2002, national edition, sec. A.

CITATION MAP 15.2: ARTICLE IN A JOURNAL, CMS STYLE

To cite an article from a journal, include the following elements.

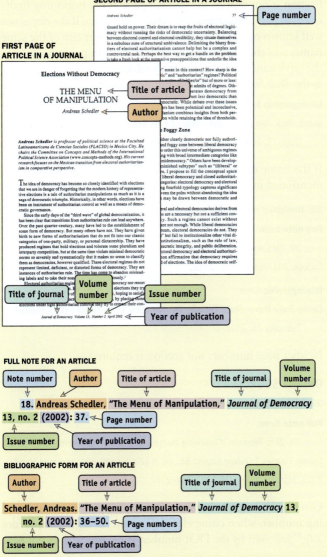

SECOND PAGE OF ARTICLE IN A JOURNAL

Page number

FIRST PAGE OF ARTICLE IN A JOURNAL

Title of article

Author

Title of journal

Volume number

Issue number

Year of publication

FULL NOTE FOR AN ARTICLE

Note number · Author · Title of article · Title of journal · Volume number

> 18. Andreas Schedler, "The Menu of Manipulation," *Journal of Democracy*
> 13, no. 2 (2002): 37.

Page number

Issue number · Year of publication

BIBLIOGRAPHIC FORM FOR AN ARTICLE

Author · Title of article · Title of journal · Volume number

> Schedler, Andreas. "The Menu of Manipulation," *Journal of Democracy* 13,
> no. 2 (2002): 36–50.

Page numbers

Issue number · Year of publication

Omit the initial *The* in the newspaper's name. If the city of publication is not part of the name, add it at the beginning (italicized) as part of the name: *St. Paul Pioneer Press*. If the city is not well known or could be confused with another city of the same name, add the state name or abbreviation in parentheses after the city's name. If the paper is a well-known national one, such as the *Wall Street Journal*, it is not necessary to add the city.

Bibliographic form

Bragg, Rick. "An Oyster and a Way of Life, Both at Risk." *New York Times*.

　　June 15, 2002, national edition, sec. A.

If the name of the newspaper and the date of publication are mentioned in your text, no bibliographic entry is needed.

22. Unsigned article in a newspaper

Full note form

　　22. "Nittany Lions Finish with a Flourish," *Centre Daily Times* (State College, PA), February 26, 2012.

Bibliographic form

Centre Daily Times (State College, PA). "Nittany Lions Finish with a Flourish."

　　February 26, 2012.

Neither page numbers nor section is required.

ONLINE SOURCES

23. Article from an online journal

Full note form

　　23. Zina Peterson, "Teaching Margery and Julian in Anthropology-Based Survey Courses," *College English* 68, no. 5 (2006): 481-501, accessed May 5, 2010, https://doi.org/10.2307/25472167.

Give the DOI (digital object identifier), a permanent identifying number, when citing electronic sources. Write "https://doi .org/" followed by the DOI number. If the source does not have a DOI, list the URL. If the material is time-sensitive or if your discipline or instructor requires it, include the access date before the DOI or URL. A URL or DOI continued on a second line may be broken *after* a colon or double slash or *before* a single slash, a comma, a period, a hyphen, a question mark, a percent symbol, a number sign (#), a tilde (~), or an underline (_). It can be broken either before or after an ampersand (&) or equals sign.

Bibliographic form

Peterson, Zina. "Teaching Margery and Julian in Anthropology-Based Survey
　　Courses." *College English* 68, no. 5 (2006): 481-501. Accessed May 5,
　　2010. https://doi.org/10.2307/25472167.

24. Article from a journal database

Full note form

　　24. Samuel Guy Inman, "The Monroe Doctrine and Hispanic America,"
Hispanic America Historical Review 4, no. 4 (1921): 635, http://www
.jstor.org/stable/2505682.

If there is no DOI, give a stable URL for the article in the online database. Place a period after a DOI or URL. If the URL can only be accessed when you are logged into the database through a library or personal subscription, provide the name of the database instead of the URL.

Bibliographic form

Inman, Samuel Guy. "The Monroe Doctrine and Hispanic America." *Hispanic
　　America Historical Review* 4, no. 4 (1921): 635-76. http://www.jstor
　　.org/stable/2505682.

25. Article from an online magazine

Full note form

　　25. Mark Frank, "Judge for Themselves: Why a Supreme Court Ruling on
Sentencing Guidelines Puts More Power Back on the Bench," *Time*, January 24,
2005, http://www.time.com/time/magazine/printout/0,8816,1018063,00.html.

CITATION MAP 15.3: ARTICLE IN A DATABASE, CMS STYLE

Include the following elements when citing an article in a database.

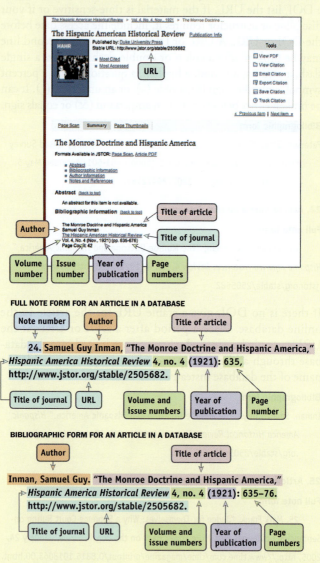

Title of article — The Monroe Doctrine and Hispanic America

Title of journal

Author

Volume number

Issue number

Year of publication

Page numbers

URL

FULL NOTE FORM FOR AN ARTICLE IN A DATABASE

Note number — **Author** — **Title of article**

24. Samuel Guy Inman, "The Monroe Doctrine and Hispanic America," *Hispanic America Historical Review* 4, no. 4 (1921): 635, http://www.jstor.org/stable/2505682.

Title of journal — **URL** — **Volume and issue numbers** — **Year of publication** — **Page number**

BIBLIOGRAPHIC FORM FOR AN ARTICLE IN A DATABASE

Author — **Title of article**

Inman, Samuel Guy. "The Monroe Doctrine and Hispanic America," *Hispanic America Historical Review* 4, no. 4 (1921): 635–76. http://www.jstor.org/stable/2505682.

Title of journal — **URL** — **Volume and issue numbers** — **Year of publication** — **Page numbers**

Bibliographic form

Frank, Mark. "Judge for Themselves: Why a Supreme Court Ruling on Sentencing Guidelines Puts More Power Back on the Bench." *Time,* January 24, 2005. http://www.time.com/time/magazine/printout/0,8816,1018063,00.html.

26. Online book

Full note form

26. Marian Hurd McNeely, *The Jumping-off Place*, illus. William Siegel (New York: Longmans, 1929), 28, http://digital.library.upenn.edu/women /mcneely/place/place.html.

Bibliographic form

McNeely, Marian Hurd. *The Jumping-off Place*. Illustrated by William Siegel. New York: Longmans, 1929. http://digital.library.upenn.edu/women /mcneely/place/place.html.

Include the same information (author, title, city, publisher, year) as for a book. Some online books provide page images of the original book, but others do not. If page numbers vary, use a chapter or other section number instead.

27. Electronic book (e-book)

Full note form

27. S. C. Gwynne, *Empire of the Summer Moon* (New York: Scribner, 2010), Kindle edition, chap. 11.

Bibliographic form

Gwynne, S. C. *Empire of the Summer Moon*. New York: Scribner, 2012. Kindle edition.

28. Website

Full note form

28. Jeremy Hylton, The Complete Works of William Shakespeare, *The Tech*, MIT, 1993, http://shakespeare.mit.edu.

Bibliographic form

Hylton, Jeremy. The Complete Works of William Shakespeare. *The Tech*. 1993.

   http://shakespeare.mit.edu.

Unless no other publication information is available, access dates are not necessary.

29. Work from a website

Full note form

   29. Eric Skalac, "BP Well to Stay Sealed after Gulf Spill, Experts Predict," *National Geographic*, last modified April 20, 2011, http://news.nationalgeographic .com/news/Energy/2011/04/110418-oil-spill-anniversary-is-bp-well-sealed/.

Bibliographic form

Skalac, Eric. "BP Well to Stay Sealed after Gulf Spill, Experts Predict."

   National Geographic, last modified April 20, 2011. http://news

   .nationalgeographic.com/news/Energy/2011/04/110418-oil-spill

   -anniversary-is-bp-well-sealed/.

30. Blog entry

Full note form

   30. Megan Slack, "What Is the Sequester?" *The White House Blog*, February 22, 2013, http://www.whitehouse.gov/blog/2013/02/22/what-sequester.

Bibliographic form

Slack, Megan. "What Is the Sequester?" *The White House Blog*. February 22,

   2013. http://www.whitehouse.gov/blog/2012/02/22/what-sequester.

If *blog* does not appear as part of the name, add it in parentheses after the name. Although all blogs can be cited in notes, only frequently cited blogs appear in the bibliography.

31. E-mail and other personal communication

Full note form

   31. Evan Michaels, e-mail message to James Smith, February 22, 2017.

CITATION MAP 15.4: WORK FROM A WEBSITE, CMS STYLE

Include the following elements when citing a short work from a website.

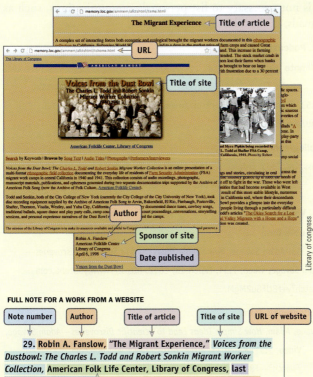

Library of congress

FULL NOTE FOR A WORK FROM A WEBSITE

Note number | Author | Title of article | Title of site | URL of website

29. **Robin A. Fanslow,** "The Migrant Experience," *Voices from the Dustbowl: The Charles L. Todd and Robert Sonkin Migrant Worker Collection,* American Folk Life Center, Library of Congress, last modified April 6, 1998, http://memory.loc.gov/ammem/afctshtml /tsme.html.

Date of publication

Sponsor of site

BIBLIOGRAPHIC FORM FOR A WORK FROM A WEBSITE

Author | Title of article | Title of site | URL of website

Fanslow, Robin A. "The Migrant Experience," *Voices from the Dustbowl: The Charles L. Todd and Robert Sonkin Migrant Worker Collection,* American Folk Life Center, Library of Congress, last modified April 6, 1998, http://memory.loc.gov/ammem/afctshtml /tsme.html.

Date of publication

Sponsor of site

It is not necessary to list personal communications, such as e-mails, in the bibliography.

32. Podcast

Full note form

32. Ira Glass, "363: Enforcers," *This American Life*, podcast audio, 57:53, February 22, 2013, http://www.thisamericanlife.org/play_full.php?play=363.

Bibliographic form

Glass, Ira. "363: Enforcers." *This American Life*. Podcast audio, 57:53. February 22, 2013. http://www.thisamericanlife.org/play_full.php?play=363.

33. Video or audio

Full note form

33. Adam Savage, *How Simple Ideas Lead to Scientific Discoveries—Adam Savage*, video, 7:31, March 13, 2012, https://www.youtube.com/watch?v+F8UFGu2MgM.

Bibliographic form

Savage, Adam. *How Simple Ideas Lead to Scientific Discoveries—Adam Savage*. Video, 7:31. March 13, 2012. https://www.youtube.com/watch?v+F8UFGu2MgM.

OTHER SOURCES

34. DVD or Blu-ray

Full note form

34. *The Girl with the Dragon Tattoo*, directed by David Fincher (Culver City, CA: Sony Pictures Entertainment, 2011), DVD and Blu-ray.

Bibliographic form

The Girl with the Dragon Tattoo. Directed by David Fincher. Culver City, CA: Sony Pictures Entertainment, 2011. DVD and Blu-ray.

35. Interviews, published and unpublished

Full note form (Published)

    35. Aldous Huxley, interview by Mike Wallace, *The Mike Wallace Interview: Aldous Huxley (1958–05–18)*, YouTube video, last modified Aug. 1, 2008, http://www.youtube.com/watch?v=KGaYXahbcL4.

Bibliographic form (Published)

Huxley, Aldous. Interview by Mike Wallace. *The Mike Wallace Interview: Aldous Huxley (1958–05–18)*. YouTube video. Last modified Aug. 1, 2008. http://www.youtube.com/watch?v=KGaYXahbcL4.

Full note form (Unpublished)

    35. John Teodori, interview by James Timothy, November 16, 2007, transcript.

Bibliographic form (Unpublished)

Unpublished interviews rarely appear in the bibliography, but, if they do, they should include the name of the person being interviewed, the interviewer, the place and date of the interview, and the availability of a transcript or recording.

36. Sound recording

Full note form

    36. Frédéric Chopin, *Nocturne Op. 9 No. 2*, with Ivan Moravec (piano), recorded in 1966, Nonesuch B000005J03, 1991, compact disc.

Bibliographic form

Chopin, Frédéric. *Nocturne Op. 9 No. 2*. Ivan Moravec (piano). Recorded in 1966. Nonesuch, B000005J03, 1991, compact disc.

37. Live performance, including lecture

Full note form

    37. *Proof*, by David Auburn, Walter Kerr Theatre, New York, New York, October 2, 2002.

    37. Jessica Enoch, "Feminist Memory Studies" (lecture, University of Maryland, College Park, MD, April 6, 2017).

CMS

Bibliographic form

Since live performances cannot be accessed again by readers, they are not usually included in the bibliography.

38. Work of art

Full note form

38. Paul Gauguin, *Ancestors of Tehamana*, 1893, oil on canvas, Art Institute of Chicago, Chicago, IL.

Bibliographic form

Gauguin, Paul. *Ancestors of Tehamana*, 1893. Oil on canvas. Art Institute of
   Chicago, Chicago, IL.

15b   Sample CMS-style paper

The following student paper, a historical research project, addresses an ongoing struggle in South Africa related to electricity usage. Because he included a full bibliography, Cristian Nuñez supplied endnotes written in short form. Only the first pages of his essay along with portions of his notes and bibliography appear here.

Local Politics and National Policy in a Globalized World:

South Africa's Ongoing Electricity Dilemma

Cristian Nuñez

Political Science 87

Professor Stone

December 15, 2016

1

This introduction establishes the importance of the topic. The thesis statement is the final sentence of the first paragraph.

Since its 1994 inception, the South African democracy has struggled to alleviate national poverty without alienating the global financial community on which it depends. Even though the government's moderate pro-business agenda is intended to reduce poverty, it continues to provide too little support for the nation's poor—an agenda harshly criticized by citizen-advocate groups. One such group is the Soweto Electricity Crisis Committee (SECC), a civic organization advocating free basic utilities for all South Africans, who charges that South Africa's government is not living up to the human rights core of its Constitution, guaranteeing all South Africans access to basic resources.[1] The SECC addresses human rights through its controversial—and illegal—practice of delivering free electricity to South Africa's poorest people.

The Electricity Crisis

In this passage, Nuñez explains how the change from apartheid to democracy inadvertently created additional economic woes for nonwhites in South Africa.

Following the 1993 end of apartheid, the majority (African National Congress [ANC]) government swept into power with a mandate to reverse the injustices prevalent in South Africa. Millions of poor nonwhites hoped that affordable housing, modern education, and basic utilities would be expanded in their long-neglected neighborhoods. However, carrying out these goals would prove to be extremely difficult for the new ANC president Nelson Mandela, who had inherited a huge financial crisis from the old National Party regime. To avert a spending crisis of any kind (one that would devalue South African currency both locally and globally), Mandela's

2

ANC government implemented broad economic reforms in the hope
of directing the foreign investment and capital inflows necessary for
growing the South African economy.[2]

Dirk Bleyer/imageBROKER/Getty Images

**Figure 1. This township settlement in Soweto typifies the poverty
and lack of access to public services for many South African citizens.**

One of the economic reforms included the plan to privatize
the nation's many parastatals (state-owned enterprises). In
preparation for privatization, each parastatal enacted cost-recovery
pricing to make itself more competitive and more attractive to
foreign investors. Unfortunately for the South African poor, such
cost-recovery measures eliminated both subsidized utilities and
rent in nonwhite neighborhoods like Soweto, which is located
just outside of Johannesburg and has long been a hotbed of
revolutionary actions and ideas. In response, a number of civics

Nuñez
outlines
the steps
Mandela
and the
new
government
took to
address the
financial
problems
they had
inherited.

CMS

3

(community action groups) protested the government's economic reforms, the most brash of them being the SECC.

By 2001, in an effort to remain financially solvent, South Africa's public utility company, the Electricity Supply Commission (Eskom), was disconnecting twenty thousand households a month for not paying their bills. In response, the SECC illegally reconnected more than three thousand Soweto households in a program called "Reconnect the Power."[3] Because no workable solutions to this problem have yet been discovered since those early disconnections, those illegal reconnections remain in place. In 2009, SECC's electricians were reconnecting nearly forty houses per week, resulting in an estimated 60 percent of Soweto residents receiving electricity without charge. For many of the SECC electricians, having electric power is a constitutional right, not a luxury. SECC electrician Levy argues that he and the electricians "are giving back what belongs to the people," thereby justifying the SECC's ongoing activism.[4]

The Legacy of Apartheid and Perceptions of Eskom
Although the SECC was established in 2000, the practice of nonpayment for basic needs has a much longer history in South Africa. During apartheid, the ANC urged residents of Soweto and other townships to stop paying their rent and their electricity and water bills (which were often higher than those of households in

4

upper-class white neighborhoods). The boycott the ANC organized was a powerful weapon against apartheid, eventually bankrupting local authorities. Many people retained this stance of resistance following the end of apartheid. "We did not expect this," said Chris Ngcobo, an organizer of the Soweto boycott under apartheid, who now helps oversee an ANC/Eskom project to reverse the culture of nonpayment. "We expected that after the elections people would just pay. But it will not be so easy."[5]

For many residents, nonpayment as protest continued as an intentional act during the Mandela years. During these early post-apartheid years, bill payment was presented as a patriotic gesture in support of the Mandela government.[6] The residents, however, wanted to see improvements first before resuming payment.

In the rest of his paper, Nuñez describes the ways in which the SECC has intervened in order to provide electricity to poor, nonwhite South Africans.

CMS

5

Notes

1. *Countries of the World.*

2. McNeil, "Shedding State Companies."

3. Bond, *Against Global Apartheid*, 170.

4. Fisher, "South Africa Crisis."

5. Daley, "In South Africa."

6. Daley.

6

Bibliography

Bond, Patrick. *Against Global Apartheid: South Africa Meets the World Bank, IMF and International Finance*. Cape Town: Univ. of Cape Town Press, 2003.

Chang, Claude V. *Privatisation and Development: Theory, Policy and Evidence*. Hampshire, UK: Ashgate, 2006.

Countries of the World and Their Leaders Yearbook 2011. 2 vols. Detroit: Gale, 2010. http://go.galegroup.com.

Daley, Suzanne. "In South Africa, a Culture of Resistance Dies Hard." *New York Times*, July 19, 1995. http://www.nytimes.com/1995/07/19/world/in-south-africa-a-culture-of-resistance-dies-hard.html.

———. "Seeing Bias in Their Utility Rates, Mixed Race South Africans Riot." *New York Times*, February 7, 1997. http://www.nytimes.com/1997/02/07/world/seeing-bias-in-their-utility-rates-mixed-race-south-africans-riot.html.

Eskom. *Annual Report 1999*. n.d. http://www.eskom.co.za/annreport/main.htm.

Fisher, Jonah. "South Africa Crisis Creates Crusading Electricians." *BBC News*, November 24, 2009. http://news.bbc.co.uk/2/hi/8376400.stm.

The bibliography begins on a new page.

Suzanne Daley is listed twice in the bibliography. Her second mention uses a 3-em dash or six hyphens.

CMS

7

Kingsnorth, Paul. *One No, Many Yeses*. Sydney, AUS: Simon and

Schuster, 2003.

McNeil, Donald G., Jr. "Shedding State Companies, if Sometimes

Reluctantly." *New York Times*, February 27, 1997. http://

www.nytimes.com/1997/02/27/business/shedding-state

-companies-if-sometimes-reluctantly.html.

16 CSE Documentation

The Council of Science Editors (CSE) has established guidelines for writers in the life and physical sciences: *Scientific Style and Format: The CSE Manual for Authors, Editors, and Publishers*, eighth edition. It presents three systems for citing and documenting research sources: the citation-sequence system, the name-year system, and the citation-name system.

16a CSE-style in-text citations

CSE's guidelines for the citation-sequence system, the name-year system, and the citation-name system differ significantly, so be sure to know which you will be expected to use before you get started. Once you know your instructor's preference, follow the guidelines in one of the following boxes as you prepare your in-text references.

TIPS FOR PREPARING CITATION-SEQUENCE IN-TEXT REFERENCES

- Place a superscript number after each mention of a source or each use of material from it. This number corresponds to the number assigned to the source in the end references.
- Be sure to place the number immediately after the material used or the word or phrase indicating the source: Herbert's original method[1] was used.
- Use the same number each time you refer to the same source.
- Order the numbers according to the sequence in which sources are introduced: Both Li[1] and Holst[2] have shown . . .

(Continued on page 235)

TIPS FOR PREPARING CITATION-SEQUENCE *(Continued)*
IN-TEXT REFERENCES

- When referring to more than one source, use commas to separate the numbers corresponding to the sources; there is no space after each comma. Use a hyphen or an en dash between two numbers to indicate a sequence of sources: The early studies[1, 2, 4-7] . . .

TIPS FOR PREPARING NAME-YEAR IN-TEXT REFERENCES

- Place the author's last name and the year of publication in parentheses after the mention of a source: In a more recent study (Karr 2017), these findings were not replicated. Using the author's last name, the reader will be able to find the corresponding entry in the alphabetized reference list.

- Omit the author's name from the parenthetical citation if it appears in the text preceding it: In Karr's study (2017), these findings were not replicated.

- If the source has two authors, use both of their last names: (Phill and Richardson 2017). If there are three or more authors, use the first author's last name and the abbreviation *et al*: (Drake et al 2016).

- Use semicolons to separate multiple citations. Order these citations chronologically when the years differ but alphabetically when the years are the same: (Li 2016; Holst 2017) but (Lamont 2016; Li 2016).

TIPS FOR PREPARING CITATION-NAME IN-TEXT REFERENCES

- Arrange your end references alphabetically. Then assign each reference a number. Use the superscript form of this number in the text immediately after the material used or the word or phrase indicating the source: Stress-related illnesses are common among college students.[1]

- Use the same number each time you refer to the same source.

- When referring to more than one source, use commas to separate the numbers corresponding to the sources; there is no space after each comma. Use a hyphen or an en dash between two numbers to indicate a sequence of sources: Recent studies of posttraumatic stress disorder[1, 2, 4-7] . . .

16b   CSE-style list of references

On the final page of your paper, list all the sources you have mentioned. The ordering of the entries will depend on which system you have chosen. Both the citation-name system and the name-year system require alphabetical ordering according to the authors' last names; the citation-sequence system requires that the sources be listed in the order they were mentioned in your text.

TIPS FOR PREPARING END REFERENCES

- Center the heading *References* or *Cited References* (not in italics) at the top of the page.

- If you are using the *citation-sequence system*, list the sources in the order in which they were introduced in the text.

- If you are using the *citation-name system*, your end references should be ordered alphabetically according to the first author's last name and then the references should be numbered.

- If you are using the *name-year system*, your end references should be ordered alphabetically.

- Entries on citation-sequence and citation-name reference lists differ only in overall organization: citation-sequence references are listed according to the order of occurrence within the text; citation-name references are listed alphabetically. The name-year system differs from both the citation-sequence and citation-name systems only in the placement of the date of publication: the name-year system calls for the date to be placed after the author's name. The citation-sequence and the citation-name systems call for the date to be placed after the publisher's name in entries for books and after the name of the periodical in entries for articles.

- When listing place of publication information, if the city is not well known or could be confused with another city, include an abbreviation for the state or country in parentheses after the name of the city. The name of a country may be spelled out.

The entries listed after the directory include examples in the citation-sequence or citation-name system, followed by examples in the name-year system.

CSE

BOOKS

1. Book with one author

Citation-sequence or citation-name system

1. King BJ. How animals grieve. Chicago: University of Chicago Press; 2013. 193 p.

Begin the entry with the author's last name and his or her first initial and middle initial (if given). Capitalize only the first word of the title and any proper nouns or adjectives. Include the place of publication, the publisher's name, and the year of publication. Provide the total page count if required, using the abbreviation *p* for "pages."

Name-year system

King BJ. 2013. How animals grieve. Chicago: University of Chicago Press. 193 p.

2. Book with two or more authors

Citation-sequence or citation-name system

2. Ohanian HC, Ruffini R. Gravitation and spacetime. 3rd ed. Cambridge (England): Cambridge University Press; 2013.

Invert the name and initials of all authors, using commas to separate the names. Do not use the word *and* or an ampersand.

Name-year system

Ohanian HC, Ruffini R. 2013. Gravitation and spacetime. 3rd ed. Cambridge (England): Cambridge University Press.

3. Book with an organization (or organizations) listed as author
Citation-sequence or citation-name system

3. American Medical Association Council on Ethical and Judicial Affairs. Code of medical ethics of the American Medical Association. Chicago: American Medical Association; 2016.

Name-year system

American Medical Association Council on Ethical and Judicial Affairs. 2016.
Code of medical ethics of the American Medical Association. Chicago:
American Medical Association.

4. Book with editor(s)

Citation-sequence or citation-name system

4. Maxfield FR, Willard JM, Shuyan L, editors. Lysosomes: biology, diseases,
and therapeutics. Hoboken (NJ): Wiley; 2016.

Include the word *editor* or *editors* after the last name.

Name-year system

Maxfield FR, Willard JM, Shuyan L, editors. 2016. Lysosomes: biology,
diseases, and therapeutics. Hoboken (NJ) Wiley.

5. Section of a book with an editor

Citation-sequence or citation-name system

5. Banich MT. Hemispheric specialization and cognition. In: Whitaker HA,
editor. Concise encyclopedia of brain and language. Oxford (England):
Elsevier; 2010. p. 224-230.

Name-year system

Banich MT. 2010. Hemispheric specialization and cognition. In: Whitaker HA,
editor. Concise encyclopedia of brain and language. Oxford (England):
Elsevier. p. 224-230.

6. Chapter or part of an edited book

Citation-sequence or citation-name system

6. Gadoth N. Free radicals: their role in brain function and dysfunction.
In: Armstrong D, Stratton RD, editors. Oxidative stress and antioxidant
protection: the science of free radical biology and disease. Hoboken
(NJ): Wiley; 2016. p. 23-38.

Name-year system

Gadoth N. 2016. Free radicals: their role in brain function and dysfunction. In:
Armstrong D, Stratton RD, editors. Oxidative stress and antioxidant protection:
the science of free radical biology and disease. Hoboken (NJ): Wiley. p. 23-38.

7. Paper or abstract in conference proceedings

Citation-sequence or citation-name system

7. Barge RA. Using standards to support human factors engineering. In:
Anderson M, editor. Contemporary ergonomics and human factors 2013:
proceedings of the International Conference on Ergonomics and Human
Factors; 2013 Apr 15–18, Cambridge, England. Croydon (England):
Taylor & Francis; 2013. p. 135-137.

Name-year system

Barge RA. 2013. Using standards to support human factors engineering. In:
Anderson M, editor. Contemporary ergonomics and human factors 2013:
proceedings of the International Conference on Ergonomics and Human
Factors; 2013 Apr 15-18, Cambridge, England. Croydon (England):
Taylor & Francis. p. 135-137.

ARTICLES

8. Article in a scholarly journal

Citation-sequence or citation-name system

8. Kao-Kniffin J, Freyre DS, Balser TC. Increased methane emissions from an
invasive wetland plant under elevated carbon dioxide levels. Appl Soil
Ecol. 2011; 48 (3):309-312.

Place a period after the abbreviated name of the journal (abbreviations can be found online by searching for "CSE journal abbreviations"). Next, list the year of publication, the volume number, and the issue number. Place a semicolon between the year of publication and the volume number. Put the issue

CITATION MAP 16.1: ARTICLE IN A JOURNAL, CSE STYLE

Include the following elements when citing an article from a journal.

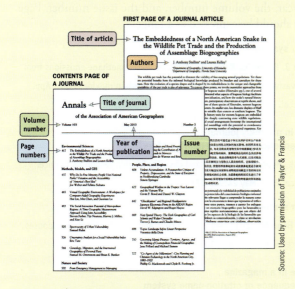

FIRST PAGE OF A JOURNAL ARTICLE

Title of article → The Embeddedness of a North American Snake in the Wildlife Pet Trade and the Production of Assemblage Biogeographies

Authors → J. Anthony Stallins[1] and Lauren Kelley[2]

CONTENTS PAGE OF A JOURNAL

Annals — Title of journal

of the Association of American Geographers

Volume number → Volume 103 · Mar 2013 · Number 2 ← Issue number

Page numbers

Year of publication

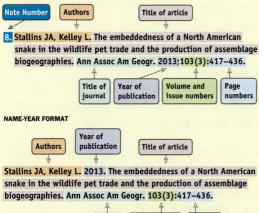

CITATION-SEQUENCE OR CITATION-NAME FORMAT

Note Number · Authors · Title of article

8. **Stallins JA, Kelley L.** The embeddedness of a North American snake in the wildlife pet trade and the production of assemblage biogeographies. Ann Assoc Am Geogr. 2013;103(3):417–436.

Title of journal · Year of publication · Volume and issue numbers · Page numbers

NAME-YEAR FORMAT

Authors · Year of publication · Title of article

Stallins JA, Kelley L. 2013. The embeddedness of a North American snake in the wildlife pet trade and the production of assemblage biogeographies. Ann Assoc Am Geogr. 103(3):417–436.

Title of journal · Volume and issue numbers · Page numbers

number in parentheses. Note that there are no spaces separating the year, the volume number, and the issue number. Page numbers should be expressed as a range.

Name-year system

Kao-Kniffin J, Freyre DS, Balser TC. 2011. Increased methane emissions from an invasive wetland plant under elevated carbon dioxide levels. Appl Soil Ecol. 48(3):309-312.

9. Article in a weekly journal
Citation-sequence or citation-name system

9. Mishra SK, Hoon MA. The cells and circuitry for itch responses in mice. Science. 2013 May 24:968-971.

Name-year system

Mishra SK, Hoon MA. 2013 May 24. The cells and circuitry for itch responses in mice. Science. 968-971.

10. Article in a magazine
Citation-sequence or citation-name system

10. Slaughter A. Our evolving sense of self. Natl Geogr. 2017;231(1):152-154.

List the volume and issue numbers when available.

Name-year system

Slaughter A. 2017. Our evolving sense of self. Natl Geogr. 231(1):152-154.

11. Article in a newspaper
Citation-sequence or citation-name system

11. Pear R. Health lobby quiet as law faces repeal. New York Times (Late Ed.) 2017 Jan 1;Sect. A:1 (col. 4).

Include the section letter, page number, and column number.

Name-year system

Pear R. 2017 Jan 1. Health lobby quiet as law faces repeal. New York Times (Late Ed.). Sect. A:1 (col. 4).

ONLINE SOURCES

12. Online book
Citation-sequence or citation-name system

12. Institute of Medicine, Committee on the Effect of Climate Change on
  Indoor Air Quality and Public Health. Climate change, the indoor
  environment, and health. Washington (DC): National Academy Press;
  2011 [accessed 2013 May 26]. Available from: http://www.nap.edu
  /catalog.php?record_id=13115.

Give the date of access in brackets after the date of publication. Provide the full URL at the end of the entry. If it must
continue on an additional line, break it after a slash or other
punctuation mark.

Name-year system

Institute of Medicine, Committee on the Effect of Climate Change on
  Indoor Air Quality and Public Health. 2011. Climate change, the
  indoor environment, and health. Washington (DC): National Academy
  Press; [accessed 2013 May 26]. http://www.nap.edu/catalog.
  php?record_id=13115.

13. Article in an online journal
Citation-sequence or citation-name system

13. Jacomb F, Marsh J, Holman L. Sexual selection expedites the evolution of
  pesticide resistance. Evol. 2016 [accessed 2017 Jan 10];70(12):2746-
  2751. http://onlinelibrary.wiley.com/doi/10.1111/evo.13074/full.

Name-year system

Jacomb F, Marsh J, Holman, L. 2016. Sexual selection expedites the evolution
  of pesticide resistance. Evol. [accessed 2017 Jan 10];70(12):2746-
  2751. http://onlinelibrary.wiley.com/doi/10.1111/evo.13074/full.

CITATION MAP 16.2: ARTICLE IN A DATABASE, CSE STYLE

Include the following elements when citing an article in a database.

RECORD FOR AN ARTICLE IN A DATABASE

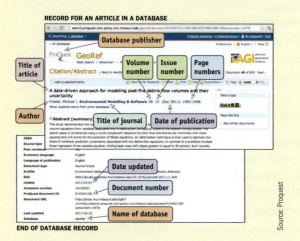

Source: Proquest

END OF DATABASE RECORD

CITATION-SEQUENCE OR CITATION-NAME FORMAT

Note number · Author · Title of article · Title of journal · Date of publication

14. Friedel M. A data driven approach for modeling post-fire debris-flow volumes and their uncertainty. Environ Model Softw. 2011 [updated 2012 Mar 1; accessed 2013 May 2];26(12):1583–1598. GeoRef. Ann Arbor (MI): ProQuest. http://dx.doi.org.proxy.mul.missouri.edu/10.1016/j.bbr.2011.03.031. Document No.: 919265108.

Date updated · URL · Volume and issue numbers · Page numbers · Name of database · Publication information for database · Document number

NAME-YEAR FORMAT

Author · Date of publication · Title of article · Title of journal · Page numbers

Friedel M. 2011. A data driven approach for modeling post-fire debris-flow volumes and their uncertainty. Environ Model Softw. [updated 2012 Mar 1; accessed 2013 May 2];26(12):1583–1598. GeoRef. Ann Arbor (MI): ProQuest. http://dx.doi.org.proxy.mul.missouri.edu/10.1016/j.bbr.2011.03.031. Document No.: 919265108.

Date updated · URL · Publication information for database · Volume and issue numbers · Document number · Name of database

CSE

14. Article in a database
Citation-sequence or citation-name system

14. Stave G, Darcey DJ. Prevention of laboratory animal allergy in the United
    States. J Occup Environ Med. 2012 [accessed 2013 May 17];54(5):558-
    563. Academic Search Complete. Ipswich (MA): EBSCO. http://web.
    ebscohost.com. Document No.: 75239696.

Because CSE does not provide specific guidelines for citing an
article retrieved from a database, this entry follows the guidelines for citing an online journal and a database.

Name-year system

Stave G, Darcey DJ. 2012. Prevention of laboratory animal allergy in
    the United States. J Occup Environ Med. [accessed 2013 May
    17];54(5):558-563. Academic Search Complete. Ipswich (MA): EBSCO.
    http://web.ebscohost.com. Document No.: 75239696.

15. Article in an online magazine
Citation-sequence or citation-name system

15. Rubanyi G. Could gene therapy cure heart disease? Sci Am. 2017
    [accessed 2017 Jan 10];316(1):38-43. https://www.scientificamerican.
    com/article/could-gene-therapy-cure-heart-disease/.

Name-year system

Rubanyi G. 2017. Could gene therapy cure heart disease? Sci Am. [accessed
    2017 Jan 10];316(1):38-43. https://www.scientificamerican.com/
    article/could-gene-therapy-cure-heart-disease/.

16. Article in an online newspaper
Citation-sequence or citation-name system

16. Singer N. Making ads that whisper to the brain. New York Times. Online
    version. 2010 Nov 13 [accessed 2010 Nov 29]. http://www.nytimes.
    com/2010/11/14/business/14stream.html?ref=health.

Name-year system

Singer N. 2010 Nov 13. Making ads that whisper to the brain. New York
Times. Online version. [accessed 2010 Nov 29]. http://www.nytimes
.com/2010/11/14/business/14stream.html?ref=health.

17. Website

Citation-sequence or citation-name system

17. Southern California Earthquake Data Center. Pasadena (CA): Caltech; c2013
[updated 2013 Jan 31; accessed 2013 Jun 3]. http://www.data.scec.org/.

Name-year system

Southern California Earthquake Data Center. c2013. Pasadena (CA): Caltech;
[updated 2013 Jan 31; accessed 2013 Jun 3]. http://www.data.scec.org/.

18. Short work from a website
Citation-sequence or citation-name system

18. National Wind Institute. Lubbock (TX): Texas Tech University; c2013.
The Enhanced Fujita scale; 2011 Aug 4 [accessed 2013 Jun 3];
[13 paragraphs]. http://www.spc.noaa.gov/efscale/.

Be sure to include both the copyright date for the site and the
publication date for the short work. In square brackets after
the date of access, provide the extent of the material used.

Name-year system

National Wind Institute. c2013. Lubbock (TX): Texas Tech University. The
Enhanced Fujita scale; 2011 Aug 4 [accessed 2013 Jun 3]; [13 paragraphs].
http://www.spc.noaa.gov/efscale/.

19. Report from a government agency
Citation-sequence or citation-name system

19. Centers for Disease Control and Prevention, US Department of Health
and Human Services. Skin cancer prevention progress report 2016.
Atlanta (GA): Centers for Disease Control and Prevention; 2016

[accessed 2017 Jan 14]. https://www.cdc.gov/cancer/skin/pdf/
skincancerpreventionprogressreport_2016.pdf.

Name-year system

Centers for Disease Control and Prevention, US Department of Health
and Human Services. 2016. Skin cancer prevention progress report
2016. Atlanta (GA): Centers for Disease Control and Prevention;
[accessed 2017 Jan 14]. https://www.cdc.gov/cancer/skin/pdf/
skincancerpreventionprogressreport_2016.pdf.

20. Online video
Citation-sequence or citation-name system

Among giants [video]. Rainhouse Cinema, 12:51 minutes. 2011 [accessed 2015
May 1]. https://vimeo.com/66173800.

Name-year system

Among giants. 2011. [video] Rainhouse Cinema. 12:51 minutes. [accessed
2015 May 1]. https://vimeo.com/66173800.

The following sample References list will show you how to organize name-year entries. The sample entries correspond to the name-year entries listed in items 1 through 8 on pages 237-239. Notice that the list is alphabetized. Citation-name entries would also be alphabetized. Citation-sequence entries, however, would be placed in the order they were introduced in the paper.

References

American Medical Association Council on Ethical and Judicial
Affairs. 2016. Code of medical ethics of the American Medical
Association. Chicago: American Medical Association.

Banich MT. 2010. Hemispheric specialization and cognition.
In: Whitaker HA, editor. Concise encyclopedia of brain and
language. Oxford (England): Elsevier. p. 224-230.

Barge RA. 2013. Using standards to support human factors engineering.
In: Anderson M, editor. Contemporary ergonomics and human
factors 2013: proceedings of the International Conference on
Ergonomics and Human Factors; 2013 Apr 15–18; Cambridge,
England. Croydon (England): Taylor & Francis. p. 135-137.

Gadoth N. 2016. Free radicals: their role in brain function and
dysfunction. In: Armstrong D, Stratton RD, editors. Oxidative
stress and antioxidant protection: the science of free radical
biology and disease. Hoboken (NJ): Wiley. p. 23-38.

Kao-Kniffin J, Freyre DS, Balser TC. 2011. Increased methane emissions
from an invasive wetland plant under elevated carbon dioxide
levels. Appl Soil Ecol. 48(3):309-312.

King BJ. 2013. How animals grieve. Chicago: University of Chicago
Press. 193 p.

Maxfield FR, Willard JM, Shuyan L, editors. 2016. Lysosomes:
biology, diseases, and therapeutics. Hoboken (NJ): Wiley.

Ohanian HC, Ruffini R. 2013. Gravitation and spacetime. 3rd ed.
Cambridge (England): Cambridge University Press.

G

GRAMMAR

Visit the MindTap® for this book for additional information and resources.

17   Sentence Essentials

When you think of the word *grammar*, you might also think of the word *rule*—a regulation you must obey. But *rule* has another meaning: "a statement of what should be done to gain some benefit," as in *An important rule to follow when you exercise is to drink plenty of water*. Grammar rules provide you with beneficial advice on how to achieve success as a writer. Because grammar rules describe how language is commonly or conventionally used, to follow grammar rules simply means to write in a way that is considered appropriate by a specific set of readers. This chapter covers concepts of grammar that will help you understand how to write clear, convincing, and conventional sentences.

17a   Parts of speech

When you look up a word in the dictionary, you will often find it followed by one or more of these labels: *adj.*, *adv.*, *conj.*, *interj.*, *n.*, *prep.*, *pron.*, and *v.* (or *vb.*). These are the abbreviations for the traditional eight parts of speech: *adjective*, *adverb*, *conjunction*, *interjection*, *noun*, *preposition*, *pronoun*, and *verb*.

(1) Verbs

Verbs that indicate action (*walk*, *drive*, *study*) are called **action verbs**. Verbs that express being or experiencing are called **linking verbs**, which link a subject to a subject complement; they include *be*, *seem*, and *become* and the sensory verbs *look*, *taste*, *smell*, *feel*, and *sound*. Both action verbs and linking verbs are frequently accompanied by **auxiliary** or **helping verbs**, which come before the main verb and add shades of meaning, such as information about time (*will* study this afternoon), ability (*can* study), or obligation (*must* study).

THINKING RHETORICALLY
VERBS

Decide which of the following sentences evokes a clearer image:

➤ The team captain **was** absolutely ecstatic.
➤ Grinning broadly, the team captain **shot** both her arms into the air.

You probably chose the sentence with the action verb *shot* rather than the sentence with *was*. When their goal is vibrant imagery, successful writers avoid using the verb *be* in any of its forms (*am, is, are, was, were*, or *been*). Instead, they use vivid action verbs.

(2) Nouns

Nouns usually name people, places, things, and ideas. **Proper nouns** are specific names: *Bill Gates, Redmond, Microsoft Corporation*. **Common nouns** refer to any member of a class or category: *person, city, company*. There are three types of common nouns.

- **Count nouns** refer to people, places, things, and ideas that can be counted. They have singular and plural forms: *boy, boys; car, cars; concept, concepts.*
- **Noncount nouns** refer to things or ideas that cannot be counted: *furniture, information.*
- **Collective nouns** are nouns that refer to groups and that can be either singular or plural, depending on the context of the sentence: *The **committee** published its report* [singular]. *The **committee** disagree about their duties* [plural].

THINKING RHETORICALLY
NOUNS

Nouns like *entertainment* and *nutrition* that refer to concepts are called **abstract nouns**. In contrast, nouns like *guitar* and *apple* that refer to things perceivable by the senses are called **concrete nouns**. When your rhetorical situation calls for the use of abstractions, balance them with tangible details conveyed through concrete nouns.

(3) Pronouns

Most pronouns (*it*, *he*, *she*, *they*, and many others) replace **antecedents**—nouns or noun phrases that have already been mentioned.

➤ My parents bought the cheap, decrepit house because **they** thought **it** had charm.

A pronoun and its antecedent may be found either in the same sentence or in separate, though usually adjacent, sentences.

➤ The students collaborated on a research project last year. **They** even presented their findings at a national conference.

The pronouns in the preceding examples are **personal pronouns**. For a discussion of other types of pronouns, see chapter **21**.

(4) Adjectives

Adjectives most commonly modify nouns: *spicy* food, *special* price. Sometimes they modify pronouns: *blue* ones, anyone *thin*. Adjectives usually answer one of these questions: Which one? What kind of . . . ? How many? What color or size or shape (and so on)? Although adjectives usually precede the nouns they modify, they occasionally follow them: *enough* time, time *enough*. Adjectives may also follow linking verbs such as *be*, *seem*, and *become*:

The <u>moon</u> is **full** tonight.   <u>He</u> seems **shy**.

Articles, *a*, *an*, and *the*, are also used before nouns. The article *a* is used before a consonant sound (**a** yard, **a** university, **a** VIP); *an* is used before a vowel sound (**an** apple, **an** hour, **an** NFL team).

MULTILINGUAL WRITERS
ARTICLE USAGE

English has two types of articles: indefinite and definite. The **indefinite articles**, *a* and *an*, indicate that a singular noun is used in a general way, as when you introduce the noun for the first time or when you define a word.

➤ Pluto is **a** dwarf <u>planet</u>.

➤ There has been **a** <u>controversy</u> over the classification of Pluto.

➤ **A** <u>planet</u> is a celestial body orbiting a star such as our sun.

The **definite article**, *the*, is used before a noun that has already been introduced or when a reference is obvious. *The* is also used before a noun that is related in form or meaning to a word previously mentioned.

➤ Scientists distinguish between planets and <u>dwarf planets</u>. One of **the** <u>dwarf planets</u> in our solar system is Pluto.

➤ Scientists are not sure how to <u>classify</u> some celestial bodies. **The** <u>classification</u> of Pluto proved to be controversial.

The definite article also appears before a noun considered unique, such as *moon*, *universe*, and *sky*.

➤ **The** <u>moon</u> is full tonight.

(5) Adverbs

Adverbs most frequently modify verbs. They provide information about time, manner, place, and frequency, thus answering one of these questions: When? How? Where? How often?

➤ The conference starts **tomorrow**. [time]

➤ I **rapidly** calculated the cost. [manner]

➤ We met **here**. [place]

➤ They **often** work late on Thursdays. [frequency]

Adverbs that modify verbs can often move from one position in a sentence to another.

➤ He **carefully** removed the radio collar.

➤ He removed the radio collar **carefully**.

Adverbs also modify adjectives and other adverbs by intensifying or otherwise qualifying the meanings of those words.

➤ I was **extremely** curious. [modifying an adjective]

➤ The team played **surprisingly** well. [modifying an adverb]

THINKING RHETORICALLY
ADVERBS

What do the adverbs add to the following sentences?

➤ The scientist **delicately** places the slide under the microscope.

➤ "You're late," he whispered **vehemently**.

➤ She is **wistfully** hopeful.

Adverbs can help you portray an action, indicate how someone is speaking, and add detail to a description.

(6) Prepositions

A **preposition** is a word that combines with a noun and any of its modifiers to provide additional detail—often answering one of these questions: Where? When?

➤ **In** the early afternoon, we walked **through** our old neighborhood. [answers the questions *When*? and *Where*?]

A preposition may also combine with a pronoun.

➤ We walked **through** it.

A grammar rule that has caused much controversy over the years advises against ending a sentence with a preposition. Most professional writers now follow this rule only when they adopt a formal tone. If their rhetorical situation calls for an informal tone, they will not hesitate to place a preposition at the end of a sentence.

➤ He found friends **on** whom he could depend. [formal]

➤ He found friends he could depend **on**. [informal]

SOME COMMON PREPOSITIONS

about	behind	for	of	to
above	between	from	on	toward
after	by	in	out	under
as	despite	into	past	until
at	during	like	since	up
before	except	near	through	with

Phrasal prepositions consist of more than one word.

➤ The coach postponed practice **because of** bad weather.

SOME COMMON PHRASAL PREPOSITIONS

according to	due to	in spite of
as for	except for	instead of
because of	in addition to	with regard to

(7) Conjunctions

Conjunctions are connectors. They fall into four categories: coordinating, correlative, subordinating, and adverbial. A **coordinating conjunction** connects similar words or groups of words; that is, it generally links a word to a word, a phrase to a phrase (17d), or a clause to a clause (17e). There are seven coordinating conjunctions. Use the made-up word *fanboys* to help you remember them.

F	A	N	B	O	Y	S
for	and	nor	but	or	yet	so

➤ tired **yet** excited [*Yet* joins two words and signals contrast.]

➤ in the boat **or** on the pier [*Or* joins two phrases and marks them as alternatives.]

➤ We did not share a language, **but** somehow we communicated. [*But* joins two independent clauses and signals contrast.]

In the example sentence above, *but* links two independent clauses and thus is preceded by a comma. A coordinating conjunction such as *but* may also link independent clauses that stand alone as sentences.

> The momentum in the direction of globalization seems too powerful to buck, the economic logic unmatchable. **But** in a region where jobs are draining away, and where an ethic of self-reliance remains a dim, vestigial, but honored memory, it seems at least an outside possibility.
>
> —BILL MCKIBBEN, "Small World"

A **correlative conjunction** (or **correlative**) consists of two parts. The most common correlatives are *both . . . and, either . . . or, neither . . . nor*, and *not only . . . but also*.

➤ **Not only** did they run ten miles, **but** they **also** swam twenty laps. [*Not only . . . but also* joins two independent clauses and signals addition.]

Generally, a correlative conjunction links similar structures. The following sentence has been revised because the correlative conjunction was linking a phrase to a clause.

➤ **Not only** ~~saving~~ *did he save* the lives of the accident victims, **but** he **also** prevented many spinal injuries.

A **subordinating conjunction** introduces a dependent clause (**17e**). It also carries a specific meaning; for example, it may indicate cause, concession, condition, purpose, or time. A dependent clause that begins a sentence is followed by a comma.

➤ **Unless** the project receives funding, the research will stop. [*Unless* signals a condition.]

➤ She studied Spanish **when** she worked in Costa Rica. [*When* signals time.]

SUBORDINATING CONJUNCTIONS

after	before	once	unless
although	even if	since	until
as if	even though	so that	when
as though	if	than	whether
because	in that	though	while

Adverbial conjunctions—such as *however, nevertheless, then,* and *therefore*—link independent clauses (**17e**). These conjunctions, also called **conjunctive adverbs**, signal relationships such as cause, condition, and contrast. Adverbial conjunctions are set off by commas. An independent clause preceding an adverbial conjunction may end in a semicolon or a period.

➤ The senator thought the plan was reasonable**; however,** the voters did not.

➤ The senator thought the plan was reasonable**. However,** the voters did not.

➤ The senator thought the plan was reasonable. The voters, **however,** did not.

➤ The senator thought the plan was reasonable. The voters did not, **however**.

ADVERBIAL CONJUNCTIONS

also	indeed	moreover	still
finally	instead	nevertheless	then
furthermore	likewise	nonetheless	therefore
however	meanwhile	otherwise	thus

(8) Interjections

Interjections most commonly express an emotion such as surprise or dread. Interjections that come before a sentence end in a period or an exclamation point.

➤ **Oh.** Now I understand.

➤ **Wow!** Your design is astounding.

Interjections that begin or interrupt a sentence are set off by commas.

➤ **Hey,** what are you doing?

➤ The solution, **alas,** was not as simple as I had hoped it would be.

EXERCISE 17.1

Identify the part of speech for each word in the sentences below.

1. Hey, are you a fan of both anime and manga?

2. If you are, you should join the University Anime and Manga Club.

3. Every Tuesday at noon, we watch current anime or swap favorite manga.

4. Memberships are free; however, donations are always welcome.

5. Whenever you have time, you can simply look for us in the Student Union.

17b Subjects and predicates

A sentence consists of two parts:

> SUBJECT + PREDICATE

The **subject** is generally someone or something that either performs an action or is described. The **predicate** expresses the action initiated by the subject or gives information that describes, identifies, or categorizes the subject.

The <u>landlord</u> + <u>renovated</u> the apartment.
[The subject performs an action; the predicate expresses the action.]

<u>They</u> + <u>had sounded</u> reasonable.
[The subject is described; the predicate gives information about the subject.]

The central components of the subject and the predicate are often called the **simple subject** (the main noun or pronoun) and the **simple predicate** (the main verb and any auxiliary verbs). They are underlined in the examples above.

    Compound subjects and **compound predicates** include a connecting word (conjunction) such as *and, or,* or *but.*

➤ <u>Republicans</u> **and** <u>Democrats</u> are debating this issue. [compound subject]

➤ The candidate <u>stated his views on climate change</u> **but** <u>did not discuss fracking</u>. [compound predicate]

17c Complements

Complements are parts of the predicate required by the verb to make a sentence complete. A complement is generally a pronoun, a noun, or a noun with modifiers.

➤ The committee chair introduced

> **her.** [pronoun]
>
> **Sylvia Holbrook.**
> [noun]
>
> **the new but well-
> known <u>member</u>.**
> [noun with modifiers]

There are four different complements: direct objects, indirect objects, subject complements, and object complements.

The **direct object** either receives the action of the verb or shows the result of the action.

➤ Steve McQueen drove **a Ford Mustang** in the movie *Bullitt*.

➤ I. M. Pei designed **the East Building of the National Gallery**.

Indirect objects typically name the person(s) receiving or benefiting from the action indicated by the verb. Verbs that often take indirect objects include *buy, give, lend, sell, send,* and *write*.

➤ The supervisor gave **the new employees** <u>computers</u>.

[*To whom* were the computers given?]

➤ She wrote **them** <u>recommendation letters</u>.

[*For whom* were the recommendation letters written?]

The **subject complement** follows a linking verb. The most common linking verb is *be* (*am, is, are, was, were, been*). Other linking verbs are *become, seem,* and *appear* and the sensory verbs *feel, look, smell, sound,* and *taste*. A subject complement can be a pronoun, a noun, or a noun with modifiers. It can also be an adjective.

➤ The winner was
- **you**. [pronoun]
- **Harry Solano**. [noun]
- **the lucky <u>person</u> with the highest score**. [noun with modifiers]
- **ecstatic**. [adjective]

The **object complement** helps complete the meaning of a verb such as *call, elect, make, name,* or *paint.* The object complement can be a noun or an adjective, along with any modifiers.

➤ Reporters called the rookie **the best <u>player</u>**. [noun with modifiers]

➤ The strike left the fans **somewhat <u>disappointed</u>**. [adjective with modifier]

EXERCISE 17.2

Identify the subject and the predicate in each sentence. Then, looking at just the predicate, identify the type of complement the sentence contains. Complements are underlined.

1. A naturalist gave <u>us</u> <u>a short lecture on the Cascade Mountains</u>.

2. He showed <u>slides of mountain lakes and heather meadows</u>.

3. Douglas fir predominates in the Cascade forests.

4. Mountaineers and artists consider <u>the North Cascades</u> <u>the most dramatic mountains in the range</u>.

5. Timberlines are <u>low</u> because of the short growing season.

6. Many volcanoes are in the Cascades.

7. Mt. Rainier is <u>the highest volcano in the range</u>.

8. Many visitors to this area hike <u>the Pacific Crest Trail</u>.

9. My friend lent <u>me</u> <u>his map of the trail</u>.

10. The trail begins in southern California, passes through Oregon and Washington, and ends in British Columbia.

17d | Phrases

A **phrase** is a sequence of grammatically related words without a subject, a predicate, or both. A phrase is categorized according to its most important word.

(1) Noun phrases

A noun phrase consists of a main noun and its modifiers. It can serve as a subject or as a complement. It can also be the object of a preposition such as *in, of, on, at,* or *to.*

➤ **The heavy frost** killed **many fruit trees**. [subject and direct object]

➤ **My cousin** is **an organic farmer**. [subject and subject complement]

➤ **His farm** is in **eastern Oregon**. [subject and object of the preposition *in*]

MULTILINGUAL WRITERS
NUMBER AGREEMENT IN NOUN PHRASES

Some words must agree in number with the nouns they precede. The words *a, an, this,* and *that* are used before singular nouns; *some, few, these, those,* and *many* are used before plural nouns.

➤ **an/that** opportunity [singular noun]

➤ **some/few/those** opportunities [plural noun]

The words *less* and *much* precede nouns representing abstract concepts or masses that cannot be counted (noncount nouns).

➤ **less** freedom, **much** water [noncount nouns]

(2) Verb phrases

A verb is essential to the predicate of a sentence. It generally expresses action or a state of being. Besides a main verb, a **verb phrase** includes one or more **auxiliary verbs**, sometimes called *helping verbs*, such as *be, have, do, will,* and *should*.

➤ The passengers **have deplaned**. [auxiliary verb + main verb]

(3) Verbal phrases

A **verbal phrase** differs from a verb phrase because it serves as a noun or a modifier rather than as a verb.

➤ He <u>was **reading**</u> the story aloud. [*Reading* is part of the verb phrase, *was reading*.]

➤ **Reading** college-level material is fundamental to academic success. [*Reading* is part of the verbal phrase, *reading college-level material*. It serves as a noun. COMPARE: **It** is fundamental to academic success.]

➤ The student **reading** aloud is an education major. [*Reading* is part of the verbal phrase, *reading* aloud. It modifies *the student*.]

Verbal phrases are divided into three types: gerund phrases, participial phrases, and infinitive phrases.

Gerund phrases include a verb form ending in *-ing* (the gerund). A gerund phrase serves as a noun, usually functioning as the subject or object in a sentence.

➤ <u>**Writing** a bestseller</u> was her only goal. [subject]

➤ My neighbor enjoys <u>**writing** about distant places</u>. [object]

Because gerund phrases act as nouns, pronouns can replace them.

That was her only goal.   My neighbor enjoys **it**.

THINKING RHETORICALLY
GERUNDS

What is the difference between the subjects in the following sentences?

➤ They bundle products together, which may result in higher consumer costs.

➤ Bundling products together may result in higher consumer costs.

In the first sentence, the subject is the actor, *they*. In the second sentence, the subject is an action, *bundling products together*. As you revise, ask yourself whether you want to emphasize actors or actions.

Participial phrases include either a present participle (a verb form ending in *-ing*) or a past participle (a verb form ending in *-ed* for regular verbs or another form for irregular verbs). Participial phrases function as modifiers.

➤ **Fearing a drought**, the farmers used less irrigation water.

➤ All the farmers in the area, **plagued by drought**, used less irrigation water.

➤ Farmers conserved water, **fearing a drought in late summer**.

Remember that gerund and participial phrases differ in function. A gerund phrase functions as a noun; a participial phrase functions as a modifier.

➤ **Working together** can spur creativity. [gerund phrase]

➤ **Working together**, the students designed their own software. [participial phrase]

A present participle (*-ing* form) cannot function alone as the main verb in a sentence. It must be accompanied by a form of *be* (*am*, *is*, *are*, *was*, or *were*).

➤ They *are* **thinking** about the future.

THINKING RHETORICALLY
PARTICIPIAL PHRASES

If some of your sentences sound monotonous or choppy, try combining them by using participial phrases.

➤ *Crowded along the city streets, fans celebrated* ~~Fans crowded along the city streets. They were celebrating~~ their team's first state championship.

Infinitive phrases serve as nouns or as modifiers. The form of the infinitive is distinct—the infinitive marker *to* followed by the base form of the verb.

➤ The company intends **to hire** **twenty new employees**. [noun]

➤ We discussed his plan **to use** **a new packing process**. [modifier of the noun *plan*]

➤ **To attract** **customers**, the company changed its advertising strategy. [modifier of the verb *changed*]

Some instructors advise against putting words between the infinitive marker *to* and the base form of the verb.

➤ *Under the circumstances, the* The jury was unable to~~, under the circumstances,~~ convict the defendant.

This is good advice to remember if the intervening words create a cumbersome sentence. However, most writers today recognize that a single word splitting an infinitive can provide emphasis.

➤ He did not expect to actually publish his work.

MULTILINGUAL WRITERS
VERBS FOLLOWED BY GERUNDS AND/OR INFINITIVES

Some verbs in English can be followed by a gerund, some can be followed by an infinitive, and some can be followed by either.

Followed by a Gerund

admit   avoid   consider   deny   dislike   enjoy   finish

➤ She **enjoys playing** the piano.

Followed by an Infinitive

agree   decide   deserve   hope   need   plan   promise   seem

➤ She **promised to play** the piano for us.

Followed by Either a Gerund or an Infinitive

begin   continue   like   prefer   remember   stop   try

➤ She **likes to play** the piano.   ➤ She **likes playing** the piano.

Although either a gerund phrase or an infinitive phrase can follow these verbs, the resulting sentences may differ in meaning.

➤ We **stopped discussing** the plan. [The discussion has ended.]

➤ We **stopped to discuss** the plan. [The discussion has not yet started.]

(4) Prepositional phrases

Prepositional phrases provide information about time, place, cause, manner, and so on. They can also answer one of these questions: Which one? What kind of . . . ?

➤ **With great feeling**, Martin Luther King expressed his dream **of freedom**.

[*With great feeling* describes the way the speech was delivered, and *of freedom* specifies the kind of dream.]

➤ King delivered his most famous speech **at a demonstration in Washington, DC**.

[Both *at a demonstration* and *in Washington, DC* provide information about place.]

A prepositional phrase consists of a **preposition** (a word such as *at*, *of*, or *in*) and a pronoun, noun, or noun phrase (called the **object of the preposition**). A prepositional phrase modifies another element in the sentence.

➤ Everyone **in class** went to the play. [modifier of the pronoun *everyone*]

➤ Some students met the professor **after the play**. [modifier of the verb *met*]

(5) Appositives

An **appositive** is most often a noun or a noun phrase that refers to the same person, place, thing, or idea as a preceding noun or noun phrase but in different words. When the appositive simply specifies the referent, no commas are used.

➤ Lin-Manuel Miranda's play ***Hamilton*** won a Pulitzer Prize. [specifies which of Miranda's plays won the award.]

When the appositive provides extra details, commas set it off.

➤ *Hamilton*, **a play by Lin-Manuel Miranda**, won a Pulitzer Prize. [provides an extra detail about the play]

(6) Absolute phrases

An **absolute phrase** is usually a noun phrase modified by a prepositional phrase, an adjective phrase, or a participial phrase.

➤ **Her guitar in the front seat**, she pulled away from the curb.

➤ **More vaccine having arrived**, the staff scheduled its distribution.

The first absolute phrase provides details; the second expresses cause.

EXERCISE 17.3

Label the underlined phrases in the following sentences as noun phrases, verb phrases, prepositional phrases, or verbal phrases. For verbal phrases, specify the type: gerund, participial, or infinitive. When a long phrase includes a shorter (embedded) phrase, identify just the long phrase. Finally, identify any appositive phrases or absolute phrases in the sentences.

1. <u>After the Second World War,</u> <u>fifty-one countries</u> formed <u>the United Nations,</u> <u>an international organization dedicated to peace, tolerance, and cooperation.</u>

2. <u>The Charter of the United Nations</u> <u>was written</u> <u>in 1945</u>.

3. <u>According to this charter,</u> the United Nations <u>may address</u> a wide range <u>of issues</u>.

4. <u>The United Nations</u> devotes most of its energies to <u>protecting human rights,</u> <u>maintaining peace,</u> and <u>encouraging social development</u>.

5. <u>To reach its goals,</u> the United Nations depends on funding <u>from its member states</u>.

6. <u>Its blue flag easily recognized everywhere,</u> the United Nations now includes <u>193 member states</u>.

7. <u>Symbolizing peace,</u> the emblem <u>on the flag</u> is a map <u>enclosed by olive branches</u>.

17e   Clauses

(1) Independent clauses

A **clause** is a group of related words that contains a subject and a predicate. An **independent clause**, sometimes called a *main clause*, has the same grammatical structure as a simple sentence: both contain a subject and a predicate.

➤ The students earned high grades.

An independent clause can stand alone as a complete sentence. Other clauses can be added to independent clauses to form longer, more detailed sentences.

(2) Dependent clauses

A **dependent clause** also has a subject and a predicate. However, it cannot stand alone as a complete sentence because of the word introducing it—usually a relative pronoun or a subordinating conjunction.

➤ The athlete **who placed first** grew up in Argentina. [relative pronoun]

➤ She received the gold medal **because she performed flawlessly**. [subordinating conjunction]

Noun clauses are dependent clauses that serve as subjects or objects. They are introduced by *if*, *that*, or a *wh-* word such as *why*, *what*, or *when*. To decide whether a clause is a noun clause, try replacing it with a pronoun such as *it* or *this*.

➤ **What the witness said** may not be true. [subject]

➤ We do not understand **why they did it**. [direct object]

When no misunderstanding would result, the word *that* can be omitted from the beginning of a clause.

➤ The scientist said **she was moving to Australia**. [*that* omitted]

However, *that* should always be retained when there are two noun clauses.

➤ The scientist said **that she was moving to Australia** and **that her research team was planning to accompany her**. [*that* retained in both noun clauses]

An **adjectival clause**, or **relative clause**, follows a pronoun, noun, or noun phrase and answers one of these questions: Which one? What kind of . . . ? Such clauses, which nearly always follow the words they modify, usually begin with a **relative pronoun** (*who, whom, that, which,* or *whose*) but sometimes start with a **relative adverb** (*when, where,* or *why*).

➤ Nobody likes news reports **that can be easily falsified**. [answers the question *What kind of news reports?*]

➤ Students **who have good study habits** begin their research early. [answers the question *Which students?*]

A relative pronoun can be omitted as long as the meaning of the sentence is still clear.

➤ Mother Teresa was someone **the whole world admired**. [*Whom*, the direct object of the clause, has been omitted: the whole world admired *whom*.]

➤ She was someone **who cared more about serving than being served**. [*Who* cannot be omitted because it is the subject of the clause.]

An **adverbial clause** usually answers one of the following questions: Where? When? Why? How? How frequently? In what manner? Adverbial clauses are introduced by subordinating conjunctions such as *because, although,* and *when*.

➤ **When the need arises**, the company hires new writers. [answers the question *How frequently does the company hire new writers?*]

➤ She acted **as though she understood the directions**. [answers the question *How did she act?*]

THINKING RHETORICALLY
ADVERBIAL CLAUSES

In an adverbial clause that refers to time or establishes a fact, both the subject and any form of the verb *be* can be omitted. Using such **elliptical constructions** will make your writing more concise.

➤ **Though tired**, they continued to study for the exam.

   [COMPARE: **Though they were tired**, they continued to study for the exam.]

Be sure that the omitted subject of an elliptical clause is the same as the subject of the independent clause. Otherwise, revise either the adverbial clause or the main clause.

                I was
➤ While ˄reviewing your report, a few questions occurred to me.

OR
                                      I thought of
➤ While reviewing your report, ˄a few questions ~~occurred to me~~.

EXERCISE 17.4

1. Identify the dependent clauses in the following paragraph.

2. Identify the underlined words as coordinating, correlative, subordinating, or adverbial conjunctions.

   [1]If you live by the sword, you might die by the sword. [2]<u>However</u>, <u>if</u> you make your living by swallowing swords, you will not necessarily die by swallowing swords. [3]At least, this is the conclusion Brian Witcombe and Dan Meyer reached <u>after</u> they surveyed forty-six professional sword swallowers. [4](Brian Witcombe is a radiologist, <u>and</u> Dan Meyer is a famous sword swallower.) [5]Some of those surveyed mentioned <u>that</u> they had experienced <u>either</u> "sword throats" <u>or</u> chest pains, <u>and</u> others who let their swords drop to their stomachs described perforation of their innards, <u>but</u> the researchers could find no listing of a sword-swallowing mortality in the medical studies they reviewed. [6]The researchers did not inquire into the reasons for swallowing swords in the first place.

CAUTION

Used carefully, a grammar checker can be a helpful tool, but keep the following advice in mind.

➤ Use a grammar checker only in addition to your own editing and proofreading.
➤ Always evaluate any sentences flagged by a grammar checker to determine whether there is, in fact, a problem.
➤ Carefully review the revisions proposed by a grammar checker before accepting them. Sometimes the proposed revisions create new errors.

18 Sentence Fragments

As its name suggests, a **sentence fragment** is only a piece of a sentence; it is not complete.

18a Recognizing sentence fragments

A sentence is considered a fragment when it is incomplete in one of three ways. It is missing a subject *or* a verb, it is missing both, or it is a dependent clause. Most fragments can be attached to adjacent sentences.

MISSING VERB   Alternative medical treatment may include
hypnosis.—̲*the*̲**The placement of a patient into a sleeplike state**.

MISSING SUBJECT	**Derived from a word meaning "nervous**
	hypnotism
	sleep.~~,~~" ~~Hypnotism~~ actually refers to a type
	of focused attention.
NO SUBJECT OR	*Contrary to popular belief, the*
VERB	~~The~~ hypnotic state differs from sleep.
	~~Contrary to popular belief~~.
DEPENDENT CLAUSE	Most people can be hypnotized easily~~.~~
	, although
	~~Although~~ the depth of the trance for each
	person varies.

18b Phrases as sentence fragments

A phrase is a group of words without a subject and/or predicate. When punctuated as a sentence (that is, with a period or other end punctuation), it becomes a fragment. To revise a phrase fragment, you can often attach it to a nearby sentence.

VERBAL PHRASE AS A FRAGMENT

, creating
➤ Early humans valued color~~.~~ ~~Creating~~ **permanent colors with natural pigments.**

PREPOSITIONAL PHRASE AS A FRAGMENT

, originally
➤ For years, the Scottish have dyed sweaters with soot~~.~~ ~~Originally~~ **from the chimneys of peat-burning stoves**.

APPOSITIVE PHRASE AS A FRAGMENT

➤ During the Renaissance, one of the most highly valued pigments
—*an*
was ultramarine~~.~~ ~~An~~ **extract from lapis lazuli.**

ABSOLUTE PHRASE AS A FRAGMENT

➤ The deciduous trees of New England are known for their brilliant autumn color. *, sugar* **Sugar maples dazzling tourists with their orange and red leaves**.

Instead of attaching a fragment to a nearby sentence, you can sometimes recast the fragment as a complete sentence.

FRAGMENT	Humans painted themselves for a variety of purposes. **To attract a mate, to hide themselves from game or predators, or to signal aggression**.
REVISION	Humans used color for a variety of purposes. For example, they painted themselves to attract a mate, to hide themselves from game or predators, or to signal aggression.

18c Dependent clauses as sentence fragments

A dependent clause is a group of words with both a subject and a predicate, but because it begins with a subordinating conjunction or a relative pronoun, it cannot stand alone as a sentence.

➤ More than two thousand people were aboard the *Titanic*. *, which* **Which was the largest ocean liner in 1912**.

➤ The iceberg was no surprise. *because* **Because the *Titanic's* wireless operators had received reports of ice in the area**.

You can also recast the fragment as a complete sentence by removing the subordinating conjunction or relative pronoun and supplying any missing elements.

➤ The iceberg was no surprise. The *Titanic's* wireless operators had received reports of ice in the area.

THINKING RHETORICALLY

FRAGMENTS

When used judiciously, fragments—like short sentences—emphasize ideas or add surprise. However, fragments are generally permitted only when the rhetorical situation allows the use of a casual tone.

> **May. When the earth's Northern Hemisphere awakens from winter's sleep and all of nature bristles with the energies of new life.** My work has kept me indoors for months now. I'm not sure I'll ever get used to it.
>
> —KEN CAREY, *Flat Rock Journal: A Day in the Ozark Mountains*

EXERCISE 18.1

Follow the guidelines in this chapter to locate and revise the fragments in the following paragraph. If you find it necessary, make other improvements as well. Be prepared to explain your revisions.

¹One of the most popular rides at any county fair or amusement park is the Ferris wheel. ²The original Ferris wheel, designed by George Washington Gale Ferris, Jr., for a national exposition in 1893. ³Rose to height of 264 feet. ⁴And accommodated 2,140 passengers. ⁵Ferris's goal was to build something that would surpass in effect the Eiffel Tower. ⁶Which was constructed just a few years earlier. ⁷Though Ferris's plans were not immediately accepted. ⁸Once they were, and the wheel opened to the public, it became an immediate success. ⁹At times carrying thirty-eight thousand passengers a day. ¹⁰Since the nineteenth century. ¹¹Engineers have designed taller and taller Ferris wheels. ¹²The 541-foot Singapore Flyer holds the record, but the Beijing Great Wheel, currently under construction. ¹³Will be over a hundred feet taller.

19 Comma Splices and Fused Sentences

A **comma splice**, or **comma fault**, refers to the incorrect use of a comma between two independent clauses (clauses including a subject and predicate that can stand alone as complete sentences).

➤ Most stockholders favored the merger, *but* the management did not.

A **fused sentence**, or **run-on sentence**, consists of two independent clauses run together without any punctuation at all.

➤ The first section of the proposal was approved *; however,* the budget will have to be resubmitted.

To revise a comma splice or a fused sentence, include appropriate punctuation and any necessary connecting words.

19a Locating comma splices and fused sentences

You can find comma splices and fused sentences by remembering that they commonly occur in certain contexts.

- With transitional words and phrases such as *however*, *therefore*, and *for example*

COMMA SPLICE   The director is unable to meet you this week*;* *however,* next week she has time on Tuesday.

- When an explanation or an example is given in the second sentence

FUSED SENTENCE   The cultural center has a new collection
of Navajo weavings , many of them were
. Many
donated by a retired anthropologist.

- When a positive clause follows a negative clause, or vice versa

COMMA SPLICE   A World Cup victory is not just an everyday
sporting event, it is a national celebration.
. It

- When the subject of the second clause is a pronoun whose antecedent is in the preceding clause

FUSED SENTENCE
. It
Lake Baikal is located in southern Russia , it
is 394 miles long. [The pronoun *it* refers to
Lake Baikal.]

19b Revising comma splices and fused sentences

If you find comma splices or fused sentences in your writing, try one of the following methods to revise them.

(1) Link independent clauses with a comma and a coordinating conjunction

By linking clauses with a comma and a coordinating conjunction (*and*, *but*, *or*, *nor*, *for*, *so*, or *yet*), you signal the relationship between the clauses.

FUSED SENTENCE   The diplomats will end their discussion on
Friday , they will submit their final decision
and
on Monday.

COMMA SPLICE   Some diplomats applauded the treaty, others
but
opposed it vehemently.

(2) Link independent clauses with a semicolon or a colon or separate them with a period

When you link independent clauses with a semicolon, the semi-colon usually indicates addition or contrast. When you link clauses with a colon, the second clause serves as an explanation or an elaboration of the first. A period indicates that each clause is a complete sentence, distinct from surrounding sentences.

COMMA SPLICE	Our division's reports are posted on our web page;∧ hard copies are available by request.
COMMA SPLICE	Our division's reports are posted on our web page.∧ Hard copies are available by request.
FUSED SENTENCE	Our mission statement is simple:∧we aim to provide good athletic gear at affordable prices.

(3) Recast an independent clause as a dependent clause or as a phrase

A dependent clause includes a subordinating conjunction such as *although* or *because*, which indicates how the dependent and independent clauses are related (in a cause-and-effect relationship, for example). A prepositional phrase includes a preposition such as *in*, *on*, or *because of* that may also signal a relationship directly. Verbal, appositive, and absolute phrases suggest relationships less directly because they do not include connecting words.

COMMA SPLICE	*Because the* ∧~~The~~ wind had blown down power lines, the whole city was without electricity for several hours. [dependent clause]
COMMA SPLICE	*Because of the downed* ∧~~The wind had blown down~~ power lines, the whole city was without electricity for several hours. [prepositional phrase]
COMMA SPLICE	*The wind having* ∧~~The wind had~~ blown down power lines, the whole city was without electricity for several hours. [absolute phrase]

(4) Integrate one clause into the other

When you integrate clauses, you will generally retain the important details but omit or change some words.

FUSED SENTENCE The proposal covers all ~~but one point it does~~ *the points except assessment procedures.*
~~not describe how the project will be assessed.~~

(5) Use transitional words or phrases to link independent clauses

Another way to revise fused sentences and comma splices is to use transitional words and phrases such as *however*, *on the contrary*, and *in the meantime*.

FUSED SENTENCE Sexual harassment is not an issue for just women *. After all,* men can be sexually harassed too.

COMMA SPLICE The word *status* refers to relative position within a group*; however,* it is often used to indicate only positions of prestige.

19c Using divided quotations

When dividing quotations with attributive tags such as *he said* or *she asked*, use a period between independent clauses.

COMMA SPLICE "Beauty brings copies of itself into being," states Elaine Scarry*. "It* makes us draw it, take photographs of it, or describe it to other people."

Both parts of the quotation are complete sentences, so the attributive tag is attached to the first, and the sentence is punctuated with a period.

EXERCISE 19.1

➤ Revise each comma splice or fused sentence in the following paragraph. Some sentences may not need revision.

[1]In *The Politics of Happiness*, Derek Bok, former president of Harvard University, discusses findings that researchers studying well-being reported in the late 2000s. [2]He mentions, for example, research showing that measurements of happiness in the United States did not rise much over a period of fifty years, people responded to survey questions about their levels of happiness in much the same way as they did fifty years earlier. [3]Even though average incomes grew, levels of happiness did not. [4]Bok believes that people become accustomed to higher standards of living they do not realize how quickly they adapt and so do not become happier. [5]Bok recognizes that not everyone's income increased but notes that, strangely enough, the disparity between rich and poor did not cause increased dissatisfaction among the poor, he cites further studies showing that citizens in countries with costly welfare programs were not necessarily happier than citizens in countries with welfare programs that were not as generous. [6]Because of these studies, Bok suggests that our government not focus on economic growth alone as an indicator of well-being but that it instead take into account current research on what makes people happy. [7]This discussion "is bound to contribute to the evolution of society and the refinement of its values," he explains, "that alone will be an accomplishment of enduring importance to humankind" (212).

20 Verbs

Choosing verbs to convey your message precisely is the first step toward writing clear sentences.

20a Verb forms

Regular verbs have four forms: a base form, an *-s* form (third-person singular in the present tense), an *-ing* form (present participle), and an *-ed* form (past participle).

VERB FORMS OF REGULAR VERBS

Base Form	-s Form (Present Tense, Third Person, Singular)	-ing Form (Present Participle)	-ed Form (Past Form or Past Participle)
work	works	working	worked
watch	watches	watching	watched
apply	applies	applying	applied
stop	stops	stopping	stopped

CAUTION

When verbs are followed by words with similar sounds, you may find their endings (*-s* or *-ed*) difficult to hear. In addition, these verb endings may seem unfamiliar because your dialect does not have them. Nonetheless, you should use *-s* and *-ed* when you write for an audience that expects you to include these endings.

➤ She ~~seem~~ *seems* satisfied with the report.

➤ We were ~~suppose~~ *supposed* to receive the results yesterday.

Irregular verbs are not as predictable as regular verbs. The past form and the past participle seldom carry the *-ed* suffix. Most irregular verbs, such as *write*, have forms similar to some of those for regular verbs: base form (*write*), *-s* form (*writes*), and *-ing* form (*writing*). However, the past form (*wrote*) and the past participle (*written*) differ from the regular forms.

VERB FORMS OF COMMON IRREGULAR VERBS

Base Form	Past Form	Past Participle
arise	arose	arisen
awake	awaked, awoke	awaked, awoken
be	was/were	been
begin	began	begun
break	broke	broken
bring	brought	brought
buy	bought	bought
choose	chose	chosen
come	came	come
dive	dived, dove	dived
do	did	done
dream	dreamed, dreamt	dreamed, dreamt
drink	drank	drunk
drive	drove	driven
eat	ate	eaten
forget	forgot	forgotten
forgive	forgave	forgiven
get	got	gotten, got
give	gave	given
go	went	gone
hang (suspend)	hung	hung
keep	kept	kept
know	knew	known

(continues on page 283)

(continued)	**VERB FORMS OF COMMON IRREGULAR VERBS**	
Base Form	**Past Form**	**Past Participle**
lay (to place)	laid	laid
lead	led	led
lie (to recline)	lay	lain
lose	lost	lost
pay	paid	paid
prove	proved	proved, proven
rise	rose	risen
say	said	said
see	saw	seen
set	set	set
sink	sank	sunk
sit	sat	sat
sneak	snuck, sneaked	snuck, sneaked
speak	spoke	spoken
stand	stood	stood
steal	stole	stolen
swim	swam	swum
take	took	taken
tell	told	told
throw	threw	thrown
wear	wore	worn
write	wrote	written

MULTILINGUAL WRITERS

OMISSION OF FORMS OF *BE* IN OTHER LANGUAGES

Forms of the verb *be* can be omitted in some languages. In English, however, they are necessary.

➤ Sentence without an auxiliary verb: The population *is* growing.

➤ Sentence without a linking verb: It *is* quite large.

A **prepositional verb** is a frequently occurring combination of a verb and a preposition. *Rely on*, *think about*, *look like*, and *ask for* are all prepositional verbs. A **phrasal verb** is a combination of a verb and a particle such as *up*, *out*, or *on*. A **particle** resembles an adverb or a preposition, but it is so closely associated with a verb that together they form a unit of meaning. *Carry out*, *make up*, *take on*, and *turn out* are common phrasal verbs. Notice that each one has a meaning that can be expressed in a single word: *do*, *form*, *accept*, and *attend*.

MULTILINGUAL WRITERS
PHRASAL VERBS

Definitions of phrasal verbs are sometimes difficult to determine. For example, *find out* means "to discover." If you are unsure of the definition of a phrasal verb, look it up in a comprehensive dictionary. Phrasal verbs are often listed at the end of an entry for a common verb such as *do*, *make*, *take*, *turn*, or *find*.

The **auxiliary verbs** *be*, *do*, and *have* combine with main verbs, both regular and irregular.

be	*am, is, are, was, were surprised*
	am, is, are, was, were writing
do	*does, do, did call*
	doesn't, don't, didn't spend
have	*has, have, had prepared*
	has, have, had read

Another type of auxiliary verb is called a **modal auxiliary**. There are nine modal auxiliaries: *can*, *could*, *may*, *might*, *must*, *shall*, *should*, *will*, and *would*.

COMMON MEANINGS OF MODAL AUXILIARIES

Meaning	Modal Auxiliary	+	Main Verb	Example
Ability	can, could		afford	They *can afford* to buy a small house.
Certainty	will		leave	We *will leave* tomorrow.
Obligation	must		return	You *must return* your books soon.
Advice	should		talk	He *should talk* with his counselor.
Permission	may		use	You *may use* the computers in the library.

CAUTION

When a modal auxiliary occurs with the auxiliary *have* (*must have forgotten, should have known*), *have* frequently sounds like the word *of*. When you proofread, be sure that modal auxiliaries are not followed by *of*.

▶ They **could ~~of~~ taken** another route.
⁀have

Most modal verbs have more than one meaning. *Could* sometimes refers to ability (*I **could** swim a mile when I was sixteen*). However, *could* can also refer to possibility (*Something good **could** happen*).

EXERCISE 20.1

Revise the following sentences. Explain any changes you make.

1. Any expedition into the wilderness suffer its share of mishaps.
2. The Lewis and Clark Expedition began in May 1804 and end in September 1806.
3. Fate must of smiled on Meriwether Lewis and William Clark, for there were no fatalities under their leadership.

4. Lewis and Clark lead the expedition from St. Louis to the Pacific Ocean and back.

5. By 1805, the Corps of Discovery, as the expedition was call, included thirty-three members.

6. The Corps might of lost all maps and specimens had Sacajawea, a Native American woman, not fish them from the Missouri River.

20b   Verb tenses

Verb tenses provide information about time. For example, the tense of a verb may indicate that an action took place in the past or that an action is ongoing. Verb tenses are labeled as present, past, or future; they are also labeled as simple, progressive, perfect, or perfect progressive. The following chart shows how these labels apply to the tenses of *walk*.

Some of the tenses have more than one form because they depend on the person and number of the subject. **Person** refers to the role of the subject. First person (*I, we*) indicates that the subject of the verb is the writer or writers. Second person (*you*) indicates that the subject is the audience. Third person (*he, she, it, they*) indicates that the subject is someone or something other than the writer or audience. **Number** indicates whether the subject is one (*I, he, she, it, you*-singular) or more than one (*we, they, you*-plural).

VERB TENSES

	Present	Past	Future
Simple	I/you/we/they **walk** He/she/it **walks**	**walked**	**will walk**
Progressive	I **am walking** You/we/they **are walking** He/she/it **is walking**	I/he/she/it **was walking** You/we/they **were walking**	**will be walking**

(continues on page 287)

(continued)	VERB TENSES		
	Present	Past	Future
Perfect	I/you/we/they **have walked**	**had walked**	**will have walked**
	He/she/it **has walked**		
Perfect progressive	I/you/we/they **have been walking**	**had been walking**	**will have been walking**
	He/she/it **has been walking**		

MULTILINGUAL WRITERS

VERBS NOT USED IN THE PROGRESSIVE FORM

Some verbs that do not express actions but rather mental states, emotions, conditions, or relationships are not used in the progressive form. These verbs include *believe*, *belong*, *contain*, *cost*, *know*, *own*, *prefer*, and *want*.

➤ The book ~~is containing~~ *contains* many Central American folktales.

20c Verb tense consistency

By using verb tenses consistently, you help your readers understand when the actions or events you are describing took place. Every verb tense has two parts: time frame and aspect. *Time frame* refers to whether the tense is present, past, or future. *Aspect* refers to whether it is simple, progressive, perfect, or perfect progressive. (See the chart in **20b**.) Consistency in the time frame of verbs, though not necessarily in their aspect, ensures that sentences reporting a sequence of events link together logically. In the following paragraph, notice that the time frame remains in the past, but the aspect may be either simple, perfect, or progressive.

past perfect

At that point, Kubrick **had finished** *Dr. Strangelove.*

simple past

Working independently, he **started** his science-fiction master-piece, *2001: A Space Odyssey* with much of Hollywood

past progressive

unaware that he **was working** in a new genre.

If you do need to shift to another time frame, you can use a time marker.

now, then, today, yesterday

in two years, during the 1920s

after you finish, before we left

simple present

➤ The Minnesota State Fair **attracts** thousands of visitors.

time marker

Last year, attendance on Labor Day weekend

simple past

exceeded 650,000.

You may be able to change time frames without including time markers when you wish (1) to explain or support a general statement with information about the past, (2) to compare and contrast two different time periods, or (3) to comment on a topic.

➤ Thomas Jefferson, author of the Declaration of Independence, **is** considered one of our country's most brilliant citizens. His achievements **were** many, as **were** his interests. [The second sentence provides evidence from the past to support the claim in the first sentence.]

Before you turn in your final draft, check your verb tenses to ensure that they are logical and consistent. Revise any that are not.

➤ The white wedding dress *came* ~~comes~~ into fashion when Queen
   Victoria wore a white gown at her wedding to Prince Albert of Saxe.
   Soon after, brides who could afford them bought stylish white
   dresses for their weddings. Brides of modest means, however,
   continued ~~continue~~ to choose dresses they could wear more than once.

EXERCISE 20.2

Revise the following paragraph so that it contains no unnecessary shifts in verb tense.

> **I had** already **been walking** for a half hour in the semidarkness of Amsterdam's early-morning streets when I **came** to a red traffic signal. I **am** in a hurry to get to the train station and no cars **were** out yet, so I **cross** over the cobblestones, passing a man waiting for the light to change. I never **look** back when he **scolds** me for breaking the law. I **had** a train to catch. I **was** going to Widnau, in Switzerland, to see Aunt Marie. I **have** not **seen** her since I **was** in second grade.

20d Voice

Voice indicates the relationship between a verb and its subject. When a verb is in the **active voice**, the subject is generally a person or thing performing an action. When a verb is in the **passive voice**, the subject is usually the *receiver* of the action.

ACTIVE   Jen Wilson **wrote** the essay.

PASSIVE   The essay **was written** by Jen Wilson.

Some passive sentences do not include a *by* phrase because the actor is unknown or unimportant.

➤ Jen Wilson's essay **was published** in the student newspaper.

The terms *active* and *passive* can sometimes cause confusion. As grammatical terms, they do not refer to the difference between action and inaction—running vs. napping. The best way to decide whether a sentence is in the passive voice is to examine its verb phrase.

(1) Verbs in the passive voice

The verb phrase in a sentence written in the passive voice consists of a form of the auxiliary verb *be* (*am, is, are, was, were, been*) and a past participle. Depending on the verb tense, other auxiliaries such as *have, will,* and *should* may appear as well. The following sentences include common forms of *call* in the passive voice.

➤ The meeting **is called** to order. [simple present]

➤ The recruits **were called** to duty. [simple past]

➤ The council **is being called** to act on the proposal. [present progressive]

➤ Ms. Jones **has been called** to jury twice already. [present perfect]

Generally, sentences that do not include both a form of the auxiliary verb *be* and a past participle are in the active voice.

(2) Choosing between the active and passive voice

To use the active voice for emphasizing an actor and an action, first make the actor the subject of the sentence; then choose verbs that will help your readers see what the actor is doing.

➤ A group of students **planned** the graduation ceremony.

Use the passive voice when you want to stress the recipient of the action, rather than the actor, or when the actor's identity is unimportant or unknown.

➤ Tuition increases **were discussed** at the board meeting.

Writers of scientific prose often use the passive voice to highlight the experiment rather than the experimenter, as in this excerpt from a student lab report:

> First, the slides **were placed** on a compound microscope under low power, a 40× magnification level. The end of the root tip **was located**; then the cells immediately behind the root cap **were examined**.

EXERCISE 20.3

Identify the voice in each sentence as active or passive.

1. Emojis, standardized digital icons or images, are used primarily in electronic communication.

2. The word *emoji* comes from two Japanese words: *e* for "picture" and *moji* for "character."

3. The first emojis were designed by Japanese companies.

4. According to Clive Thompson, who writes and blogs about technology, emojis are employed by 92 percent of people communicating online.

5. Like emoticons, emojis convey shades of feeling.

6. Should emojis be considered a language?

20e Mood

The **mood** of a verb expresses the writer's attitude toward the factuality of what is being expressed. The **indicative mood** is used for statements and questions regarding fact or opinion. The **imperative mood** is used to give commands or directions. The **subjunctive mood** is used to state requirements, make requests, and express wishes.

INDICATIVE	We will be on time.
IMPERATIVE	Be on time!
SUBJUNCTIVE	The director insists that we be on time.

The subjunctive mood is also used to signal hypothetical situations (situations that are not real or not currently true): *If I **were** president, I'd protect national parks.*

Verb forms in the subjunctive mood serve a variety of functions. The **present subjunctive** is the base form of the verb. It is used to express necessity.

➤ The doctor recommended that he **go** on a diet. [active voice]

➤ We demanded that you **be reimbursed**. [passive voice]

The **past subjunctive** has the same form as the simple past (for example, *had, offered, found,* or *wrote*). However, the past subjunctive form of *be* is *were* for all subjects, regardless of person or number. This form is used to present hypothetical situations.

➤ If they **offered** me the job, I would take it. [active voice]

➤ Even if he **were promoted**, he would not change his mind. [passive voice]

The **perfect subjunctive** verb has the same form as the past perfect tense: *had* + past participle. The perfect subjunctive signals that a statement is not factual.

➤ I wish **I had known** about the scholarship competition. [active voice]

➤ If she **had been awarded** the scholarship, she would have quit her part-time job. [passive voice]

TIPS FOR USING THE SUBJUNCTIVE

- In clauses beginning with *as if* and *as though*, use the past subjunctive or the perfect subjunctive:

  ➤ He acts as if he ∧was the owner.
     were

  ➤ She looked at me as though she ∧heard this story before.
     had

(Continued on page 293)

| **TIPS FOR USING THE SUBJUNCTIVE** | *(Continued)* |

- In nonfactual dependent clauses beginning with *if*, use the past subjunctive or the perfect subjunctive. Avoid using *would have* in the *if* clause.

  ➤ If I ~~was~~ rich, I would buy a yacht.
      were

  ➤ If the driver ~~would have checked~~ his rearview mirror, the accident would not have happened.
      had

- In dependent clauses following verbs that express wishes, use the past subjunctive or the perfect subjunctive.

  ➤ I wish I ~~was~~ taller.
      were

  ➤ My brother wishes he ~~studied~~ harder years ago.
      had

- In *that* clauses expressing suggestions or demands, following verbs such as *ask*, *insist*, or *recommend*, use the base form of the verb in the *that* clause.

  ➤ The director asks that fans ~~are~~ patient for the next film in the popular series.
      be

EXERCISE 20.4

Use subjunctive verb forms to revise the following sentences.

1. The planners of Apollo 13 acted as if the number 13 was a lucky number.

2. Superstitious people think that if NASA changed the number of the mission, the astronauts would have had a safer journey.

3. They also believe that if the lunar landing would have been scheduled for a day other than Friday the Thirteenth, the crew would not have encountered any problems.

(continued)

(Continued)

4. The crew used the lunar module as though it was a lifeboat.

5. After the successful splashdown, NASA administrators required that an investigative board was established.

6. If NASA ever plans a space mission on Friday the Thirteenth again, the public would object.

20f   Subject-verb agreement

To say that a verb *agrees* with a subject means that the form of the verb (*-s* form or base form) is appropriate for the subject. For example, if the subject refers to one person or thing (*an athlete, a car*), the *-s* form of the verb (*runs*) is appropriate. If the subject refers to more than one person or thing (*athletes, cars*), the base form of the verb (*run*) is appropriate. Notice in the following examples that the singular third-person subjects in the first line take a singular verb (*-s* form) and all the other subjects take the base form.

He, she, it, Joe, a student	has, looks, writes
I, you, we, they, the Browns, the students	have, look, write

The verb *be* does not follow this pattern. It has three different present-tense forms and two different past-tense forms.

I	am/was
He, she, it, Joe, a student	is/was
You, we, they, the Browns, the students	are/were

(1) Words between the subject and the verb

When phrases such as the following occur between the subject and the verb, they do not affect the number of the subject or the form of the verb.

| along with | in addition to | not to mention |
| as well as | including | together with |

➤ Her **salary**, <u>together with</u> tips, **is** just enough to live on.

➤ **Tips**, <u>together with</u> her salary, **are** just enough to live on.

(2) Subjects joined by *and*

A compound subject (two nouns joined by *and*) that refers to a single person or thing takes a singular verb.

➤ The **founder and president** of the art association **was** elected to the board of the museum.

(3) Subjects joined by *or* or *nor*

When singular subjects are linked by *or, either . . . or*, or *neither . . . nor*, the verb is singular as well.

➤ The **provost or** the **dean** usually **presides** at the meeting.

➤ **Either** his **accountant or** his **lawyer has** the will.

If the linked subjects differ in number, the verb agrees with the subject closer to the verb.

➤ Neither the basket nor the **apples were** expensive. [plural]

➤ Neither the apples nor the **basket was** expensive. [singular]

(4) Inverted order

In most sentences, the subject precedes the verb.

➤ The large **cities** of the Northeast **were** the hardest hit by the winter storms.

The subject and verb can sometimes be inverted for emphasis; however, they must still agree.

➤ The hardest hit by the winter storms **were** the large **cities** of the Northeast.

When *there* begins a sentence, the subject and verb are always inverted; the verb still agrees with the subject, which follows it.

➤ There **are** several **cities** in need of federal aid.

(5) Clauses with relative pronouns

In an adjectival (relative) clause, the subject is generally a relative pronoun (*that, who,* or *which*). To determine whether the relative pronoun is singular or plural, you must find its antecedent (the word or words it refers to). When the antecedent is singular, the relative pronoun is singular; when the antecedent is plural, the relative pronoun is plural. In essence, the verb in the adjectival clause agrees with the antecedent.

➤ **The person who reviews** proposals is out of town this week.

➤ The director met with the **students who are** studying abroad next quarter.

➤ The Starion is one of the new **models that include** a DVD player as standard equipment.

(6) Indefinite pronouns

The indefinite pronouns *each, either, everybody, everyone,* and *anyone* are considered singular and so require singular verb forms.

➤ **Either** of them **is willing** to lead the discussion.

➤ **Everybody** in our apartment building **has** a parking place.

All, any, some, none, half, and *most* can be either singular or plural, depending on whether they refer to a unit or quantity (singular) or to individuals (plural).

➤ My sister collects antique **jewelry**; **some** of it **is** quite valuable.

> My sister collects comic **books**; <u>**some**</u> *pl v* **are** quite valuable.

When an indefinite pronoun is followed by a prepositional phrase beginning with the preposition *of*, the verb agrees in number with the object of the preposition.

> <u>**None**</u> of *pl obj* **those** *pl v* **are** spoiled.

> <u>**None**</u> of the *sing obj* **food** *sing v* **is** spoiled.

(7) Collective nouns and measurement words

Collective nouns and measurement words require singular verbs when they refer to groups or units. They require plural verbs when they refer to individuals or parts.

SINGULAR (REGARDED AS A GROUP OR UNIT)	PLURAL (REGARDED AS INDIVIDUALS OR PARTS)
The **majority rules**.	The **majority** of us **are** in favor.
Ten million gallons of oil **is** more than enough.	**Ten million gallons** of oil **were spilled**.

(8) Words ending in -s

Titles of works that are plural in form (for example, *Star Wars* and *Dombey and Son*) are treated as singular because they refer to a single book, movie, recording, or other work.

> ***Love & Friendship* is** one of the films she discussed in her paper.

Some nouns ending in *-s* are singular: *linguistics*, *news*, and *Niagara Falls*.

> The **news is** encouraging.

Nouns such as *athletics*, *politics*, and *electronics* can be either singular or plural, depending on their meanings.

| SINGULAR | **Statistics is** an interesting subject. |
| PLURAL | **Statistics are** often misleading. |

(9) Subjects and subject complements

Some sentences may have a singular subject and a plural subject complement, or vice versa. In either case, the verb agrees with the subject.

➤ Her primary **concern is** rising health-care costs.

➤ **Croissants are** the bakery's specialty.

THINKING RHETORICALLY

AGREEMENT OF RELATED SINGULAR AND PLURAL NOUNS

When a sentence has two or more nouns that are related, use either the singular form or the plural form consistently.

➤ The **student** raised her **hand**. The **students** raised their **hands**.

Occasionally, you may have to use a singular noun to retain an idiomatic expression or to avoid ambiguity.

➤ **They** kept their **word**.

(10) Subjects beginning with *what*

When *what* may be understood as "the thing that," the verb in the main clause is singular.

➤ What we need **is** a new policy. [*The thing that* we need is a new policy.]

If *what* is understood as "the things that," the verb in the main clause is plural.

➤ What we need **are** new guidelines. [*The things that* we need are new guidelines.]

EXERCISE 20.5

Choose the correct form of the verb in parentheses.

1. There (is/are) at least two good reasons for changing motor oil: risk of contamination and danger of additive depletion.

2. Reasons for not changing the oil (include/includes) the cost to the driver and the inconvenience of the chore.

3. What I want to know (is/are) the number of miles I can drive before I have to change my oil.

4. My older brother says three thousand miles (is/are) not long enough.

5. Each of the car manuals I consulted (recommends/recommend) five-thousand-mile intervals.

6. Neither the automakers nor the oil station attendants (know/knows) how I drive.

21 Pronouns

When you use pronouns effectively, you add clarity and coherence to your writing.

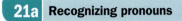

21a Recognizing pronouns

A **pronoun** is commonly defined as a word that refers to a noun or noun phrase already mentioned—its **antecedent**.

➤ <u>John</u> said **he** would guide the trip.

➤ <u>The participant with the most experience</u> said **he** would guide the trip.

Most pronouns refer to nouns, but some such as *this*, *that*, *my*, and *their* come before nouns.

➤ **This** <u>man</u> is our guide.   **My** map is over there.

Pronouns are categorized as personal, reflexive/intensive, relative, interrogative, demonstrative, or indefinite.

(1) Personal pronouns

Personal pronouns are like nouns: they refer to people, places, things, ideas, and so on.

SINGULAR	I, me, you, he, him, she, her, it
PLURAL	we, us, you, they, them

(2) Possessive pronouns

Possessive pronouns are personal pronouns that indicate ownership and similar relationships.

SINGULAR	my, mine, your, yours, his, her, hers, its
PLURAL	our, ours, your, yours, their, theirs

Avoid confusing possessive forms with common contractions: *it's* (*it is*), *they're* (*they are*), and *who's* (*who is*).

(3) Reflexive/Intensive pronouns

Reflexive pronouns direct the action back to the subject (*I saw myself*); intensive pronouns are used for emphasis (*I myself questioned the judge*).

SINGULAR	myself, yourself, himself, herself, itself
PLURAL	ourselves, yourselves, themselves

Avoid using a reflexive pronoun as a subject.

➤ Ms. Palmquist and ~~myself~~ ᴵ discussed our concern with the senator.

Hisself, themself, and *theirselves* are inappropriate in academic or professional writing. Instead, use *himself* and *themselves.*

(4) Relative pronouns

An adjectival clause (or relative clause) ordinarily begins with a relative pronoun: *who, whom, which, that,* or *whose.* To provide a link between this type of dependent clause and the main clause, the relative pronoun corresponds to a word or words in the main clause called the **antecedent**.

➤ The students talked to **a reporter** *(ant)* **who** *(rel pro)* had just returned from overseas.

Who, whose, and *whom* ordinarily refer to people; *which* refers to things; *that* refers to things and, in some contexts, people. The possessive *whose* (used in place of the awkward *of which*) usually refers to people but sometimes refers to things.

Knowing the difference between an essential clause and a nonessential clause will help you decide whether to use *which* or *that.* A clause that a reader needs in order to identify the antecedent correctly is an **essential clause**.

➤ **The person** *(ant)* **who presented the award** *(ess cl)* was last year's winner.

If the essential clause were omitted from this sentence, the reader would not know which person was last year's winner.

A **nonessential clause** is *not* needed for correct identification of the antecedent and is thus set off by commas. A nonessential clause often follows a proper noun (a specific name).

➤ **Andrea Bowen,** *(ant)* **who presented the award,** *(noness cl)* was last year's winner.

If the nonessential clause were removed from this sentence, the reader would still know the identity of last year's winner.

According to a traditional grammar rule, *that* is used in essential adjectival clauses, and *which* is used in nonessential adjectival clauses.

➤ I need a job **that** pays well.

➤ For years, I have had the same job, **which** pays well enough.

However, some professional writers use *which* in essential clauses. Nonetheless, if you are following APA guidelines, use *which* only in nonessential clauses.

(5) Interrogative pronouns

The interrogative pronouns *what, which, who, whom,* and *whose* are question words.

➤ **Who** won the award?   **Whom** did you see?

(6) Demonstrative pronouns

The demonstrative pronouns *this* and *these* indicate that someone or something is close by in time, space, or thought. *That* and *those* signal remoteness.

➤ **These** issues will be addressed in the next section.

➤ He envied **those** people who could live simply.

(7) Indefinite pronouns

Indefinite pronouns usually do not refer to specific persons, objects, ideas, or events.

anyone	anybody	anything
everyone	everybody	everything
someone	somebody	something
no one	nobody	nothing
each	either	neither

Indefinite pronouns do not refer to an antecedent. In fact, some indefinite pronouns *serve* as antecedents.

➤ **Someone** forgot **her** purse.

21b Pronoun case

To understand the uses of pronouns, you must first be able to recognize person and number. **Person** indicates whether a pronoun refers to the writer (**first person**), to the reader (**second person**), or to another person, place, thing, or idea (**third person**). **Number** reveals whether a pronoun is singular or plural.

Case refers to the form a pronoun takes to indicate its relationship to other words in a sentence. There are three cases relevant to understanding pronouns: subjective, objective, and possessive (also called genitive).

➤ **He** [subjective] wants **his** [possessive] legislators to help **him** [objective].

CASE:	Subjective		Objective		Possessive	
NUMBER:	Singular	Plural	Singular	Plural	Singular	Plural
First person	I	we	me	us	my, mine	our, ours
Second person	you	you	you	you	your, yours	your, yours
Third person	he, she, it	they	him, her, it	them	his, her, hers, its	their, theirs

(1) Pronouns in the subjective case

A pronoun that is the subject of a sentence is in the **subjective case**. To determine which pronoun form is correct in a compound subject (a noun and a pronoun joined by *and*), say the sentence using the pronoun alone, omitting the noun. For the following sentence, notice that "*Me* solved the problem" seems strange, but "*I* solved the problem" is fine.

➤ ~~Me and~~ Marisa *and I* solved the problem.

Place the pronoun *I* last in the sequence. If the compound subject contains two pronouns, test each one by itself.

➤ *He* ~~Him~~ and I joined the club in July.

Pronouns following a *be* verb (*am, is, are, was, were, been*) should also be in the subjective case.

➤ The first to arrive were Kevin and ~~me~~ *I*.

MULTILINGUAL WRITERS
NOUN OR PRONOUN AS SUBJECT

In some languages, a noun in the subject position may be followed by a pronoun. In Standardized English, though, such a pronoun should be omitted.

➤ My roommate ~~he~~ works in the library for three hours a week.

(2) Pronouns in the objective case

Whenever a pronoun follows an action verb or a preposition, it takes the **objective case**.

The whole staff admired **him**. [direct object]

The staff sent **him** a card. [indirect object]

The staff depended on **him**. [object of a preposition]

Pronouns joined by *and* or *or* are also in the objective case when they follow a verb (other than the linking verb *be*) or a preposition.

➤ They will appoint you or ~~I~~ *me*. [direct objects]

➤ They lent Tom and ~~I~~ *me* money for tuition. [indirect objects]

➤ Jan sat between my brother and ~~I~~ *me*. [objects of the preposition]

To determine whether to use the subjective or objective case, remember to say the sentence with just the pronoun. Notice that "They will appoint *I*" does not sound right.

(3) Possessive forms

Pronouns in the **possessive case** can be divided into two groups based on whether they are followed by nouns. *My*, *your*, *his*, *her*, *its*, *our*, and *their* are all followed by nouns; *mine*, *yours*, *his*, *hers*, *ours*, and *theirs* are not. (Note that *his* is in both groups.)

➤ **Their** budget is higher than **ours**. [*Their* is followed by a noun; *our*s is not.]

(4) Appositive pronouns

Appositive pronouns are in the same case as the nouns they rename.

➤ Our group—Becky, Lee, and ~~me~~ *I*—argued for the new policy. [subjective]

➤ My grandmother gave her old art books to her grandchildren—Josh, Evan, Kayla, and ~~I~~ *me*. [objective]

(5) *Who/whoever* and *whom/whomever*

To choose between *who* and *whom* or between *whoever* and *whomever*, you must first determine whether the word is functioning as a subject or an object. A pronoun functioning as the subject takes the subjective case.

➤ **Who** won the award? [COMPARE: **She** won the award.]

➤ The teachers knew **who** won the award.

➤ The student **who** won the award was quite surprised.

➤ **Whoever** won the award deserved it.

When the pronoun is an object, use *whom* or *whomever*.

➤ **Whom** did they hire? [COMPARE: They hired **him**.]

➤ I do not know **whom** they hired.

➤ The student **whom** they hired graduated in May.

➤ **Whomever** they hired will have to work hard this year.

Whom may be omitted in sentences when no misunderstanding would result.

➤ The friend he relied on moved away. [*Whom* has been omitted after *friend*.]

(6) Pronouns with infinitives and gerunds

A pronoun grouped with an infinitive (*to* + the base form of a verb) takes the objective case.

➤ The director wanted **me** to help **him**.

A gerund (*-ing* verb form functioning as a noun) is preceded by a possessive pronoun in formal writing.

➤ I appreciated **his** helping Denise. [COMPARE: I appreciated **Mike's** helping Denise.]

Notice that a possessive pronoun is used before a gerund but not before a present participle (*-ing* verb form functioning as an adjective).

➤ I saw **him** helping Luke.

(7) Pronouns in elliptical constructions

The words *as* and *than* frequently introduce **elliptical constructions**—clauses in which the writer has intentionally omitted words. To check whether you have used the correct case in an elliptical construction, read the written sentence aloud, inserting any words that have been omitted from it.

➤ She admires Clarice as much as **I**. [subjective case]
  Read aloud: She admires Clarice as much as *I do*.

➤ She admires Clarice more than **me**. [objective case]

Read aloud: She admires Clarice more than *she admires me*.

EXERCISE 21.1

Revise the following paragraph, using appropriate pronouns. Some sentences may not require editing.

¹When me and my brother were in middle school, we formed a band with our friends Jason and Andrew. ²My grandmother had given Jake a guitar and I a drum kit for Christmas. ³We practiced either alone or together for the rest of the winter. ⁴Then, in the spring, we met up with Jason, who we had known for years. ⁵Him and his cousin Andrew, whom we later called Android, were excited to join me and Jake. ⁶Jason already had a guitar, and Andrew could sing. ⁷After we played together one afternoon, we decided to call ourself *The Crash*. ⁸Jason and Andrew came over to our house to jam whenever they're parents let them—which was most of the time. ⁹Our parents did not mind our noise at all. ¹⁰My dad said us playing reminded him of his own teenage garage band.

EXERCISE 21.2

Correct the pronoun errors in the following sentences. Not all sentences have errors.

1. The board of directors has asked you and I to conduct a customer survey.

2. They also recommended us hiring someone with extensive experience in statistical analysis.

3. Whomever understands statistics should take the lead on this project.

4. Although the board asked me to be in charge, I would like you to recruit and interview candidates.

5. The directors recognize your expertise and will surely approve of you taking the lead.

21c Pronoun-antecedent agreement

A pronoun and its antecedent (the word or word group to which it refers) agree in number (both are singular or both are plural).

➤ The **supervisor** said **he** would help.
   [Both antecedent and pronoun are singular.]

➤ My **colleagues** said **they** would help.
   [Both antecedent and pronoun are plural.]

MULTILINGUAL WRITERS
POSSESSIVE PRONOUNS

A possessive pronoun (*his, her, its, their, my, our,* or *your*), also called a **possessive determiner**, agrees with its antecedent, not with the noun it precedes.

➤ Ken Carlson brought ^*his* ~~her~~ young daughter to the office today.
   [The possessive pronoun *his* agrees with the antecedent, *Ken Carlson*, not with the following noun, *daughter*.]

(1) Indefinite pronouns

An indefinite pronoun such as *everyone, someone,* or *anybody* takes a singular verb form.

➤ Everyone **has** [not *have*] the right to an opinion.

Difficulties arise, however, because words like *everyone* and *everybody* seem to refer to more than one person even though they take a singular verb. Thus, the definition of grammatical number and our everyday notion of number conflict. In conversation and informal writing, a plural pronoun (*they, them,* or *their*) is often used with the singular *everyone*. Nonetheless, when you write for an audience that expects you to follow traditional grammar rules, make sure to use a third-person singular pronoun.

➤ Everyone has the combination to ^*his or her* ~~their~~ private locker.

You can avoid the awkwardness of using *his* or *her* by using an article instead, making both the antecedent and the possessive pronoun plural, or rewriting the sentence using the passive voice (the *be* auxiliary + the past participle).

➤ Everyone has the combination to **a** private locker. [article]

➤ **Students** have combinations to **their** private lockers. [plural antecedent and plural possessive pronoun]

➤ The combination to a private locker **is issued** to everyone. [passive voice]

(2) Two antecedents joined by *or* or *nor*

If a singular and a plural antecedent are joined by *or* or *nor*, place the plural antecedent second and use a plural pronoun.

➤ Either the senator **or** her <u>assistants</u> will explain how <u>they</u> devised the plan for tax reform.

➤ Neither the president **nor** the <u>senators</u> stated that <u>they</u> would support the proposal.

(3) Collective nouns

When an antecedent is a collective noun such as *team*, *faculty*, or *committee*, determine whether you intend the noun to be understood as singular or plural. Then, make sure that the pronoun agrees in number with the noun.

➤ The choir decided that ^*it* ~~they~~ would tour during the winter.
[Because the choir decided as a group, *choir* should be considered singular.]

➤ The committee disagree on methods, but ^*they* ~~it~~ agree on basic aims.
[Because the committee members are behaving as individuals, *committee* is regarded as plural.]

EXERCISE 21.3

Revise the following sentences so that pronouns and antecedents agree. Some verb forms will have to change as well.

1. A researcher relies on a number of principles to help them make ethical decisions.

2. Everyone should have the right to participate in a study only if they feel comfortable doing so.

3. A team of researchers should provide its volunteers with consent forms, in which they describe to the volunteers the procedures and risks involved in participation.

4. Every participant should be guaranteed that the information they provide will remain confidential.

5. Institutions of higher education require that a researcher address ethical issues in their proposals.

21d Clear pronoun reference

The meaning of each pronoun in a sentence should be immediately obvious. In the following sentence, the pronoun *he* clearly refers to the antecedent, *Jack*.

➤ **Jack** has collected shells since **he** was eight years old.

(1) Ambiguous pronoun reference

Revise sentences in which a pronoun can refer to either of two antecedents.

➤ Anna told her sister ~~that she had~~ to call home.

(2) Remote pronoun reference

To help readers understand your meaning, place relative pronouns as close to their antecedents as possible.

that was originally written in 1945
➤ The **poem** ^ has been published in a new book. ~~that was~~
~~originally written in 1945.~~

[A poem, not a book, was first published in 1945.]

Notice, however, that a relative pronoun does not always have to follow its antecedent directly. In the following example, there is no risk of misunderstanding.

➤ We slowly began to notice <u>changes</u> in our lives **that** we had never expected.

(3) Broad pronoun reference

Pronouns such as *it*, *this*, *that*, and *which* sometimes refer to the sense of a whole clause, sentence, or paragraph.

➤ Large corporations may seem stronger than individuals, but **that** is not true. [*That* refers to the sense of the whole first clause.]

In academic situations, revise sentences that do not have specific antecedents.

➤ When class attendance is compulsory, some students feel that
perception
education is being forced on them. This ^ is unwarranted. [In the

original sentence, *this* had no clear antecedent.]

(4) Implied reference

Express an idea explicitly rather than merely implying it.

Teaching music
➤ My father is a music teacher. ^ It is a profession that requires much patience. [In the original sentence, *it* had no expressed antecedent.]

Be especially careful to provide clear antecedents when referring to the work or possessions of others. The following sentence requires revision because *she* can refer to someone other than Jen Norton, who could be an editor instead of an author.

her   *Jen Norton*
➤ In ~~Jen Norton's~~ new book, ~~she~~ argues for election reform.
     ^   ^

(5) The use of *it* without an antecedent

The expletive *it* does not have a specific antecedent. Instead, it is used to postpone, and thus give emphasis to, the subject of a sentence. If a sentence that begins with this expletive is wordy or awkward, replace *it* with the postponed subject.

> ➤ It was no use trying to repair the car.

Trying to repair the car ... *useless.*

EXERCISE 21.4

Edit the following sentences to make all references clear.

1. A singer, songwriter, and human rights activist, it is no wonder that Joan Baez is one of today's most inspirational public figures.

2. Baez's father worked for the United Nations Education, Scientific and Cultural Organization (UNESCO), which meant that as a young girl, she lived in many different countries.

3. Though you might find it hard to believe, Baez recorded her first album when she was only nineteen years old.

4. Baez had a younger sister, Mimi Fariña, who was also a singer-songwriter; sometimes she joined her on tour.

5. In 2011, at a general meeting of the human-rights organization Amnesty International, they gave Baez a special award for her inspirational activism.

6. In 2017, Baez was inducted into the Rock and Roll Hall of Fame; this will recognize that her work strongly influenced the development of rock in the 1960s.

21e Pronoun consistency

Whenever you write, you must establish your point of view (perspective). Your point of view will be evident in the pronouns you choose. *I* or *we* indicates a first-person point of view, which is appropriate for writing that includes personal views or experiences. If you decide to address the reader as *you*, you are adopting a second-person point of view. However, because a second-person point of view is rare in academic writing, avoid using *you* unless you need to address the reader. If you select the pronouns *he*, *she*, *it*, *one*, and *they*, you are writing with a third-person point of view. The third-person point of view is the most common point of view in academic writing.

Although you may find it necessary to use different points of view, especially if you are comparing or contrasting other people's views with your own, be careful not to confuse readers by shifting perspective unnecessarily.

To an observer, a sleeping person appears passive, unresponsive, and essentially isolated from the rest of the world and its barrage of stimuli. While it is true that ~~you are~~ *someone asleep is* unaware of most surrounding noises ~~when you are asleep, our~~ *, that person's* brain is far from inactive. In fact, the brain can be as active during sleep as it is ~~when you are awake.~~ *in a waking state* When ~~our brains are~~ *it is* asleep, the rate and type of electrical activity change.

EXERCISE 21.5

Revise the following paragraph so that there are no unnecessary shifts in point of view.

[1]Benjamin Franklin proposed the idea of moving clocks ahead during the summer to conserve energy. [2]We did not adopt Daylight Savings Time until 1918 as a fuel-saving measure during World War I. [3]I believe that today most, but not all, states set their clocks forward in March. [4]Most people hate when you have to reset the clocks in the spring but enjoy the extra hour of sleep in November.

| **21f** | **Use of first-person and second-person pronouns** |

Using *I* is appropriate when you are writing about personal experience. In academic and professional writing, the use of the first-person singular pronoun is also a clear way to distinguish your own views from those of others. However, if you frequently repeat *I feel* or *I think*, your readers may suspect that you do not understand much beyond your own experience.

We, the first-person plural pronoun, is trickier to use correctly. When you use it, make sure that your audience can tell which individuals are included in this plural reference. For example, if you are completing a course assignment, does *we* mean you and the instructor, you and your fellow students, or some other group (such as all Americans)? Because you may inadvertently use *we* in an early draft to refer to more than one group of people, as you edit, check to see that you have used this pronoun consistently.

If you address readers directly, you will undoubtedly use the second-person pronoun *you* (as we, the authors of this handbook, have done). There is some disagreement, though, over whether to permit the use of the indefinite *you* to mean "a person" or "people in general." If your instructor tells you to avoid using the indefinite *you*, recast your sentences. For example, use *one* instead of *you*.

➤ Even in huge, anonymous cities, ~~you find~~ *one finds* community spirit.

If the use of *one* is too formal, try changing the word order or using different words.

➤ Community spirit is found even in huge, anonymous cities.

EXERCISE 21.6

Revise the following paragraph to eliminate the use of the first- and second-person pronouns.

¹In my opinion, some animals should be as free as we are. ²For example, I think orangutans, African elephants, and Atlantic bottlenose dolphins should roam freely rather than be held in captivity. ³We should neither exhibit them in zoos nor use them for medical research. ⁴If you study animals such as these, you will see that, like us, they show emotions, self-awareness, and intention. ⁵You might even find that some use language to communicate. ⁶It is clear to me that they have the right to freedom.

22 Modifiers

Modifiers are words, phrases, or clauses that modify; that is, they qualify or limit the meaning of other words. When used effectively, modifiers enliven writing with details and enhance its coherence.

22a Recognizing modifiers

You can distinguish an adjective from an adverb by determining what type of word is modified. **Adjectives** modify nouns and pronouns; **adverbs** modify verbs, adjectives, and other adverbs.

ADJECTIVES	ADVERBS
She looked **curious**.	She looked at me **curiously**.
[modifies pronoun]	[modifies verb]
productive meeting	**highly** productive meeting
[modifies noun]	[modifies adjective]
a **quick** lunch	**very** quickly
[modifies noun]	[modifies adverb]

In addition, consider the form of the modifier. Many adjectives end with one of these suffixes: *-able*, *-al*, *-ful*, *-ic*, *-ish*, *-less*, or *-y*.

accept**able**   rent**al**   event**ful**   angel**ic**   sheep**ish**   effort**less**   sleep**y**

Present participles (verb + *-ing*) and past participles (verb + *-ed*) can also be used as adjectives.

a **determining** factor   a **determined** effort

Be sure to include the *-ed* ending of a past participle.

➤ Please see the ~~enclose~~ *enclosed* documents for more details.

MULTILINGUAL WRITERS
ADJECTIVE SUFFIXES IN OTHER LANGUAGES

In some languages, adjectives and nouns agree in number. In Spanish, for example, when a noun is plural, the adjective is plural as well: *vistas claras*. In English, however, adjectives do not have a plural form: *clear views*.

The easiest type of adverb to identify is the adverb of manner. It is formed by adding *-ly* to an adjective.

careful**ly**   unpleasant**ly**   silent**ly**

Although you may not hear the *-ly* ending when you speak, be sure to include it when you write.

➤ They bought only ~~local~~ grown vegetables.
 locally

However, not all words ending in *-ly* are adverbs. Certain adjectives related to nouns also end in *-ly* (*friend, friendly; hour, hourly*). In addition, not all adverbs end in *-ly*. Adverbs that indicate time or place (*today, tomorrow, here,* and *there*) do not have the *-ly* ending. A few words—for example, *fast, right,* and *well*—can function as either adjectives or adverbs.

➤ They like **fast** cars. [adjective]

➤ They ran **fast** enough to catch the bus. [adverb]

(1) Modifiers of linking verbs and action verbs

An adjective used after a sensory linking verb (*look, smell, taste, sound,* or *feel*) modifies the subject of the sentence. A common error is to use an adverb after this type of verb.

➤ I felt ~~badly~~ about missing the rally. [The adjective *bad* modifies *I.*]
 bad

However, when *look, smell, taste, sound,* or *feel* is used as an action verb, it can be modified by an adverb.

➤ She looked **angrily** at the referee. [The adverb *angrily* modifies *looked.*]

 BUT

 She looked **angry**. [The adjective *angry* modifies *she.*]

Good is an adjective and so is not used with action verbs.

➤ The whole team played ~~good~~.
 well

> **EXERCISE 22.1**
>
> Revise the following sentences to include adjectives and adverbs considered conventional in academic writing.
>
> 1. Relaxation techniques have been developed for people who feel uncomfortably in some way.
> 2. Meditation is one technique that is real helpful in relieving stress.
> 3. People searching for relief from tension have found that a breathing meditation works good.
> 4. They sit quiet and concentrate on both inhaling and exhaling.
> 5. They concentrate on breathing deep.

(2) Nouns as modifiers

Adjectives and adverbs are the most common modifiers, but nouns can also be modifiers (***movie*** *critic*, ***reference*** *manual*). A string of noun modifiers can be cumbersome. The following example shows how a sentence with too many noun modifiers can be revised.

➤ The ~~Friday afternoon~~ Student Affairs Committee meeting has *scheduled for Friday afternoon* been postponed.

(3) Phrases and clauses as modifiers

Participial phrases, prepositional phrases, and some infinitive phrases are modifiers.

➤ **Growing in popularity every year**, mountain bikes now dominate the market. [participial phrase]

➤ Mountain bikes first became popular **in the 1980s**. [prepositional phrase]

➤ Some people use mountain bikes **to commute to work**. [infinitive phrase]

Adjectival and adverbial clauses are both modifiers.

➤ BMX bicycles have frames **that are relatively small**.
[adjectival clause]

➤ **Although mountain bikes are designed for off-road use**, many people use them on city streets. [adverbial clause]

22b Comparatives and superlatives

Many adjectives and adverbs have three forms. The **positive form** is the word you would look for in a dictionary. The **comparative form**, which either ends in -*er* or is preceded by *more* or *less*, compares two elements. The **superlative form**, which either ends in -*est* or is preceded by *most* or *least*, compares three or more elements:

POSITIVE	COMPARATIVE	SUPERLATIVE
hard	harder	hardest
deserving	more/less deserving	most/least deserving

Flat adverbs and their corresponding adjectives share the same form:

➤ He was driving too **fast**. [flat adverb]

➤ He likes **fast** cars. [adjective]

Some adverbs have a positive form and a flat form. They can often be used interchangeably: *dig deep, dig deeply*. Other flat adverbs include *slow, quick, bright, tight*, and *straight*.

(1) Complete and logical comparisons

When using the comparative form of an adjective or an adverb, be sure to indicate what two elements you are comparing.

➤ A diesel engine is **heavier**/ *than a gas engine.*

Occasionally, the second element in a comparison is implied.

➤ She wrote **two** papers; the instructor gave her a **better** grade on the second [paper].

A comparison should also be logical. The following example illogically compares *population* and *Wabasha*.

➤ The **population** of Winona is larger than ^*that of* **Wabasha**.

(2) Double comparatives or superlatives

Use either an ending or a preceding qualifier, not both, to form a comparative or superlative.

➤ The first bridge is ~~more~~ narrower than the second.

➤ The ~~most~~ narrowest bridge is in the northern part of the state.

Comparative and superlative forms of modifiers that have absolute meanings, such as *a more perfect society* and *the most unique campus*, are rarely used in academic writing.

EXERCISE 22.2

Provide the comparative or superlative form of each modifier.

1. Amphibians can be divided into three groups. Frogs and toads are in the (common) group.

2. Because they do not have to maintain a specific body temperature, amphibians eat (frequently) than mammals do.

3. Reptiles may look like amphibians, but their skin is (dry).

4. During the Devonian period, the (close) ancestors of amphibians were fish with fins that looked like legs.

22c Double negatives

The term **double negative** refers to the use of two negative words to express a single negation. Consider revising any sentences that include *not* and another negative word such as *no*, *nothing*, *nobody*, *hardly*, *barely*, or *scarcely*.

➤ He did**n't** keep ~~**no**~~ *any* records.

➤ I could**n't hardly** quit in the middle of the job.

MULTILINGUAL WRITERS
NEGATION IN OTHER LANGUAGES

The use of two negative words in one sentence is common in languages such as Spanish:

➤ *Yo* **no** *compré* **nada**. ["I didn't buy anything."]

If your native language allows this type of negation, be sure to revise any double negatives you find in your academic and professional writing.

22d Placement of modifiers

Effective placement of modifiers will improve the clarity and coherence of your sentences. A **misplaced modifier** obscures the meaning of a sentence.

(1) Placing modifiers near the words they modify

Readers expect phrases and clauses to modify the nearest grammatical element.

➤ ~~Crouched and ugly, the~~ *The* young boy gasped at the *crouched and ugly* phantom moving across the stage. [The repositioned modifiers *crouched* and *ugly* describe the phantom, not the boy.]

(2) Using limiting modifiers

Place the limiting modifiers *almost*, *even*, *hardly*, *just*, and *only* before the words or word groups they modify. Altering placement can alter meaning.

➤ The committee can **only** nominate two members for the position. [The committee cannot *appoint* the two members to the position.]

➤ The committee can nominate **only** two members for the position. [The committee cannot nominate more than two members.]

➤ **Only** the committee can nominate two members for the position. [No person or group other than the committee can nominate members.]

(3) Revising squinting modifiers

A **squinting modifier** can be interpreted as modifying either what precedes it or what follows it. To avoid such lack of clarity, you can reposition the modifier, add punctuation, or revise the entire sentence.

SQUINTING

Even though Erikson lists some advantages **overall** his vision of a successful business is faulty.

REVISED

Even though Erikson lists some **overall** advantages, his vision of a successful business is faulty. [modifier repositioned; punctuation added]

REVISED

Erikson lists some advantages; **however**, **overall**, his vision of a successful business is faulty. [sentence revised]

EXERCISE 22.3

Improve the clarity of the following sentences by moving the modifiers.

1. Alfred Joseph Hitchcock was born the son of a poultry dealer in London.

2. Hitchcock was only identified with thrillers after making his third movie, *The Lodger*.

3. Hitchcock's most famous movies revolved around psychological improbabilities that are still discussed by movie critics today.

4. Although his movies are known for suspense sometimes moviegoers also remember Hitchcock's droll sense of humor.

5. Hitchcock just did not direct movie thrillers; he also produced two television series.

6. Originally a British citizen, Queen Elizabeth II knighted Alfred Hitchcock in 1980.

22e Dangling modifiers

Dangling modifiers do not clearly modify anything in the rest of the sentence. If a sentence begins with an introductory modifier, be sure that what follows—namely, the subject of the sentence—is actually being modified.

➤ Lying on the beach, *we found that* time became irrelevant. [Time cannot lie on a beach.]

➤ When *you are* exercising strenuously, it is important to drink plenty of water. [subject added to the modifier; "it" is not exercising]

Although you will most frequently find a dangling modifier at the beginning of a sentence, you may sometimes find one at the end of a sentence.

➤ Adequate lighting is a necessity *for anyone* ~~when~~ studying.
   [Lighting cannot study.]

EXERCISE 22.4

Revise any misplaced or dangling modifiers.

1. Climbing a mountain, fitness becomes all-important.

2. In determining an appropriate challenge, considering safety precautions is necessary.

3. Even when expecting sunny weather, rain gear should be packed.

4. Although adding extra weight, climbers should not leave home without a first-aid kit.

5. By taking pains at the beginning of a trip, agony can be averted at the end of a trip.

S

EFFECTIVE SENTENCES

Visit the MindTap® for this book for additional information and resources.

23 Sentence Unity

Effective academic and professional writing is composed of sentences that are consistent, clear, and complete.

23a Choosing and arranging details

Well-chosen details (of time, location, or cause) add interest and credibility to your writing.

MISSING IMPORTANT DETAIL	An astrophysicist from the Harvard-Smithsonian Center has predicted a galactic storm.
WITH DETAIL ADDED	An astrophysicist from the Harvard-Smithsonian Center has predicted **that** a galactic storm **will occur within the next ten million years**.

The added detail about time clarifies the sentence and helps readers accept the information. Every word and every detail you use should contribute to your central thought, as in the following description of brain activity:

A given mental task may involve a complicated web of circuits, which interact in varying degrees with others throughout the brain—not like the parts in a machine, but like the instruments in a symphony orchestra combining their tenor, volume, and resonance to create a particular musical effect.

—JAMES SHREEVE, "Beyond the Brain"

23b Revising mixed metaphors

When you use language that evokes images, make sure that the images are meaningfully related. Revise sentences that create **mixed metaphors**—combinations of images that do not make sense together—by replacing the words that evoke conflicting images.

➤ As he climbed the corporate ladder, he ~~sank into a sea of~~ *incurred a large* debt.

The odd image of a man hanging onto a ladder as it disappears into the water can easily be revised with the removal of one conflicting image.

23c Revising mixed constructions

A sentence that begins with one kind of grammatical structure and shifts to another is a **mixed construction**.

➤ *Practicing* ~~By practicing~~ a new language daily will help you become proficient. [*Practicing a new language* (a gerund phrase) replaces the prepositional phrase, *By practicing a new language*, which cannot serve as the subject of the verb *will help*.]

➤ *Her scholarship award* ~~Although she won a scholarship~~ does not give her the right to skip classes. [*Although she won a scholarship* (an adverbial clause) cannot serve as the subject. The editing makes the noun phrase *Her scholarship award* the subject.]

You can revise a mixed construction by changing the subject or using the beginning of the current sentence as a modifier and adding a new subject after it.

➤ Although she won a scholarship (an adverbial dependent clause), **she** does not have the right to skip classes (an independent clause). [The adverbial dependent clause now modifies the independent clause.]

23d   Relating sentence parts

When the subject of a sentence is described as being or doing the logically impossible, the sentence has **faulty predication**. Similarly, mismatches between a verb and its complement can obscure meaning.

(1) Mismatch between subject and verb

A sentence's subject and verb must create a meaningful idea.

MISMATCH	The absence of detail screams out at the reader. [An *absence* cannot scream.]
REVISION	The reader immediately notices the absence of detail.

When a form of the verb *be* joins two parts of a sentence, these two parts should be logically related.

Free speech

➤ ⌃~~The importance of free speech~~ is essential to a democracy. [*Importance* cannot be essential.]

(2) Mismatch of verbs and complements

A verb and its complement should fit together meaningfully.

MISMATCH	Only a few students used the incorrect use of *there*. [To "use an incorrect use" is not logical.]
REVISION	Only a few students used *there* correctly.

Verbs used to report the words of others appear in attributive tags and are followed by specific types of complements. A few common verbs and their complements follow.

VERBS FOR ATTRIBUTIVE TAGS AND THEIR COMPLEMENTS

Verb + *that* noun clause

agree	claim	report	suggest
argue	demonstrate	state	think

➤ The researcher <u>reported</u> that the weather patterns had changed.

Verb + noun phrase + *that* noun clause

convince   remind   tell

➤ He <u>told</u> the reporters that he was planning to resign.

Verb + *wh-* noun clause

demonstrate	discuss	report	suggest
describe	explain	state	wonder

➤ She <u>described</u> what had happened.

EXERCISE 23.1

Revise the following sentences so that each verb is followed by a conventional complement. When you use reporting verbs before clauses, be sure the clauses follow one of these patterns.

1. The speaker discussed that applications had specific requirements.

2. He convinced that mass transit was affordable.

3. The two groups agreed how the problem could be solved.

4. Hickey described that changes had been made to the farming operation.

5. They wondered that such a catastrophe could happen.

23e Avoiding *is when*, *is where*, and *the reason . . . is because* constructions

Some common structures in our spoken language are considered faulty in academic writing because of their mismatched sentence parts.

(1) Mismatches in definitions

In a definition, the term being defined should be followed by a noun or a noun phrase, not an adverbial clause. Avoid using *is when* or *is where*.

➤ Ecology is ~~when you~~ study the relationships among living organisms and between living organisms and their environment.
  (the ... of)

➤ Exploitative competition is ~~where~~ two or more organisms ~~vie~~ for a limited resource such as food.
  (the contest between ... vying)

(2) Mismatch of *the reason* with *is because*

In academic writing, avoid the construction *the reason . . . is because*. The word *because* means "for the reason that." Saying "the reason is for the reason that" is redundant.

➤ The ~~reason the~~ old train station was closed ~~is~~ because it had fallen into disrepair.

23f Including necessary words

Take care to include all necessary small words such as articles, prepositions, verbs, and conjunctions.

➤ Graduation will take place in the Bryce Jordan Center.

When a sentence has a compound verb (two verbs linked by a conjunction), you may need to supply a preposition for each verb.

➤ He neither **believes** *in* nor **approves of** exercise. [The verb *believes*
does not work with *of*.]

All verbs, both auxiliary and main, should be included to
make sentences complete.

➤ Voter turnout has never *been* and will never be 100 percent.

When a sentence consists of two short clauses and the verb in
both clauses is the same, the verb in the second clause can be
omitted.

➤ The wind **was** fierce and the thunder [was] deafening.

Include the word *that* before a clause when it makes the sentence easier to read.

➤ The paleontologists discovered *that* the fossil provided a link
between the dinosaur and the modern bird.

That should always be retained when a sentence has two parallel clauses.

➤ The graph indicated **that the population had increased** but **that
the number of homeowners had not**.

23g Completing comparisons

A comparison has two parts: someone or something is compared to someone or something else. Comparisons should
include all necessary words to make the comparison complete.

➤ Printers today are markedly different *from those sold in the early 1990s*.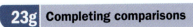

➤ His first novel was better *than the one just published*.

Complete comparisons must also be logical so that the meaning
is clear.

UNCLEAR	Her test scores are higher than the other students.

Are the *scores* being compared to *students*?

CLEAR	Her test scores are higher than **those of** the other students.
CLEAR	Her test scores are higher than the other **students' scores**.

23h Completing intensifiers

In speech, the intensifiers *so*, *such*, and *too* are used to mean "very," "unusually," or "extremely."

➤ That movie was **so** funny.

In academic and professional writing, however, the intensifiers *so*, *such*, and *too* require a completing phrase or clause.

➤ That movie was **so** funny that I watched it twice.

EXERCISE 23.2

Revise each of the following sentences to make them clear and complete.

1. Ralph McQuarrie sketched designs for R2D2 and Darth Vader, including his mask. Iain McCaig wanted to create something scarier for *The Phantom Menace*.

2. He drew generic male face with metal teeth and long red ribbons of hair falling in front of it.

3. He designed a face that looked as though it been flayed.

4. The evil visage of Darth Maul was so horrible. To balance the effect, McCaig added elegant black feathers.

24 Subordination and Coordination

Subordination and coordination indicate relationships between ideas and add variety to sentences.

24a Using subordination effectively

Using subordination allows you to clarify the relationships among the ideas in a sentence. Subordinate grammatical structures (dependent clauses, phrases, even single words) cannot stand alone; they are attached to or embedded in an independent (or main) clause.

(1) Subordinating conjunctions

A **subordinating conjunction** specifies the relationship between a dependent clause and an independent clause. For example, it might signal a causal relationship.

➤ Our team won the swim meet **because the members inspire one another**.

Some Frequently Used Subordinating Conjunctions

Cause	*because*
Concession	*although, even though*
Condition	*if, unless*
Effect	*so that*
Sequence	*before, after*
Time	*when*

By using subordinating conjunctions, you can combine short sentences and indicate how they are related.

➤ *After we* We spent all day Saturday studying. *, we* We went to hear Kofi Annan at Schwab Auditorium.

(2) Relative pronouns

Dependent clauses can begin with a **relative pronoun** (*who, whom, which, that,* or *whose*).

➤ The Roman temple has a portico **that opens to the morning sun.**

➤ Steven Spielberg produced and directed a film about Abraham Lincoln. *, which won many awards, including the Oscar for best actor* [Adding a dependent clause (beginning with the relative pronoun *which*) embeds multiple details into the sentence without sacrificing conciseness.]

CAUTION

A relative clause beginning with *which* can modify a specific word or phrase—or refer to an entire independent clause. Take care to make your reference explicit.

➤ *Because he* He is a top graduate of our prestigious business school, *he will have* ~~which should guarantee him~~ many interviews.

24b Using coordination effectively

Coordinate means "being of equal rank." Use coordination to link elements that have the same grammatical form. For example, they may be two words that are both adjectives, two phrases that are both prepositional, or two clauses that are both independent.

a **stunning** and **satisfying** conclusion [adjectives]

in the attic or **in the basement** [prepositional phrases]

The company was losing money, yet **the employees suspected nothing.** [independent or main clauses]

To indicate the relationship between coordinate words, phrases, or clauses, choose an appropriate coordinating conjunction.

Coordinating Conjunctions

Addition	*and*
Alternative	*or, not*
Cause	*for*
Contrast	*but, yet*
Result	*so*

➤ The hike to the top of Angels Landing has countless
switchbacks. ~~It also has~~ dangerous drop-offs. [Using
    ^*and*
coordination helps avoid unnecessary repetition.]

You can also link two independent clauses with a semicolon, a semicolon and an adverbial conjunction (such as *however* or *nevertheless*), or a colon. Each connection indicates a specific relationship between the two clauses.

➤ Hikers follow the path; climbers scale the cliff wall.

The careful punctuation of two independent clauses will help you avoid comma splices and fused sentences (chapter **19**).

MULTILINGUAL WRITERS
CHOOSING CONJUNCTIONS

In English, use either a coordinating conjunction or a subordinating conjunction (but not both) to signal a connection between clauses.

➤ **Because** he had a headache, ~~so~~ he went to the health center.

➤ *He*
   ^ ~~Because~~ had a headache, **so** he went to the health center.

EXERCISE 24.1

Using subordination and coordination, revise the sentences in the following paragraph so that they emphasize the ideas you think are important.

¹The Lummi tribe lives in the Northwest. ²The Lummis have a belief about sorrow and loss. ³They believe that grief is a burden. ⁴According to their culture, this burden should not be carried alone. ⁵After the terrorist attack on the World Trade Center, the Lummis wanted to help shoulder the burden of grief felt by others. ⁶Some of the Lummis carve totem poles. ⁷These carvers crafted a healing totem pole. ⁸They gave this pole to the citizens of New York. ⁹Many of the citizens of New York had family members who were killed in the terrorist attacks. ¹⁰The Lummis do not believe that the pole itself heals. ¹¹Rather, they believe that healing comes from the prayers and songs said over it. ¹²For them, healing is not the responsibility of a single person. ¹³They believe that it is the responsibility of the community.

24c Avoiding faulty or excessive subordination and coordination

(1) Choosing precise conjunctions

Because subordinating conjunctions specify a relationship between ideas, choose them carefully.

➤ *Because*
   ~~As~~ time was running out, I randomly filled in the remaining circles on the exam sheet. [The use of *as* is distracting because it can mean either "because" or "while."]

Your choice of coordinating conjunction should also convey your meaning precisely.

➤ The rain continued to fall, ~~and~~ the concert was canceled. [To

so

indicate a cause-and-consequence relationship, *so* is more
precise than *and*, which indicates that the rain and concert are
equally significant.]

(2) Excessive subordination and coordination

Subordination and coordination are less effective when overused. In the following sentence, two dependent clauses compete for the reader's focus.

INEFFECTIVE SUBORDINATION
Although researchers used to believe that ancient Egyptians
were the first to domesticate cats, they now think that cats may
have provided company for humans five thousand years earlier
because the intact skeleton of a cat has been discovered in a
Neolithic village on Cyprus.

The revision is clearer than the original sentence because it
eliminates one of the dependent clauses.

REVISED
Although researchers used to believe that ancient Egyptians
were the first to domesticate cats, they now think that cats may
have provided company for humans five thousand years earlier.
They base their revised estimate on the discovery of an intact
cat skeleton in a Neolithic village on Cyprus.

Overuse of coordination results in a rambling sentence that is
difficult to follow.

INEFFECTIVE	The lake was surrounded by forest, and it
COORDINATION	was large and clean, so it looked refreshing.
REVISED	Surrounded by forest, the large, clean lake
	looked refreshing.

EXERCISE 24.2

Revise the following sentences to eliminate faulty or excessive coordination and subordination.

1. Duct tape was invented for the U.S. military during World War II to keep the moisture out of ammunition cases because it was strong and waterproof.

2. Duct tape was originally called "duck tape" as it was waterproof and ducks are like that too and because it was made of cotton duck, which is a durable, tightly woven material.

3. When the war was over, house builders used duck tape to connect ductwork together, and the builders started to refer to duck tape as "duct tape" and eventually the color of the tape changed from the green that was used during the war to silver, which matched the ducts.

4. Many new colorful forms of duct tape are available, although they are more expensive and less practical than standard silver.

25 Parallelism

Parallelism is the use of grammatically equivalent structures to clarify meaning and to emphasize ideas. Two or more elements are considered parallel when they have similar grammatical forms—when, for example, all are nouns or all are prepositional phrases.

25a Using coordinating conjunctions

Parallel elements are frequently joined by a **coordinating conjunction** (*and, but, or, yet, so, nor,* or *for*).

➤ My exam was <u>challenging</u> **but** invigorating. [two adjectives joined by *but*]

➤ Her goals include <u>publicizing student and faculty research,</u> <u>increasing research funding,</u> **and** <u>improving research</u> <u>facilities.</u> [three gerund phrases joined by *and*]

➤ Our instructor explained <u>what the project had entailed</u> **and** <u>how the</u> <u>researchers had used the results.</u> [two noun clauses joined by *and*]

25b   **Repeating words and grammatical forms for paired ideas**

Parallel structures allow you to pair ideas and create connections in sentences. By repeating a preposition, the infinitive marker *to*, or the introductory word of a clause, you can create parallel structures that are clear, succinct, and emphatic.

➤ My embarrassment stemmed not **from** the money lost
from
but shame.

➤ She wanted her audience **to remember** the protest song and
to understand
~~be understanding of~~ its origin.

➤ The team vowed **that** they would support each other, **that** they
that
would play their best, and they would win the tournament.

Repeating a pattern emphasizes the relationship of ideas. The following example includes the *-ing* form (present participle) of two different verbs.

remodeling
➤ Many Detroit homeowners are selling their houses or ~~should remodel~~ to enhance value.

Two or three structures joined by *and*, *but*, or *or* should be parallel, as in the following sentence.

rise,
➤ Mortgage rates ~~are rising,~~ and building codes change, but the real estate market remains strong.

THINKING RHETORICALLY
PARALLELISM

Parallel elements make your writing easy and pleasurable to read. But consider breaking from the parallel pattern to emphasize a point. For example, to describe a friend, you could start with two adjectives and then switch to a noun phrase.

➤ My friend Alison is **kind, modest**, and **the smartest mathematician in the state.**

25c Creating parallelism in lists, headings, and outlines

Each item in a list or formal outline should be parallel to emphasize consistency and connectedness (**2c**). Headings in any document should be in parallel form whenever possible (**7a**).

➤ People all around me are **buying, remodeling**, or **selling** their houses.

➤ In his speech, the president charged his generation with lofty goals: (1) reigniting economic growth, (2) restoring the American dream, and (3) *putting* ~~to make~~ government *to* work for average citizens.

25d Using correlative conjunctions

Correlative conjunctions (or **correlatives**) are pairs of words that link other words, phrases, or clauses, including *both … and, either … or, neither … nor, not only … but also*, and *whether … or*. Always use the same grammatical structures following each conjunction in the pair.

➤ **Whether** <u>at home</u> **or** <u>at school</u>, he is always busy.

    His team practices not only

➤ ~~Not only practicing~~ at 6 a.m. during the week, but ~~his team~~ also ~~scrimmages~~ on Sunday afternoons. [The editing makes the elements after the correlative conjunctions *not only . . . but also* parallel.]

EXERCISE 25.1

Rewrite the following sentences to create parallel structures.

1. Helen was praised by the vice president, and her administrative assistant admired her.

2. When she hired new employees for her department, she looked for applicants who were accomplished, able to work hard, and able to speak clearly.

3. At meetings, Helen was always prepared, participating actively yet politely, and generated innovative responses to department concerns.

4. In her annual report, she wrote that her most important achievements were attracting new majors and scholarship donations were higher.

5. When asked about her leadership style, Helen said that she preferred collaborating with others rather than to work alone in her office.

6. Whether in the department's meetings or conventions, Helen prepared her remarks in advance.

26   Emphasis

In any piece of writing, some of your ideas are more important than others. You can use emphasis to make those ideas stand out.

26a   Placing words and using punctuation

In every sentence, some words receive more emphasis than others. In general, the major stress of any sentence comes at the end or toward the end of a sentence. When you read aloud the brief sentence *We discussed the film*, you will likely stress *film*. Take advantage of this tendency by finishing a sentence with the most important information—usually an idea that is new to the reader.

➤ ~~The film's stop-motion animation was~~ raved about ~~by many viewers~~.
    ^*Many viewers*   ^*the film's stop-motion animation*

To ensure that readers focus on the end of the sentence, use an occasional colon or dash to set off the information (**32b**, **35d**).

➤ The everyday episodes of online cruelty, added together, became what he was warned about: bullying.

26b   Ordering ideas from least to most important

By arranging your ideas in **climactic (or emphatic) order**—from least important to most important—you build up suspense. In the following example, the writer emphasizes a doctor's desire to help the disadvantaged and then implies that this desire has been realized through work with young Haitian doctors:

> While he was in medical school, the soon-to-be-doctor discovered his calling: to diagnose infectious diseases, to find ways of curing people with these diseases, and **to bring the lifesaving knowledge of modern medicine to the disadvantaged**. Most recently, he has been working with a small group of young doctors in Haiti.

26c Repeating important words

Repetition used deliberately emphasizes key words or ideas (25b).

> We **forget** all too soon the things we thought we could never **forget**. We **forget** the loves and betrayals alike, **forget** what we whispered and what we screamed, **forget** who we are.
>
> — JOAN DIDION, "On Keeping a Notebook"

26d Inverting word order

Most sentences begin with a subject and end with a predicate (27c). When you move words out of their normal order, you draw attention to them. Notice the inverted word order in the second sentence of the following passage.

> [1]The Library Committee met with the City Council on several occasions to persuade them to fund the building of a library annex. [2]So successful were their efforts that a new wing will be added by next year. [3]This wing will contain archival materials that were previously stored in the basement.

The modifier *so successful* appears at the beginning of the sentence, rather than in its normal position, after the verb: Their efforts were *so successful* that . . . . The inverted word order emphasizes the committee's accomplishment.

MULTILINGUAL WRITERS
INVERTING WORD ORDER

Although most English sentences take the form of subject-verb-object, more interesting ones involve inversions of various types. Sometimes the main verb in the form of a participle is placed at the beginning of the sentence. The subject and the auxiliary verb(s) are then inverted.

➤ *part* **Carved** into the bench *aux v* **were** *s* **someone's initials**.

[COMPARE: Someone's initials were carved into the bench.]

An adjective may also begin a sentence. In this type of sentence, the subject and the linking verb are inverted.

➤ *adj* **Crucial** to our success *link v* **was** *s* **the dedication of our employees**.

[COMPARE: The dedication of our employees was crucial to our success.]

26e Using an occasional short sentence

In a paragraph of long or complicated sentences, a short sentence works well for emphasis, especially when it appears immediately after an especially long sentence.

➤ After organizing the kitchen, buying the groceries, slicing the vegetables, mowing the lawn, weeding the garden, hanging the decorations, and setting up the grill, I was ready to have a good time when my guests arrived. **Then the phone rang**.

Take care not to use too many short sentences; the overall effect is choppy (27a).

EXERCISE 26.1

Use the strategy in parentheses to add emphasis in the following sentences. You may add or delete words as necessary.

1. (climactic order) In the 1960 Olympics, Wilma Rudolph tied the world record in the 100-meter race, she tied the record in the 400-meter relay, she won the hearts of fans from around the world, and she broke the record in the 200-meter race.

2. (inversion) Rudolph's Olympic achievement is impressive, but her victory over a crippling disease is even more spectacular.

3. (occasional short sentence) Rudolph was born prematurely, weighing only four and one-half pounds. As a child, she suffered from double pneumonia, scarlet fever, and then polio.

4. (inversion) Her siblings' willingness to help was essential to her recovery, as were her mother's vigilant care and her own determination.

5. (climactic order) Rudolph set a scoring record in basketball, she set the standard for future track and field stars, and she set an Olympic record in track.

27 Variety

A variety of sentence types and lengths makes your writing lively and distinctive.

27a Varying sentence length and form

Avoid the choppy effect of a series of short sentences by combining some of them into longer sentences. You can combine sentences by using coordinating conjunctions (such as *and*, *but*, and *or*) to show a connection.

➤ Minneapolis ~~is one of~~ the Twin Cities. ~~St. Paul is the other.~~ ~~They~~ differ in many ways.

and St. Paul are called / *, but* / *they*

You can also combine sentences by using subordinating conjunctions (such as *because*, *although*, and *when*) or relative pronouns (such as *who*, *that*, and *which*).

➤ Legislation on space tourism has not been passed. ~~Plans~~ for a commercial rocket service are going forward anyway. [Adding *although* creates a dependent clause and clarifies the logical relationship between ideas.]

Although legislation / *, plans*

➤ Today, lawmakers discussed some new legislation. ~~This legislation~~ would promote the safety of rocket passengers. [The editing puts emphasis on the first clause. The relative pronoun *that* introduces a description of the legislation.]

that

27b Varying sentence openings

Many writers begin their sentences with a subject. Although this pattern is common, relying on it too heavily—especially in too many sentences in a row—can make writing sound dull. Experiment with the following alternatives for beginning your sentences.

BEGINNING WITH AN ADVERB

➤ *Immediately, the* ~~The~~ dentist stopped drilling ~~immediately~~ and asked me how I was doing.

BEGINNING WITH A PHRASE

➤ *Reflecting* ~~The reporter, reflecting~~ on the election, *the reporter* understood clearly how the incumbent defeated the challenger. [participial phrase]

➤ **A town of historic interest,** Santa Fe also has many art galleries. [appositive phrase]

BEGINNING WITH A TRANSITIONAL EXPRESSION

In each of the following examples, the transitional expression shows the relationship between the ideas in the pair of sentences.

➤ Many restaurants close within a few years of opening. **But** others, which offer good food at reasonable prices, become well established.

➤ Independently owned restaurants struggle to get started for a number of reasons. **First of all,** they have to compete against successful restaurant chains.

BEGINNING WITH A DEPENDENT CLAUSE

➤ When I was twelve years old, I started my own babysitting service. [COMPARE: I started my own babysitting service when I was twelve years old.]

27c   Using cumulative and periodic sentences

In a cumulative sentence, the idea expressed in the independent clause comes first, followed by supporting ideas and details.

➤ **Dr. Jones was what people once referred to as "a lady,"** and in that sense reminded me of my grandmother, who was a single mother in the projects but always spoke as though she had nice things.

—TA-NEHISI COATES, *Between the World and Me*

In a **periodic sentence**, however, the independent clause comes last, emphasized just before the period.

➤ Because the scar resulting from the burn is typically much larger than the original lesion, allowing for less intricacy, **the designs tend to be much simpler than those used in tattoos**.

— NINA JABLONSKI, *Skin: A Natural History*

Both of these types of sentences can be effective. Because cumulative sentences are more common, however, the less common periodic sentence tends to provide emphasis.

27d   Using questions, exclamations, and commands

You can vary the sentences in a paragraph by introducing an occasional question, exclamation, or command.

QUESTION

How was the creativity of the black woman kept alive, year after year and century after century, when for most of the years black people have been in America, it was a punishable crime for a black person to read or write? And the freedom to paint, to sculpt, to expand the mind with action did not exist. Consider, if you can bear to imagine it, what might have been the result if singing, too, had been forbidden by law. Listen to the voices of Bessie Smith, Billie Holiday, Nina Simone, Roberta Flack, and Aretha Franklin, among others, and imagine those voices muzzled for life.

— ALICE WALKER, *In Search of Our Mothers' Gardens*

You can either answer the question or let readers answer it for themselves, in which case it is called a **rhetorical question**.

EXCLAMATION

But at other moments, the classroom is so lifeless or painful or confused—and I so powerless to do anything about it—that my claim to be a teacher seems a transparent sham. Then the enemy is everywhere: in those students from some alien planet, in the subject I thought I knew, and in the personal pathology that keeps me earning my living this way. *What a fool I was to imagine that I had mastered this occult art—harder to divine than tea leaves and impossible for mortals to do even passably well!*

—PARKER PALMER, *The Courage to Teach*

COMMAND

Now I stare and stare at people shamelessly. *Stare.* It's the way to educate your eye.

— WALKER EVANS, *Unclassified*

In this case, a one-word command, "Stare," provides variety.

EXERCISE 27.1

Use the strategy in parentheses to revise the following sentences for variety. You may want to combine, invert, shorten, or lengthen some of the sentences. Add or delete words as needed to provide clarification, relationships, and emphasis.

1. (combine) The civil rights activist and the conservative pundit appear to have little in common. They both take pleasure in addressing audiences.

2. (combine) Their ideologies could not be more different. Both see the Bible as a moral foundation. The well-being of the United States should be reconstructed from that biblical foundation.

3. (combine) Both liberal and conservative activists argue that their agenda is best for America's future. Neither group mentions the power and potential of working together.

EXERCISE 27.2

Rewrite each sentence so that it does not begin with a subject.

1. (begin with a prepositional phrase) John Spilsbury was an engraver and mapmaker from London who made the first jigsaw puzzle in about 1760.

2. (begin with a dependent clause) He pasted a map onto a piece of wood and used a fine-bladed saw to cut around the borders of the countries.

3. (begin with a transitional expression) The jigsaw puzzle was first an educational toy and has been a mainstay in households all over the world ever since its invention.

4. (begin with a dependent clause) The original puzzles were quite expensive because the wooden pieces were cut by hand.

5. (begin with an adverb) Most puzzles are made of cardboard today.

6. (periodic sentence) Lee's passion became mountain biking after he recovered, built up his strength, and gained self-confidence.

7. (cumulative sentence) He received donations and help from the community. His neighbors walked his two dogs. His coworkers brought precooked meals for the week.

8. (change one sentence to a question) There are multiple activities that can help survivors of traumatic brain injury toward recovery. Advocates believe that reviewing and practicing conversation and people skills are both essential to success.

L

EFFECTIVE LANGUAGE

Visit the MindTap® for this book for additional information and resources.

28 Good Usage

Using the right words at the right time can make the difference between having your ideas taken seriously or seeing them brushed aside. The right words make your writing easy and pleasurable to read; they achieve a clear style that your audience understands and the occasion requires. Sentences that are ornate—including flowery or fancy language—may not be understood by a broad audience.

ORNATE	The majority believes that achievement derives primarily from the diligent pursuit of allocated tasks.
CLEAR	Most people believe that success results from hard work.

28a Appropriate word choice

You may find yourself writing for an audience that you know will welcome slang and colloquial expressions or for a specialized audience who will immediately understand technical jargon. Otherwise, the following advice can help you determine which words to use and which to avoid. A good dictionary will also help you. Words labeled *dialect, slang, colloquial, nonstandard*, or *unconventional* are generally inappropriate for academic and professional writing. If a word has no label, you can safely assume that it can be used in writing for school or work.

(1) Slang

Slang covers a wide range of words or expressions that are considered casual or fashionable by people in a particular age group, locality, or profession. Although such expressions are used in conversation or in writing intended to mimic conversation, terms such as *totally*, *on fleek*, *turnt*, and *bae* are usually out of place in academic or professional writing.

(2) Conversational (or colloquial) words

Words labeled *colloquial* in a dictionary are fine for casual conversation and for written dialogues or personal essays on a light topic. Such words are sometimes used for special effect in academic writing, but you should usually replace them with more appropriate words. For example, conversational words such as *dumb* and *kid around* could be replaced by *illogical* and *tease*.

(3) Regionalisms

Regionalisms—such as *red up* for "tidy up," *pop* for "soda," and *sweeper* for "vacuum cleaner"—can make essay writing lively and distinctive, but they are often considered too informal for most academic and professional writing.

(4) Technical words or jargon

When writing for a diverse audience, an effective writer will not refer to the need for bifocals as *presbyopia*. However, technical language is appropriate when the audience can understand it (as when one physician writes to another about tachycardia) or when the audience (heart patients, for example) would benefit by learning the terms in question. As computer use has grown, technical terms such as *application* (*app*) and *cloud computing* have become commonly used and widely understood.

28b Inclusive language

By choosing words that are inclusive rather than exclusive, you invite readers into your writing. Prejudiced or derogatory language about skin color, cultural-ethnic background, body size or shape, physical or mental ability, or sexual orientation has no place in academic or professional writing; using it undermines your authority and credibility.

(1) Nonsexist language

Effective writers show equal respect for all people. For example, they avoid using *man* to refer to people in general because they understand that the word excludes many other people, mostly women.

➤ ~~Man's~~ *Achievements [OR Human achievements]* ~~achievements~~ in science and technology are impressive.

➤ The university offers free tuition to ~~wives~~ *partners* of faculty.

TIPS FOR AVOIDING SEXIST LANGUAGE

When reviewing drafts, revise the following types of sexist language.

- **Generic *he/his*.** Revise by changing *he* to *he or she*, using a plural form, or rewriting the sentence.

  ➤ By listening to constituents, **senators** obtain important information on the consequences of ~~his or her~~ *their* votes and decisions. [elimination of *his* by revising the sentence]

  ➤ *Senators* ~~A senator~~ should listen to ~~his or her~~ *their* constituents. [use of plural forms]

- **Terms such as *man* and *mankind*** and those with *-ess* or *-man* endings (*stewardess, chairman*). Replace such terms with gender-neutral terms, such as *flight attendant* and *chair*.

  ➤ Universal health care would benefit ~~mankind~~ *all Americans*. [Replace *mankind* with a gender-neutral term.]

- Using *they* and *their* as a third-person singular pronoun has fallen into acceptable usage as a way to avoid using singular gendered pronouns (*he, she, his, her, him, her*).

  ➤ Every attendee must relinquish their cell phone.

- **Occupational stereotypes.** Use gender-neutral terms.

  ➤ *Nurses* ~~Every nurse~~ must focus ~~his or her~~ *their* attention on ~~his or her~~ *their* patients.

  ➤ Glenda James, a ~~female~~ *an* engineer at Howard Aviation, won the best-employee award.

TIPS FOR AVOIDING SEXIST LANGUAGE

- **Inconsistent use of titles.** Use titles or full names, but do so consistently.

  Peter and Mary Holmes   or *Mr. and Ms. [or Mrs.] Holmes*
  ➤ ~~Mr. Holmes and his wife, Mary,~~ took a long trip to China.
  [title removed]

- **Unstated gender assumption.** Avoid stereotypical language and assumptions.

  an adult provide
- Have ~~your mother make~~ your costume for the school pageant.

EXERCISE 28.1

Revise the following sentences to eliminate sexist language.

1. A special code of ethics guides a nurse in fulfilling her responsibilities.

2. According to the weatherman, this spring will be unseasonably cold and wet.

3. Dr. William Avery and his wife donated money to the scholarship fund.

4. Professor Garcia mapped the evolutionary journey of man.

5. She worked her way through college as a waitress.

(2) Nonracist language

Rarely is it necessary to identify anyone's race or ethnicity in academic or professional writing except, for example, if you are writing a demographic report, an argument against existing racial inequities, or a historical account of a particular event involving ethnic groups. Determining which terms a particular group prefers can be difficult because preferences sometimes vary within a group and change over time. One conventional way to refer to Americans of a specific descent is to include an adjective before the word *American*: *African American, Asian*

American, European American, Latin American, Mexican American, Native American. In addition to *African American* and *European American*, *Black* (or *black*) and *White* (or *white*) have long been used. People of Spanish-speaking descent may prefer *Chicano/Chicana, Hispanic, Latino/Latina, Puerto Rican,* or other terms. Members of cultures that are indigenous to North America may prefer a specific name such as *Cherokee* or *Haida,* though some also accept *American Indian, indigenous peoples,* or *Native Peoples.*

(3) Writing about any difference respectfully

If a writing assignment requires you to distinguish people based on age, physical or mental ability, geographical area, religion, or sexual orientation, show respect to the human beings you discuss by using the terms they prefer.

(a) Referring to age Although some people object to the term *senior citizen,* a better alternative has not emerged. When used respectfully, the term refers to a person who has reached the age of retirement (but may have decided not to retire) and is eligible for certain privileges granted by society. However, if you know your audience would object to the term *senior citizen,* find out which alternative is preferred.

(b) Referring to disability or illness A current recommendation for referring to disabilities and illnesses is "to put the person first." Place focus on the individual rather than on the limitation: *persons with disabilities* is preferred over *disabled persons, that teenager with autism* rather than *that autistic.* You can find out whether such person-first expressions are preferred by noting whether they are used in the articles and books (or by the people) you consult.

(c) Referring to geographical areas Certain geographical terms need to be used with special care. Though most frequently used to refer to people from the United States, the term *American* may also refer to people from Canada, Mexico, and Central or South America. If your audience may be confused by this term, use *people from the United States* or *US citizens* instead.

The term *Arab* refers to people who speak Arabic. If you cannot use specific terms such as *Iraqi* or *Saudi Arabian*, be sure you know that a country's people speak Arabic, not another language. For instance, because Iranians speak Farsi, they are not Arabs.

(d) Referring to religion Reference to a person's religion should be made only if it is relevant. Because religions have both conservative and liberal followers, be careful not to make generalizations about the political stances of a religious group.

(e) Referring to sexual orientation If your purpose for writing makes it necessary to identify sexual orientation, choose terms used by the people you are discussing. For instance, *LGBTQIAPK* includes preferred terms for all the people who are not firmly heterosexual: lesbian, gay, bisexual, transgender, or queer/questioning, intersexed, asexual, pansexual/ polygamous/polyamorous, or kink.

29 Precise Word Choice

Make words work for you. By choosing the right word and putting it in the right place, you can communicate exactly what you mean and make your writing memorable to your intended audience.

29a Accurate and precise word choice

(1) Denotations and connotations

Denotations are definitions of words, such as those that appear in dictionaries. For example, the noun *beach* denotes a sandy or pebbly shore. Select words whose denotations convey your point exactly.

➤ Padre Island National Seashore ~~is really great~~.
          astounds even an indifferent tourist like me

[Because *great* can mean "extremely large" as well as "outstanding" or "powerful," its use in this sentence is imprecise.]

Connotations are the associations evoked by a word. *Beach*, for example, may connote natural beauty, surf, shells, swimming, tanning, sunburn, and crowds. The context in which a word appears affects the associations it evokes. In a report on shoreline management, *beach* has scientific and geographic connotations; in a fashion magazine, this word is associated with bathing suits, sunglasses, and sunscreen. The challenge for writers is to choose the words that are most likely to spark the appropriate connotations in their readers' minds.

➤ The *resilience* ~~obstinacy~~ of the Kemp's ridley sea turtle has delighted park rangers.

[*Obstinacy* has negative connotations, which make it an unlikely quality to cause delight.]

(2) Specific, concrete words

A **general word** is all-inclusive, indefinite, and sweeping in scope. A **specific word** is precise, definite, and limited in scope.

General	Specific	More Specific/Concrete
food	fast food	cheeseburger
place	city	Atlanta

An **abstract word** refers to a concept or idea, a quality or trait, or anything else that cannot be touched, heard, or seen. A **concrete word** signifies a particular object, a specific action, or anything that can be touched, heard, or seen.

ABSTRACT   democracy, evil, strength, charity

CONCRETE   mosquito, hammer, plastic, fog

Ask yourself questions about what you want to say: Exactly who? Exactly what? Exactly when? Exactly where? Exactly how? In the following example, notice what a difference Louise Erdrich's concrete words and details make in expressing and developing an idea.

VAGUE   She has kept no reminders of performing in her youth.

SPECIFIC   She has kept no sequined costume, no photographs, no fliers or posters from that part of her youth.

—LOUISE ERDRICH, "The Leap"

(3) Figurative language

Figurative language is the use of words in an imaginative rather than a literal sense. Similes and metaphors are the chief **figures of speech**. A **simile** is a comparison of dissimilar things that includes *like* or *as*. A **metaphor** is an implied comparison of dissimilar things without *like* or *as*.

SIMILE

When **her body was hairless as a baby's**, she adjusted the showerhead so that the water burst forth in pelting streams.

—LOIDA MARITZA PÉREZ, *Geographies of Home*

METAPHOR

Making tacos is a graceful dance.

—DENISE CHÁVEZ, *A Taco Testimony*

29b   Clichés and euphemisms

When forced or overused, certain expressions lose their impact. For example, the expressions *made of money*, *ace up his sleeve*, and *make no bones about it* were once striking and thus effective. Excessive use, though, has drained them of their original force and made them **clichés**. Newer expressions such as *above board* and *think outside the box* have also lost their vitality because of overuse. Nonetheless, clichés are so much a part of the language that nearly every writer uses them from time to time. But effective writers often give a fresh twist to an old saying.

> I seek a narrative, a fiction, to order days like the one I spent several years ago, on a gray June day in Chicago, when I took a roller-coaster ride on the bell curve of my experience.
> —GAYLE PEMBERTON, " The Zen of Bigger Thomas"

[Notice how much more effective this expression is than a reference to "being on an emotional roller coaster."]

Sometimes writers coin new expressions called **euphemisms** to substitute for words that have coarse or unpleasant connotations. To avoid the word *dying*, for example, a writer might say that someone is *passing on*. However, euphemisms sometimes obscure facts. Euphemisms such as *revenue enhancement* for *tax hike* and *pre-owned* for *used* are considered insincere or deceitful. And a euphemism such as *ethnic cleansing* is a frightening camouflage for actual *genocide*.

EXERCISE 29.1

Replace the following overused expressions with carefully chosen words. Then use the replacements in sentences.

1. reality check
2. bottom line
3. to air dirty laundry
4. mail it in

29c Idioms and collocations

Idioms are fixed expressions whose meanings cannot be entirely determined by knowing the meanings of their parts— *bear in mind, fall in love, stand a chance.* **Collocations** are common combinations of words (*strong coffee, fast plane*). Unlike idioms, they have meanings that *can* be determined by knowing the meanings of their parts—*depend on, fond of, little while, right now.* Regardless of whether you are using an idiom or a collocation, if you make even a small inadvertent change to the expected wording, you may distract or confuse your readers.

➤ She tried to keep a ~~small~~ *low* profile.

➤ They had ~~an invested~~ *a vested* interest in the project.

As you edit your writing, keep an eye out for idioms or collocations that might not be worded correctly. Then check a dictionary or the **Glossary of Usage** at the end of the book to ensure that your usage is appropriate. Writers sometimes have trouble with the following collocations, all of which contain prepositions.

CHOOSING THE RIGHT PREPOSITION

Instead of	Use
according **with**	according **to** the source
accused **for**	accused **of** the crime
based **off of**	based **on** the novel
in accordance **to**	in accordance **with** policy
independent **to**	independent **of** his family
happened **on**	happened **by** accident
superior **than**	superior **to** others

| **29d** | **Clear definitions** |

When words have more than one meaning, establish which meaning you have in mind in a particular piece of writing. A definition can set the terms of the discussion.

➤ In this essay, I use the word *communism* **in the Marxist sense of social organization based on the holding of all property in common.**

A **formal definition** first states the term to be defined, then puts it into a class, and finally differentiates it from other members of that class.

➤ A *phosphene* [term] is **a luminous visual image** [class] **that results from applying pressure to the eyeball** [differentiation].

A synonym or examples can easily clarify the meaning of a term.

➤ *Machismo*, **confidence with an attitude,** can be a pose rather than a reality.

➤ Many homophones **(such as *be* and *bee*, *in* and *inn*, or *see* and *sea*)** are not spelling problems.

30 Conciseness

Effective writers convey their thoughts clearly and efficiently, choosing each word wisely, making sure their readers understand them. Clear and effective sentences are sometimes short, but they are always wisely constructed.

30a Eliminating wordiness and other redundancies

After writing a first draft, review your sentences to make sure that they contain only the words necessary to make your point.

(1) Redundancy

Restating a key point in different words can help readers understand it. But if you rephrase readily understood terms, your work will suffer from **redundancy**—repetition for no good reason.

➤ Ballerinas auditioned ~~in the tryouts~~ for *The Nutcracker*.

➤ Each student had a unique talent *for* ~~and ability that he or she used in his or her~~ acting.

MULTILINGUAL WRITERS
USING RELATIVE PRONOUNS

Review your sentences to make sure that no clause includes both a personal pronoun (*I, me, he, him, she, her, it*) and a relative pronoun (*who, that, which*) referring to the same antecedent.

➤ The drug **that** we were testing ~~it~~ has not been approved by the Food and Drug Administration.

➤ The professor **who** directs the program ~~she~~ likes to meet with students.

(2) Wordiness

As you edit a draft, delete words that add no meaning to adjacent words and shorten wordy expressions.

➤ Some unscrupulous brokers are *cheating* ~~taking money and savings from~~ elderly people *out of their pensions* ~~who need that money because they planned to use it for their retirement~~.

> *If*
> ~~In the event that~~ taxes are raised, ~~expect complaints on the part of the voters~~.
>
> *voters will complain*

In addition, watch for vague words such as *area, aspect, factor, feature, kind, situation, thing,* and *type.* They may signal wordiness.

> *Effective*
> ~~In an employment situation, effective~~ communication is essential at work. [*Employment situation* and *at work* are redundant.]

REPLACEMENTS FOR WORDY EXPRESSIONS

Instead of	Use
at this moment (point) in time	now, today
due to the fact that	because
for the purpose of	for
it is clear (obvious) that	clearly (obviously)
without a doubt	undoubtedly
in the final analysis	finally
in my opinion	[can be omitted]
in today's society	today

USELESS WORDS IN COMMON PHRASES

yellow [in color]	connect [up together]
at 9:45 a.m. [in the morning]	[really and truly] fearless
[basic] essentials	circular [in shape]
[make an] estimate	large [in size]

---

(3) *There are* and *it is*

There or *it* may function as an **expletive**—a word that signals that the subject of the sentence will follow the verb, usually a form of *be*. Writers use expletives to emphasize words that would not be emphasized in the typical subject-verb order.

➤ Three children were playing in the yard. [typical order]

➤ There were three children playing in the yard. [use of expletive]

However, if you find that you have drafted several sentences that begin with expletives, revise a few of them.

➤ ~~There were~~ *Hundreds* ~~hundreds~~ of fans *were* crowding onto the field.

➤ *Joining the crowd* ~~It was~~ frightening ~~to join the crowd.~~

(4) Relative pronouns

The relative pronouns *who*, *which*, or *that* can frequently be deleted without affecting the meaning of a sentence. If one of these pronouns is followed by a form of the verb *be* (*am*, *is*, *are*, *was*, *were*), you can often omit the pronoun and some-times the verb as well.

➤ The change ~~that~~ the young senator proposed yesterday angered most legislators.

➤ The Endangered Species Act, ~~which is~~ passed in 1973, protects the habitats of endangered plants and animals.

30b Using elliptical constructions

An **elliptical construction** is one that deliberately omits words that can be understood from the context.

➤ Speed is the goal for some swimmers, endurance ~~is the goal~~ for others, and relaxation ~~is the goal~~ for still others.

Sometimes, as an aid to clarity, commas mark omissions in elliptical constructions.

➤ My family functioned like a baseball team: my mom was the coach; my brother, the pitcher; and my sister, the shortstop. [Use semicolons to separate items with internal commas.]

EXERCISE 30.1

Rewrite the following sentences to eliminate wordiness.

1. Founded in the year 1967, *Rolling Stone* has become well known for covering culture and politics considered popular.

2. Back in the day, the *Rolling Stone* magazine's original focus was rock and roll.

3. In its first year, I think it helped popularize musicians such as John Lennon, Mick Jagger, and also the guitarist Pete Townshend.

4. Cover photographs featured the Beatles, Jimi Hendrix, Tina Turner, and the vocalist Jim Morrison, among others.

5. The magazine also carried news reports related to the music of the 1960s period.

6. Since that day and age, the magazine has become a mainstay on newsstands everywhere all over the world.

P

PUNCTUATION

Visit the MindTap for this book for additional information and resources.

31 The Comma

Pauses are often signaled by commas, but pauses are not a reliable guide for comma placement. Commas are often called for where speakers do not pause, and speakers may pause when no comma is necessary. Better guidance for using commas comes from some basic principles for comma usage.

31a Joining clauses with coordinating conjunctions

Use a comma before a coordinating conjunction (*and*, *but*, *for*, *nor*, *or*, *so*, or *yet*) to join independent clauses.

➤ George H. W. Bush served as president from 1989 to 1993**,** **and** his son George W. Bush served from 2001 to 2009.

➤ Presidents Andrew Johnson and Lyndon Johnson shared the same last name**,** **but** they were not related.

Without the conjunctions, the sentences above would be considered comma splices; without both the conjunctions and the commas, the sentences would be considered fused sentences (see chapter 19).

When clauses are short, commas may be omitted.

➤ His grandson ran for president but his son did not.

EXERCISE 31.1

Insert commas where needed.

1. When people get goose bumps, they may be reacting to a sudden drop in the temperature or they may be responding to a strong emotion.

2. In general, people notice goose bumps on their forearms but some people also report having goose bumps on their legs.

3. When a goose is plucked, its flesh protrudes and these protrusions are what goose bumps supposedly resemble but the technical term for goose bumps is *piloerection*.

4. The German and Italian languages also have words that refer to goose flesh but French and Spanish translations refer to hens.

5. Many people report that they get goose bumps when they hear about heroic behavior yet it is not uncommon for people to have a similar response to beauty in nature or art.

6. Not only humans experience piloerection but other mammals do as well.

31b Setting off introductory words, phrases, or clauses

Place a comma after a word, phrase, or clause that comes before the main clause of a sentence.

➤ **Clearly,** the project deserves additional funding.

➤ **Despite a downturn in the national economy,** the number of students enrolled in this university has increased.

➤ **Because many students cannot afford tuition,** they find part-time jobs or apply for loans.

If there is more than one introductory word, phrase, or clause, set each off separately.

➤ Fortunately, because of a news article, the buildings in the old neighborhood drew the attention of architects interested in restoring them.

A comma may be omitted after a short introduction as long as the sentence is still clear.

➤ **In 2017** the enrollment at the university increased.

EXERCISE 31.2

Insert necessary commas in the following paragraph. Explain why each comma is needed. Some sentences may not require commas.

[1]Although its uses may not be as well known as those of the comma the hashtag serves a variety of functions. [2]However while the comma may indicate pauses or grammatical boundaries (or sometimes both) the uses of the hashtag differ. [3]In this century the hashtag found in social media signals a reference to a topic, theme, or idea that is or will become a searchable term. [4]Once this meta-data tag has been clicked the viewer accesses posts that feature the tagged word. [5]In previous centuries writers relied on the hashtag for other purposes. [6]The first use may have been to indicate weight. [7]In fact according to Keith Houston's *Shady Characters: The Secret Life of Punctuation* the hashtag may have arisen from the abbreviation for pound: *lb.* from the Latin word *libra*. [8]Initially scribes added a horizontal stroke through the top halves of each letter in the abbreviation. [9]Other uses of the hashtag include indicating a number and designating that a space should be inserted in a text.

31c   Separating elements in a series

A comma appears after each item in a series except the last one.

➤ Ethics are based on **moral, social,** or **cultural values.** [words]

➤ The company's code of ethics encourages **seeking criticism of work, correcting mistakes,** and **acknowledging the contributions of everyone.** [phrases]

Following a tradition in print and online journalism, some writers omit the comma between the final two items in a series. But omitting the comma can lead to confusion, and including it is never wrong.

THINKING RHETORICALLY
COMMAS AND CONJUNCTIONS IN A SERIES

How do the following sentences differ?

➤ We discussed them all: life, liberty, **and** the pursuit of happiness.

➤ We discussed them all: life **and** liberty **and** the pursuit of happiness.

➤ We discussed them all: life, liberty, the pursuit of happiness.

The first sentence follows conventional guidelines; that is, a comma and a conjunction precede the last element in the series. The less conventional second and third sentences do more than convey information. Having two conjunctions and no commas, the second sentence slows down the pace of the reading, causing stress to be placed on each of the three elements in the series. In contrast, the third sentence, with commas but no conjunctions, speeds up the reading, as if to suggest that the rights listed do not need to be stressed because they are so familiar. To get a sense of how your sentences will be read and understood, try reading them aloud to yourself.

31d Separating coordinate adjectives

Two or more adjectives that precede the same noun are called **coordinate adjectives**. To test whether adjectives are coordinate, either interchange them or put *and* between them. If the altered version of the phrase is acceptable, the adjectives are coordinate and should be separated by a comma.

➤ Crossing the **rushing, shallow** creek, I slipped off a rock and fell into the water. [COMPARE: a rushing and shallow creek OR a shallow, rushing creek]

The adjectives in the following sentence are not separated by a comma. Notice that they cannot be interchanged or joined by *and*.

➤ Sitting in the water, I saw an **old wooden** bridge. [NOT a wooden old bridge OR an old and wooden bridge]

31e | Setting off nonessential elements

Words, phrases, and clauses are considered nonessential when the information they convey is unnecessary for identifying who or what is being described or discussed. All nonessential elements should be set off by commas. No commas are used when the information answers the question *Which*?

ESSENTIAL WORD	The mountaineer **Walter Harper** was the first to summit Denali. [Which mountaineer? Walter Harper—no commas are needed]
NONESSENTIAL WORD	The first mountaineer to summit Denali**,** **Walter Harper,** was an Alaska Native. [Which first mountaineer? does not make sense—commas are needed]
ESSENTIAL PHRASE	The mountain **towering above** us brought to mind our abandoned plan for climbing it. [Which mountain? the one towering above us—no commas are needed]
NONESSENTIAL PHRASE	Denali**, towering above us,** brought to mind our abandoned plan for climbing it. [Which Denali? does not make sense—commas are needed]

ESSENTIAL CLAUSE	They climbed a mountain **that is over fifteen thousand feet high**. [Which mountain? one that is over fifteen thousand feet high—no comma is needed]
NONESSENTIAL CLAUSE	They climbed Denali, **which is over fifteen thousand feet high**. [Which Denali? does not make sense—a comma is needed]

31f Setting off transitions, parenthetical expressions, and contrasted elements

Commas customarily set off transitional expressions such as *for example, that is, however,* and *namely.*

➤ Travelers, **for example,** must be prepared for the unexpected.

Because they generally indicate little or no pause in reading, transitional expressions such as *also, too, at least,* and *thus* need not be set off by commas.

➤ Traveling to exotic places **thus** requires planning.

Use commas to set off parenthetical elements, such as words or phrases that provide commentary you wish to stress.

➤ Over the past year, my flights have, **miraculously,** been on time.

Commas set off sentence elements in which words such as *never* and *unlike* express contrast.

➤ A planet, **unlike** a star, reflects rather than generates light.

EXERCISE 31.3

Set off nonessential elements with commas.

1. Maine Coons long-haired cats with bushy tails are known for their size.

2. The largest cat on record for example was forty-eight inches long.

3. These animals which are extremely gentle despite their large size often weigh twenty pounds.

4. Most Maine Coons have exceptionally high intelligence for cats which enables them to recognize language and even to open doors.

5. Unlike most cats Maine Coons will play fetch with their owners.

6. According to a legend later proven to be false Maine Coons are descendants from Turkish Angora cats owned by Marie Antoinette.

31g Setting off dates, place names, and elements in an address

Use commas to make dates, place names, and addresses easy to read.

➤ Martha left for Peru on **Wednesday, February 12, 2017,** and returned on March 12.

➤ **Nashville, Tennessee,** is the largest country-and-western music center in the United States.

➤ I had to write to **Ms. Melanie Hobson, Hobson Computing, 2873 Central Avenue, Orange Park, FL 32065**. [No comma is used between the state abbreviation and the zip code.]

31h Setting off quotations

Many sentences containing direct quotations also contain attributive tags (or signal phrases) such as *The author claims* or *According to the author*. Whether they appear at the beginning, in the middle, or at the end of a sentence, attributive tags should be set off with commas.

➤ According to Jacques Barzun, "It is a false analogy with science that makes one think latest is best."

➤ "It is a false analogy with science, "claims Jacques Barzun, "that makes one think latest is best."

➤ "It is a false analogy with science that makes one think latest is best," claims Jacques Barzun.

31i Unnecessary commas

Commas are not used between the following elements.

SUBJECT AND VERB	**Rain** at frequent intervals **produces** mosquitoes.
TWO VERBS THAT AGREE WITH THE SAME SUBJECT	**I read** the comments carefully and then **started** my revision.
REPORTING VERB AND *THAT*	The author **noted** that the results of the study were not conclusive.
CONJUNCTION AND SUBJECT	We worked very hard on her campaign for state representative, **but** the **incumbent** was too strong to defeat in the northern districts.

SUCH AS OR *LIKE* AND THE EXAMPLE THAT FOLLOWS	Many university applicants take entrance exams **such as the ACT or the SAT**.
ESSENTIAL ELEMENT AND THE REST OF THE SENTENCE	Everyone **who has a mortgage** is required to have fire insurance.
MONTH OR HOLIDAY AND YEAR	The class reunion is tentatively planned for June 2022.
	The last time she saw them was on Thanksgiving Day 2015.
EXCLAMATION POINT OR QUESTION MARK AND CLOSING QUOTATION MARKS	"Dave, stop. Stop, will you? Stop, Dave. Will you stop?" implores the supercomputer HAL in *2001: A Space Odyssey*.

EXERCISE 31.4

Revise the following sentences, inserting commas where they are needed and deleting commas when they are unnecessary.

1. Alvar Nuñez Cabeza de Vaca unlike most other Spanish conquistadors came to perceive Native Americans as equals.

2. On February 15, 1527 Cabeza de Vaca was appointed to an expedition, headed for the mainland of North America.

3. The expedition landed near what is now Tampa Bay, Florida sometime in March, 1528.

4. Devastated by misfortune the expedition dwindled rapidly.

5. Cabeza de Vaca and three other members however survived.

6. His endurance now tested Cabeza de Vaca lived as a trader and healer among Native Americans of the Rio Grande Basin learning from them and eventually speaking on their behalf to the Spanish crown.

32 The Semicolon and the Colon

The semicolon and the colon both mark boundaries within a sentence and indicate how ideas are linked. They are not interchangeable, however.

32a The semicolon

The semicolon most frequently connects two independent clauses, but it can be used for other purposes as well.

(1) Connecting independent clauses

A semicolon placed between two independent clauses indicates that they are closely related. The second of the two clauses generally supports or contrasts with the first.

➤ For many cooks, basil is a key ingredient; it appears in recipes worldwide. [support]

➤ Sweet basil is used in many Mediterranean dishes; Thai basil is used in Asian and East Indian recipes. [contrast]

Sometimes, a transitional expression such as *for example* (**3d(4)**) or an adverbial conjunction such as *however* (**17a(7)**) accompanies a semicolon and further establishes the relationship between the ideas.

➤ Basil is omnipresent in the cuisine of some countries; **for example**, Italians use basil in salads, soups, and many vegetable dishes.

➤ The culinary uses of basil are well known; **however**, this herb also has medicinal uses.

A comma is usually inserted after a transitional expression, though it can be omitted if doing so will not lead to a misreading.

(2) Separating elements that contain commas

In a series of phrases or clauses that contain commas, semicolons indicate where each phrase or clause ends and the next begins.

➤ To survive, mountain lions need a large area in which to range; a steady supply of deer, skunks, raccoons, foxes, and opossums; and the opportunity to find a mate, establish a den, and raise a litter.

Semicolons do not set off phrases or dependent clauses. Use commas for this purpose.

➤ We consulted Alinka Kibukian;, the local horticulturalist.
                                ^

➤ Our trees survived;, even though we live in a harsh climate.
                      ^

EXERCISE 32.1

Revise the following sentences, using semicolons to separate independent clauses or elements that contain internal commas.

1. Soccer is a game played by two opposing teams on a rectangular field, each team tries to knock a ball, roughly twenty-eight inches in circumference, through the opponent's goal.

2. The game is called *soccer* only in Canada and the United States, elsewhere it is known as *football*.

3. Generally, a team consists of eleven players: defenders (or fullbacks), who defend the goal by trying to win control of the ball, midfielders (or halfbacks), who play both defense and offense, attackers (or forwards), whose primary responsibility is scoring goals, and a goalkeeper (or goalie), who guards the goal.

4. In amateur matches, players can be substituted frequently, however, in professional matches, the number of substitutions is limited.

32b The colon

A colon calls attention to what follows. It also separates titles from subtitles. The colon also has special uses in business correspondence and scriptural or bibliographic references.

(1) Directing attention to an explanation, a summary, or a quotation

When a colon appears between two independent clauses, it signals that the second clause will explain or expand on the first.

➤ No one expected the game to end as it did: after seven extra innings, the favored team collapsed.

A colon is also used after an independent clause to introduce a direct quotation.

➤ Marcel Proust explained the importance of mindfulness: "The true journey of discovery consists not in seeking new landscapes but in having fresh eyes."

CAUTION

Style manuals differ with regard to the use of an uppercase or a lowercase letter to begin an independent clause following a colon.

MLA CSE	The first letter should be lowercase unless (1) it begins a word that is normally capitalized, (2) the independent clause is a quotation, or (3) the clause expresses a rule or principle.
APA	The first letter should be uppercase.
CMS	The first letter should be lowercase unless (1) it begins a word that is normally capitalized, (2) the independent clause is a quotation, or (3) two or more related sentences follow the colon.

(2) Signaling that a list follows

A colon can be used to introduce a list. Note that an independent clause precedes the list.

➤ The website provides statistics for three states: Washington, Oregon, and Idaho.

Avoid placing a colon between a verb and its complement or after the words *including* and *such as*.

➤ The website provides statistics for many states including Washington, Oregon, and Idaho.

➤ The website provides statistics on topics such as population and education.

(3) Separating a title and a subtitle

Use a colon between a work's title and its subtitle.

The Sixth Extinction: *An Unnatural History*

(4) Specialized uses in business correspondence

A colon follows the salutation of a business letter and any notations.

Dear Dr. Horner: Enc:

A colon introduces the headings in a memo.

To: From: Subject: Date:

(5) Separating elements in reference numbers

Colons are often used between numbers in scriptural references.

Psalms 3:5   Gen. 1:1

However, MLA requires the use of periods instead of colons.

Psalms 3.5   Gen. 1.1

EXERCISE 32.2

Insert colons where they are needed in the following sentences.

1. Before we discuss marketing, let's define the behavior of consumers consumer behavior is the process individuals go through as they select, buy, or use products or services to satisfy their needs and desires.

2. The process consists of six stages recognizing a need or desire, finding information, evaluating options, deciding to purchase, purchasing, and assessing purchases.

3. When evaluating alternatives, a house hunter might use some of the following criteria price, location, size, age, style, and landscaping design.

4. The post-purchase assessment has one of two basic results satisfaction or dissatisfaction with the product or service.

33 The Apostrophe

Apostrophes serve a number of purposes. For example, you can use them to show that someone owns something (*my neighbor's television*), that someone has a specific relationship with someone else (*my neighbor's children*), or that someone has produced or created something (*my neighbor's recipe*). Apostrophes are also used in contractions (*can't, don't*) and in certain plural forms (*x's* and *y's*).

33a Indicating ownership and other relationships

An apostrophe, often followed by an *s*, signals the **possessive case** of nouns. Possessive nouns are used to express a variety of meanings.

OWNERSHIP	**Fumi's** computer, the **photographer's** camera
ORIGIN	**Einstein's** ideas, the **student's** decision
HUMAN RELATIONSHIPS	**Linda's** sister, the **employee's** supervisor
POSSESSION OF PHYSICAL OR PSYCHOLOGICAL TRAITS	**Mona Lisa's** smile, the **team's** spirit
ASSOCIATION BETWEEN ABSTRACTIONS AND ATTRIBUTES	**democracy's** success, **tyranny's** influence
IDENTIFICATION OF DOCUMENTS	**driver's** license, **bachelor's** degree
IDENTIFICATION OF THINGS OR DAYS NAMED AFTER PEOPLE	**St. John's** Cathedral, **Valentine's** Day
SPECIFICATION OF AMOUNTS	a **day's** wages, an **hour's** delay

(1) Singular nouns, indefinite pronouns, abbreviations, and acronyms

Add an apostrophe and an *s* to indicate the possessive case of singular nouns, indefinite pronouns such as *everyone* and *nobody* (21a(7)), abbreviations, and acronyms.

the dean**'s** office [noun]

Yeats**'s** poems [noun]

anyone**'s** computer [indefinite pronoun]

the NFL**'s** reputation [abbreviation]

OPEC**'s** price increase [acronym]

Walter Bryan Jr.**'s** letter [abbreviation]

When a singular proper noun ends in *s*, you will have to consult the style guide for your discipline. Some style guides recommend always using *'s* (*Illinois's legislature* and *Dickens's novels*). CMS allows exceptions to this rule. An apostrophe without an *s* may be acceptable when a singular common noun ends in *s* (*physics' contribution*) and when the name of a place or an organization ends in *s* but refers to a single entity (*United States' foreign aid*).

Possessive pronouns (*my, mine, our, ours, your, yours, his, her, hers, its, their, theirs,* and *whose*) are not written with apostrophes.

➤ The committee concluded **its** discussion.

(2) Plural nouns ending in *s*

Add only an apostrophe to indicate the possessive case of plural nouns that end in *s*.

➤ the boys' game　　the babies' toys　　the Joneses' house

Plural nouns that do not end in *s* need both an apostrophe and an *s*.

➤ men's lives　　women's health　　children's projects

According to the *U.S. Government Publishing Office Style Manual,* two holidays are spelled without an apostrophe: Veterans Day and Presidents Day.

CAUTION

An apostrophe is not needed to make a noun plural. To make most nouns plural, add *s* or *es*. Add an apostrophe only to signal ownership, origin, and other similar relationships.

➤ The ~~protesters'~~ *protesters* met in front of the conference center.
➤ The protesters' meeting was on Wednesday.

To form the plural of a family name, use *s* or *es*, not an apostrophe.

➤ The ~~Johnson's~~ *Johnsons* participated in the study.
　[COMPARE: The Johnsons' participation in the study was crucial.]

(3) To show collaboration or joint ownership

An apostrophe and an *s* follow the second of two singular nouns. Just an apostrophe follows the second of two plural nouns that already ends in *s*.

➤ the carpenter and the **plumber's** decision [They made the decision collaboratively.]

➤ the Becks and the **Lopezes'** cabin [They own one cabin jointly.]

(4) To show separate ownership or individual contributions

Each plural noun is followed by an apostrophe; each singular noun is followed by *'s*.

➤ the **Becks'** and the **Lopezes'** cars [Each family owns a car.]

➤ the **carpenter's** and the **plumber's** proposals [They each made a proposal.]

(5) Compound nouns

An apostrophe and an *s* follow the last word of a compound noun.

➤ my brother-in-**law's** friends, the attorney **general's** statements [singular]

➤ my brothers-in-**law's** friends, the attorneys **general's** statements [plural]

To avoid awkward constructions such as the last two, consider using a prepositional phrase beginning with *of* instead: *the statements of the attorneys general.*

(6) Nouns preceding gerunds

Depending on its number, a noun that precedes a gerund takes either an apostrophe and an *s* or just an apostrophe.

➤ Lucy**'s having** to be there seemed unnecessary. [singular noun preceding gerund]

➤ The family appreciated the lawyers**'** **handling** of the matter. [plural noun preceding gerund]

Sometimes you may find it difficult to distinguish between a gerund and a participle. A good way to tell the difference is to note whether the emphasis is on an action or on a person. In a sentence containing a gerund, the emphasis is on the action; in a sentence containing a participle, the emphasis is on the person.

➤ The completion of the project depends on **Tim's providing** the illustrations. [gerund]

➤ I heard **Tim discussing** his plans. [participle]

(7) Names of products and geographical locations

Follow an organization's preference for its name or the name of a product; follow local conventions for a geographical location.

Consumers Union	Actors' Equity	Taster's Choice
Devil's Island	Devils Tower	Lands' End

EXERCISE 33.1

Following the pattern of the example, change the modifier after each noun to a possessive form that precedes the noun.

EXAMPLE

proposals made by the committee   *the committee's proposals*

1. the holiday celebrated on January 1
2. a drive lasting an hour
3. the position taken by HMOs
4. the report given by the eyewitness
5. the generosity of the Lees
6. a new book coauthored by Pat and Alan
7. the weights of the children
8. the spying done by the neighbor

33b Marking omissions in contractions

Apostrophes mark omissions in contractions.

they're [they are]   who's [who is]

it's [it is]   you're [you are]

Apostrophes also mark omissions in numbers and in words mimicking speech.

class of '14 [class of 2014]

y'all [you all]   singin' [singing]

CAUTION

Be careful not to confuse possessive pronouns (such as *its, their, whose, your*) with contractions (*it's, they're, who's, you're*). Whenever you write a contraction, you should be able to substitute the complete words for it without changing the meaning.

POSSESSIVE PRONOUN	CONTRACTION
Its motor is small.	**It's** [It is] a small motor.
Whose turn is it?	**Who's** [Who is] representing us?

33c Forming certain plurals

These plurals are generally formed by adding *s* only:

1990s   fours and fives   YWCAs

two *and*s   the three *R*s   PhDs

Lowercase letters are made plural by adding both an apostrophe and an *s*: *p*'s and *q*'s. MLA differs from this style in recommending the use of apostrophes for the plurals of uppercase letters (four A's) as well as lowercase letters (the *x*'s and *y*'s in an equation). Note that letters used as letters, rather than as grades or abbreviations, are italicized (**38b**).

EXERCISE 33.2

Insert apostrophes where needed, delete them when unnecessary, and correct any misspellings.

1. Who's responsibility was it?

2. Hansons book was published in the early 1920s.

3. NPRs fund drive begins in five days'.

4. More students' enrolled during the academic year 16–17.

5. They're were more maybes than nos in the survey results.

6. They hired a rock n roll band for they're engagement party.

7. Only three of the proposals are still being considered: your's, our's, and the Craigs.

8. Youll have to include the ISBNs of the books' your going to purchase.

34 Quotation Marks

Quotation marks enclose direct quotations, including those in a dialogue. They are also used to set off the title of a short work.

34a Direct quotations

Double quotation marks set off direct quotations. Single quotation marks enclose a quotation within a quotation.

(1) Direct quotations

When using direct quotations, reproduce all quoted material exactly as it appears in the original.

Double quotation marks enclose only quotations, not expressions such as *she said* or *he replied*. When a sentence ends with quoted material, place the period inside the quotation marks.

> ➤ "I believe that we learn by practice," writes Martha Graham. "Whether it means to learn to dance by practicing dancing or to learn to live by practicing living, the principles are the same."

Be careful not to insert dropped quotations (11d). Quotations that begin and end with quotation marks should include an attributive tag, or they should link to a previous statement, as in the Graham example.

(2) Quotations within quotations

Use single quotation marks for any quotation embedded in another quotation.

> ➤ According to Anita Erickson, "when the narrator says, 'I have the right to my own opinion,' he means that he has the right to his own delusion" (22).

However, if the embedded quotation appears in a block quotation, use double quotation marks. (Note that double quotation marks are not used to mark the beginning and end of a block quotation.)

> ➤ Anita Erickson claims that the narrator uses the word *opinion* deceptively:

> Later in the chapter, when the narrator says, "I have the right to my own opinion," he means that he has the right to his own delusion. Although it is tempting to believe that the narrator is making decisions based on a rational belief system, his behavior suggests that he is more interested in deception. (22)

(3) Dialogue

When creating a dialogue, enclose in quotation marks what each person says. Begin a new paragraph whenever the speaker changes.

Farmer looked up, smiling, and in a chirpy-sounding voice he said, "But that feeling has the disadvantage of being . . ." He paused a beat. "Wrong."

"Well," I retorted, "it depends on how you look at it."

—**TRACY KIDDER**, *Mountains Beyond Mountains*

When quoting more than one paragraph by a single speaker, put quotation marks at the beginning of each paragraph but only at the end of the last paragraph.

(4) Short excerpts of poetry included within a sentence

When quoting fewer than four lines of poetry, enclose them in quotation marks.

➤ After watching a whale swim playfully, the speaker in "Visitation" asks, "What did you think, that joy / was some slight thing?"

34b Titles of short works

Quotation marks enclose the title of a short work, such as a story, an essay, or a song. The title of a larger work, such as a book, play, website, film, television program, magazine, or newspaper, should be italicized.

SHORT STORIES	"The Lottery"	"A Worn Path"
ESSAYS	"Walden"	"Play-by-Play"
ARTICLES	"Small World"	"Number Crunch"
BOOK CHAPTERS	"Rain"	"Cutting a Dash"
SHORT POEMS	"Orion"	"Mending Wall"
SONGS	"Lazy River"	"Imagine"
TV EPISODES	"Show Down!"	"The Last Time"

Use single quotation marks for a title within a longer title that is enclosed in double quotation marks.

"Irony in 'The Sick Rose'" [article about a poem]

34c   With other punctuation marks

To decide whether to place another punctuation mark inside or outside quotation marks, note whether the punctuation mark is part of the quotation or part of the surrounding text.

(1) With commas and periods

When your sentence starts with an expression such as *she said* or *he replied*, use a comma to separate it from the quotation (**31h**). Place a period inside the closing quotation marks.

➤ She replied, "There's more than one way to slice a pie."

If your sentence starts with the quotation instead, place a comma inside the closing quotation marks.

➤ "There's more than one way to slice a pie," she replied.

When quoting material from a source, provide the relevant page number(s).

➤ According to Diane Ackerman, "Love is a demanding sport involving all the muscle groups, including the brain" (86).

CAUTION

Do not put a comma after *that* when it precedes a quotation.

➤ Diane Ackerman claims that "[l]ove is a demanding sport involving all the muscle groups, including the brain" (86).

(2) With semicolons and colons

Place semicolons and colons outside quotation marks.

➤ His favorite song was "Cyprus Avenue"; mine was "Astral Weeks."
➤ Stereotypical themes can be easily found in "The Last One": love, lust, and revenge.

(3) With question marks, exclamation points, and dashes

If the direct quotation includes a question mark, an exclamation point, or a dash, place that punctuation *inside* the closing quotation marks.

➤ Jeremy asked, "What is truth?"

➤ Gordon shouted, "Congratulations!"

➤ Laura said, "Let me tell—" just as Dan walked into the room.

Use just one question mark inside the quotation marks when a question ends with a quoted question.

➤ Why does the protagonist ask, "Where are we headed?"

If the punctuation is not part of the quoted material, place it *outside* the closing quotation marks.

➤ Who wrote "The Figure a Sentence Makes"?

EXERCISE 34.1

Revise sentences in which quotation marks are used incorrectly and insert quotation marks where they are needed. Do not alter sentences that are written correctly.

1. Have you read On Women's Right to Vote by Susan B. Anthony?

2. In a speech delivered after she was arrested for casting an illegal vote, Anthony asked this question: Are women persons?

3. She acknowledges that she has been indicted for "the alleged crime of having voted in the last presidential election."

4. Anthony suggests that not allowing women to vote is a violation of 'the supreme law of the land'.

5. According to the author, "We, the whole people, . . . formed the Union."

6. She points out that Webster, Worcester, and Bouvier all define a citizen to be a person in the United States, entitled to vote and hold office.

7. Anthony maintains, Being persons, then, women are citizens; and no state has a right to make any law . . . that shall abridge their privileges or immunities.

34d Misused quotation marks

Avoid using quotation marks to enclose **indirect quotations**, material that restates or reports someone's words. Paraphrases and summaries generally include indirect quotations.

➤ Concluding his review of the album, Wilson said that ~~"~~he was confounded by its mixed messages.~~"~~

Quotation marks are also not used around words to add emphasis or to call attention to slang or other colloquial expressions. Instead, take the time to choose suitable words.

➤ Funny clips from late night talk shows often ~~"go viral"~~ *spread through social-networking sites* the next day.

35 The Period and Other Punctuation Marks

To indicate the end of a sentence, you can use one of three punctuation marks: the period, the question mark, or the exclamation point. Other punctuation marks—along with commas, semicolons, and colons—are used within sentences for such purposes as setting off elements or marking omissions. This chapter covers the use of dashes, parentheses, square brackets, ellipsis points, and slashes.

Leave one space after a period, a question mark, or an exclamation point unless your assignment calls for two spaces. APA recommends including two spaces to make the reading of drafts easier.

35a The period

(1) At the end of a sentence

Use a period at the end of a sentence.

➤ Many adults in the United States are overfed yet undernourished.

In addition, place a period at the end of an instruction or recommendation.

➤ Eat plenty of fruits and vegetables.

(2) After some abbreviations

Dr.　　Jr.　　a.m.　　p.m.　　vs.　　etc.　　et al.

Only one period follows an abbreviation that ends a sentence.

➤ The tour begins at 1:00 p.m.

35b The question mark

Place a question mark after a direct question.

➤ How does the atomic clock work? Who invented this clock?

➤ The question asked at the meeting was, how does the clock work?

Use a period after an indirect question (a question embedded in a statement).

➤ The article answers the question of how the clock was developed?
                                                              ∧

MULTILINGUAL WRITERS

INDIRECT QUESTIONS

In English, the subject and verb in indirect questions are not inverted as they would be in the related direct question.

➤ We do not know when ~~will~~ the meeting $_\wedge^{will}$ end.

➤ [COMPARE: When will the meeting end?]

Place a question mark after each question in a series of related questions, even when they are not full sentences.

➤ Can the atomic clock be used in cell phones**?** Word processors**?** Car navigation systems**?**

35c   The exclamation point

An exclamation point often marks the end of a sentence, but its primary purpose is rhetorical—to create emphasis.

➤ Whoa**!** They broke the record**!**

Use the exclamation point sparingly so that you do not diminish its value. If you do not intend to signal strong emotion, place a comma after an interjection and a period at the end of the sentence.

➤ Well**,** no one seriously expected this victory**.**

35d   The dash

A dash marks a break in thought or tone, sets off a nonessential element for emphasis or clarity, or follows an introductory list or series. To create a dash (also called an em dash), type two hyphens with no spaces between, before, or after them.

(1) Marking a break in the normal flow of a sentence

➤ I was awed by the almost superhuman effort Stonehenge represents——but who wouldn't be?

(2) Setting off a nonessential element

Use a dash or a pair of dashes to set off extra comments or details.

➤ Dr. Kruger's specialty is mycology——the study of fungi.

➤ The Grandview Trail——steep and unmaintained——is tough even for experienced hikers.

(3) Following an introductory list or series

After the dash, the main part of the sentence sums up the meaning of the list.

➤ Eager, determined to succeed, and scared to death——all of these describe how I felt on the first day at work.

THINKING RHETORICALLY
COMMAS, DASHES, AND COLONS

Although a comma, a dash, or a colon may be followed by an explanation, an example, or an illustration, the impact varies.

➤ He never failed to mention what was most important to him, the bottom line.

➤ He never failed to mention what was most important to him——the bottom line.

➤ He never failed to mention what was most important to him: the bottom line.

The comma, one of the most common punctuation marks, barely draws attention to what follows it. The dash, in contrast, signals a longer pause and so places more emphasis on the information that follows. The colon is more direct and formal than either of the other two punctuation marks.

35e Parentheses

Use parentheses to set off information that is not closely related to the main point of a sentence or paragraph but that provides an interesting detail, an explanation, or an illustration.

> The 5-foot-2-inch dynamo ("I act tall," she says) has piloted her career with dazzling audacity.
>
> —ANNE STOCKWELL, "Salma Hayek"

Note that the parenthetical sentence embedded in the sentence above does not end in a period. A stand-alone parenthetical sentence, however, does include end punctuation.

> We started here in the attic—a long time ago now, it seems—when I clambered up through the loft hatch to look for the source of the leak. (It turned out to be a slipped tile that was allowing rain through.)
>
> –BILL BRYSON, *At Home: A Short History of Private Life*

In addition, place parentheses around an acronym or an abbreviation when introducing it after its full form.

➤ The Search for Extraterrestrial Intelligence (SETI) uses the Very Large Array (VLA) outside Socorro, New Mexico, to scan the sky.

If you use numbers or letters in a list within a sentence, set them off by placing them within parentheses.

➤ Your application should include (1) a current résumé, (2) a statement of purpose, and (3) two letters of recommendation.

DASHES AND PARENTHESES

Dashes and parentheses are both used to set off part of a sentence, but they differ in the amount of emphasis they signal. Whereas dashes call attention to the material that is set off, parentheses usually deemphasize such material.

➤ Her grandfather——born during the Great Depression——was appointed to the Securities and Exchange Commission.

➤ Her grandfather (born in 1930) was appointed to the Securities and Exchange Commission.

35f Square brackets

Square brackets set off additions or alterations inserted to clarify direct quotations or to integrate them into a sentence.

➤ Thomas L. Friedman states, "It [opting to pause and reflect] is not a luxury or a distraction—it is a way to increase the odds that you'll better understand, and engage productively with, the world around you" (4).

➤ Thomas L. Friedman believes that "[i]t's no surprise so many people feel fearful or unmoored these days" (3).

To avoid the awkwardness of using brackets in this way, you may be able to quote only part of a sentence so that no change in capitalization is needed.

➤ Thomas L. Friedman states that taking time to reflect "is not a luxury or a distraction—it is a way to increase the odds that you'll better understand, and engage productively with, the world around you" (4).

Use brackets to set off material that is itself set within parentheses.

➤ The importance of reflection cannot be overstated (See for example, Thomas L. Friedman's *Thank You for Being Late: An Optimist's Guide to Thriving in the Age of Accelerations* [New York: Farrar, Straus and Giroux, 2016].)

35g Ellipsis points

Ellipsis points, three equally spaced periods, indicate an omission from a quoted passage or a reflective pause or hesitation.

(1) Marking an omission from a quoted passage

ORIGINAL

But we come to Roman history with different priorities—from gender identity to food supply—that make the ancient past speak to us in a new idiom.

                              MARY BEARD, *SPQR: A History of Ancient Rome*

OMISSION FROM THE MIDDLE OF THE SENTENCE

Beard states that we approach "Roman history with different priorities . . . that make the ancient past speak to us in a new idiom" (16).

Note that ellipsis points are not used to indicate an omission from the beginning of the quotation.

To indicate omitted words from the end of a quotation, put a space between the last word and the ellipsis points. Then add the end punctuation mark (a period, a question mark, or an exclamation point). If the quoted material is followed by a parenthetical source or page reference, the end punctuation comes after the second parenthesis.

OMISSION FROM THE END OF THE SENTENCE

Beard states that we approach "Roman history with different priorities—from gender identity to food supply . . ." (16).

To signal the omission of a sentence or more (even a paragraph or more), place an end punctuation mark before the ellipsis points, with one space before and after the ellipsis points.

OMISSION OF A SENTENCE OR MORE

According to Beard, "Roman victory was undoubtedly vicious. . . . But Rome expanded into a world not of communities living at peace with one another but of endemic violence . . ." (16–17).

(2) Indicating an unfinished sentence or marking a pause

Use ellipsis points to indicate that you are intentionally leaving a sentence incomplete or to signal a reflective pause.

➤ Keith saw four menacing youths coming toward him . . . and ran.

35h The slash

A slash between words, as in *and/or* and *he/she*, indicates that either word is applicable in the given context. There are no spaces before and after a slash used in this way. Because extensive use of the slash can make writing choppy, use it judiciously. (If you are following APA or MLA guidelines, avoid using *he/she*, *him/her*, and so on.)

When quoting poetry, use the slash to mark line divisions and include a space before and after the slash.

➤ Wallace Stevens refers to the listener who, "nothing himself, beholds / Nothing that is not there and the nothing that is."

EXERCISE 35.1

Add punctuation as indicated in square brackets.

1. The United Nations Educational, Scientific and Cultural Organization UNESCO was established in 1945. [parentheses]

2. Encouraging cultural diversity, fostering intercultural discussions, and promoting peace these are just a few of UNESCO's goals. [dash]

3. The organization routinely responds to global concerns such as the HIV AIDS epidemic. [slash]

4. According to a recent policy statement, the "Millennium Summit of Heads of State New York, September 2010 recognized the value of cultural diversity for the enrichment of humankind . . . " (UNESCO 4). [square brackets]

M

MECHANICS

Visit the MindTap® for this book for additional information and resources.

36 Spelling and the Hyphen

Proofreading for spelling mistakes is essential as you near the end of the writing process. Your teachers, employers, or supervisors will expect you to submit polished work.

TIPS FOR USING A SPELL CHECKER

A spell checker makes proofreading easier, though you must use it with care.

- Proofread your work carefully, even if you are using a spell checker. Spell checkers will not catch all typos, such as *form* instead of *from*.

- Double-check words you frequently misspell. If you often misspell homophones such as *there/their* (**36b**), check for these words after using the spell checker.

- If a spell checker regularly flags a word that is not in its dictionary but that is spelled correctly (such as a proper noun, specialized term, or foreign word), add that word to the dictionary.

- Use a dictionary to look up unfamiliar words that are highlighted by the spell checker. Evaluate the alternative words or spellings the spell checker provides because some of them may change the meaning of your sentence.

- Do not automatically accept changes the spell checker suggests. Reject any offers the spell checker makes to correct all instances of a particular error.

36a Spelling and pronunciation

Many words in English are not spelled the way they are pronounced, so pronunciation is not a reliable guide to correct spelling. Here are a few words typically misspelled because they include unpronounced letters:

condem*n*   foreign   lab*o*ratory   mus*c*le   solem*n*

Here are a few that include letters that are often not heard in rapid speech:

can*d*idate   diff*e*rent   gover*n*ment   sep*a*rate   libr*a*ry   Feb*r*uary

You can teach yourself the correct spellings of words by pronouncing each letter mentally so that you "hear" even silent letters.

CAUTION

The words *and*, *have*, and *than* are often not stressed in speech and are thus frequently misspelled.

➤ They would rather ⌄of written two papers ⌄then taken midterm ⌄an final exams.

(have) *(than)* *(and)*

36b Words that sound alike

Words that sound alike but are spelled differently (*aid/aide*, *principle/principal*) are frequently confused. Consult the **Glossary of Usage** for help with many of these commonly confused words. Also troublesome are two-word sequences that carry different meanings depending on whether they are written as one word or as two separate words.

Everyday life was grueling.   She attended class **every day**.

They do not fight **anymore**.   They could not find **any more** evidence.

Other examples include *awhile/a while*, *everyone/every one*, *maybe/may be*, and *sometime/some time*.

Singular nouns ending in *-nce* and plural nouns ending in *-nts* are also easily confused.

Assistance is available.	I have two **assistants**.
His **patience** wore thin.	Some **patients** waited for hours.

Be sure to include an apostrophe in contractions but not in possessive pronouns. (Before including contractions, find out whether your assignment permits their use.)

CONTRACTIONS   it's, you're, there's, who's
POSSESSIVES   its, your, theirs, whose

36c Prefixes and suffixes

When a prefix is added to a base word (often called the **root**), the spelling of the base word is unaffected.

necessary, **un**necessary   moral, **im**moral

However, adding a suffix to the end of a base word often changes the spelling.

(1) Dropping or retaining a final e

- If a suffix begins with a vowel, the final *e* of the base word is dropped: bride, brid**al**; come, com**ing**. However, to keep the *s* sound of *ce* or the *j* sound of *ge*, retain the final *e* before *-able* or *-ous*: notice**able**, courag**eous**.
- If a suffix begins with a consonant, the final *e* of the base word is retained: entire, entire**ly**; rude, rude**ness**. Some exceptions are *argument*, *ninth*, *truly*, and *wholly*.

(2) Doubling a final consonant

- If a consonant ends a one-syllable word with a single vowel or ends a stressed syllable with a single vowel, double the final consonant: stop, sto**pped**; omit, omi**tted**.
- If there are two vowels before the consonant, the consonant is not doubled: remain, remain**ed**, remain**ing**.

- If the final syllable is not stressed, the consonant is not doubled: edit, edit**ed**, edit**ing**; comment, comment**ed**, comment**ing**.

(3) Changing or retaining a final *y*

- Change a final *y* following a consonant to *i* when adding a suffix (except *-ing*): lazy, laz**ily**; defy, def**ied**, BUT def**ying**.
- Retain the final *y* when it follows a vowel: gray, gray**ish**; stay, stay**s**, stay**ed**; obey, obey**s**, obey**ed**.
- Some verb forms are irregular and thus can cause difficulties. For a list of irregular verbs, see pages 286–287.

(4) Retaining a final *l*

The letter *l* at the end of a word is retained when *ly* is added.

cool, coo**lly**   formal, forma**lly**   real, rea**lly**   usual, usua**lly**

EXERCISE 36.1

Add the specified suffix to the words that follow it.

Example
-ly: late, casual, psychological
    lately casually psychologically

1. *-ing*: put, admit, write, use, try, play
2. *-able*: desire, read, trace, knowledge
3. *-ly*: true, sincere, normal, general

---

(5) Forming plurals

- Add *es* to most nouns ending in *s*, *z*, *ch*, *sh*, or *x*: box, box**es**.
- If a noun ends in a consonant and *y*, change the *y* to *i* and add *es*: company, compan**ies**; ninety, ninet**ies**.

- If a noun ends in a consonant and *o*, add *es*: hero, hero**es**. Note that sometimes just *s* is added (photo, photo**s**) and other times either *s* or *es* can be added (motto**s**, motto**es**).
- Certain nouns have irregular plural forms: woman, wom**en**; child, child**ren**; foot, f**ee**t.
- Add *s* to most proper nouns: the Kennedy**s**. Add *es* to most proper nouns ending in *s*, *z*, *ch*, *sh*, or *x*: the Jones**es**.

Words borrowed from Latin or Greek generally form their plurals as they did in the original language.

SINGULAR

criterion	alumnus, alumna	analysis	datum	species

PLURAL

criteria	alumni, alumnae	analyses	data	species

Sometimes two different forms are acceptable: the plural form of *syllabus* is either *syllabuses* or *syllabi*.

36d Confusion of *ei* and *ie*

An old rhyme will help you remember the order of letters in most words containing *e* and *i*:

Put *i* before *e*

Except after *c*

Or when sounded like *a*

As in *neighbor* and *weigh*.

Words with *i* before *e*: bel**ie**ve, ch**ie**f, pr**ie**st, y**ie**ld

Words with *e* before *i*, after *c*: conc**ei**t, perc**ei**ve, rec**ei**ve

Words with *ei* sounding like *a* in *cake*: **ei**ght, r**ei**n, th**ei**r, h**ei**r

Words that are exceptions to the rules in the rhyme include *either*, *neither*, *species*, *foreign*, and *weird*.

36e Hyphens

Hyphens link two or more words functioning as a single word and separate word parts to clarify meaning. They also have many conventional uses in numbers, fractions, and measurements.

(1) Linking two or more words

If two or more words serve as a single adjective before a noun, they should be hyphenated. If the words follow the noun, they are not hyphenated.

> You submitted an **up-to-date** report.

> The report was **up to date**.

When the second word in a hyphenated expression is omitted, the first word is still followed by a hyphen.

> They discussed both **private-** and **public-sector** partnerships.

A hyphen is not used after adverbs ending in *ly* (*poorly planned event*).

(2) Other uses of hyphens

A hyphen is also used after certain prefixes and in certain numbers.

BETWEEN REPEATED LETTERS	anti-intellectual
FOR CLARITY	re-sign (NOT resign) the petition
AFTER *SELF-* OR *EX-*	self-esteem, ex-wife
BEFORE CAPITALIZED WORDS	un-American, non-Mexican
IN NUMBERS TWENTY-ONE THROUGH NINETY-NINE	one hundred thirty-two
IN FRACTIONS	three-fourths, one-half

When you form a compound modifier that includes a number and a unit of measurement, place a hyphen between them: *two-year-old boy*.

EXERCISE 36.2

Convert the following word groups into hyphenated compounds.

Example

a movie lasting two hours   *a two-hour movie*

1. a supervisor who is well liked
2. a television screen that is forty-eight inches across
3. a highway with eight lanes
4. a painting from the seventeenth century
5. a chemist who won the Nobel Prize
6. a virus that is food borne

(37) Capitals

Capital letters draw attention to significant details—for example, the beginnings of sentences or the names of particular people, places, and products.

37a Proper nouns

Proper nouns are capitalized, even when they are used as modifiers (*Mexico, Mexican government*). Words such as *college, company, park,* and *street* are capitalized only if they are part of a name (*a university* but *Oregon State University*).

The following names and titles should be capitalized: personal names, including titles; names of deities, religions, religious followers, and sacred works; names of awards, products, and companies; names of countries, ethnic or cultural groups, and languages; names of bridges, buildings, monuments, and geographical features or regions; names of universities and specific courses; names of days of the week, months, and holidays (but not seasons); names of historical documents, periods, and events; names of political parties and government agencies; and military terms.

CAPITALIZED	NOT CAPITALIZED
Noam Chomsky, Chomskyan	a linguist, a theoretical perspective
Uncle Rory	my uncle
President Lincoln	the president of the United States
God (a name)	a god
Bible, Koran, Talmud	sacred works
Academy Award	an award
Nike, Nike Free	a company, a running shoe
Japan, Japanese	a country, a language
Empire State Building	a building
Grand Canyon	a canyon
the West	a western state
Howard University	a university
Biology 101	a biology course
Fourth of July	a holiday
May	a month
Bill of Rights	a historical document
Renaissance	the sixteenth century
Great Depression	a recession
Democratic Party	democratic process
Internal Revenue Service	a government agency
Gulf War	a war
U.S. Army	an army

37b Titles and subtitles

The first and last words in titles and subtitles are capitalized, as are major words—that is, all words other than articles (*a*, *an*, and *the*), coordinating conjunctions (*and*, *but*, *for*, *nor*, *or*, *so*, and *yet*), prepositions (such as *in*, *on*, and *of*), and the infinitive marker *to*.

> *Dictation: A Quartet*

> "To Be a Student or Not to Be a Student"

> "Stop-and-Go Signals"

The American Psychological Association (APA) has two sets of guidelines: one for titles in the body of a paper and one for titles on a reference list. In the body of the paper, all words that have four letters or more are capitalized. On the reference list, only the first word of the title and proper nouns are capitalized.

> *Southwestern Pottery From Anasazi to Zuni* [APA, body of paper]

> *Southwestern pottery from Anasazi to Zuni* [APA, reference list]

> *Southwestern Pottery from Anasazi to Zuni* [MLA and CMS]

37c Beginning a sentence

The first letter of a sentence begins with a capital letter, but there are certain types of sentences that deserve special note.

(1) A quoted sentence

Capitalize only the first word in a quoted sentence, even if you interrupt the sentence with commentary.

➤ When asked to name the books she found most influential, Nadine Gordimer responded, "In general, the works that mean most to one—change one's thinking and therefore maybe one's life—are those read in youth."

➤ "**O**ddly," states Ved Mehta, "like my earliest memories, the books that made the greatest impression on me were the ones I encountered as a small child."

(2) A freestanding parenthetical sentence

Capitalize the first word of a freestanding sentence inside parentheses.

➤ The recordings used in the study were made in the 1980s. (**T**itles of the recordings can be found in the appendix.)

If the sentence inside the parentheses occurs within a sentence of your own, the first word should not be capitalized.

➤ The recordings used in the study were made in the 1980s (**t**itles of the recordings can be found in the appendix).

(3) An independent clause following a colon

If you are following CMS guidelines, lowercase the first letter of an independent clause (a clause with a subject and a predicate) following a colon.

➤ Wearable sensors continue to gain in popularity: **m**any of these help people with chronic diseases monitor their condition.

However, if two or more independent clauses (or sentences) follow the colon, capitalize the first word of each clause.

➤ Some wearable sensors help people stay safe: **S**ensors in helmets and body armor can indicate whether a soldier may have brain injuries. **S**ensors placed in purses can prevent theft.

The APA manual recommends capitalizing the first word of *any* independent clause following a colon. The MLA manual advises capitalizing the first word only when the independent clause that follows is a rule or principle.

➤ Think of fever as a symptom, not as an illness: **I**t is the body's response to infection. [APA]

➤ He has two basic rules for healthy living: **E**at sensibly and exercise strenuously at least three times a week. [APA and MLA]

(4) An abbreviated question

Capitalize the first words of all abbreviated questions.

➤ How do researchers distinguish the legal codes for families? **F**or individuals? **F**or genetic research?

37d **Computer keys, menu items, and icon names**

Capitalize each word in the names of specific computer keys, menu items, and icons.

➤ For more information, select **C**linical **T**rials from the **R**esearch menu.

EXERCISE 37.1

Edit the capitalization errors in the following paragraph. Be prepared to explain any changes that you make.

[1]Swimmer michael phelps holds the record as the most decorated olympian. [2]By the end of the 2016 olympics in rio de janeiro, brazil, he had earned twenty-eight medals (The previous record holder had eighteen). [3]In the 2008 summer olympic games in beijing, china, phelps finished first eight times. [4]Afterward, with a bonus he was given by the sports company speedo, phelps established a Foundation to promote healthy lifestyles and the sport of swimming, especially among children. [5]According to phelps, the swimming pool provided a place for him "To have fun, stay healthy, set goals, work hard and gain confidence."

38 Italics

Italics indicate that a word or a group of words is being used in a special way, for example, to indicate titles or foreign words.

38a Titles of works published or produced separately

Italics indicate the title of a work published or produced as a whole rather than as part of a larger work. A newspaper, for example, is a separate work, but an editorial in a newspaper is not; thus, the title of the newspaper is italicized, and the title of the editorial is enclosed in quotation marks.

The titles of the following kinds of separate works are italicized:

BOOKS	*Homegoing*	*Born to Run*
MAGAZINES	*Wired*	*National Geographic*
NEWSPAPERS	*USA Today*	*The Wall Street Journal*
PLAYS, FILMS	*Vietgone*	*La La Land*
TELEVISION SHOWS	*Atlanta*	*Game of Thrones*
RADIO SHOWS	*Morning Edition*	*Fresh Air*
RECORDINGS	*Kind of Blue*	*Hello*
WORKS OF ART	*American Gothic*	*David*
LONG POEMS	*Paradise Lost*	*The Divine Comedy*
PAMPHLETS	*Saving Energy*	*Tips for Gardeners*

According to CMS guidelines, an initial *the* in a newspaper or periodical title is not italicized or capitalized when the title is mentioned in a sentence. MLA guidelines call for an initial *the* to be italicized and capitalized.

➤ The story was published in the *New York Times*.

➤ The story was published in *The New York Times*.

When an italicized title includes the title of a separate work within it, the embedded title is not italicized.

➤ *Modern Interpretations of* Paradise Lost

The following titles are *not* italicized.

HISTORICAL DOCUMENTS	Bill of Rights, U.S. Constitution, Declaration of Independence
RELIGIOUS TEXTS	Bible, Koran, Torah, Book of Genesis
WEBSITES	Mayo Clinic, Reuters

However, if you are following MLA guidelines, italicize the names of websites.

38b Other uses of italics

Use italics for foreign words; genus and species names; legal cases; names of ships, submarines, aircraft, and spacecraft; words, letters, or figures referred to as such; and emphasized words.

FOREIGN WORD	*fútbol*
GENUS AND SPECIES	*Homo sapiens*
LEGAL CASE	*Miranda v. Arizona*
NAME OF SHIP, AIRCRAFT, OR SPACECRAFT	USS *Enterprise, Enola Gay, Orion*
REFERENCE TO WORD	The word *love* is hard to define.
REFERENCE TO LETTER OR FIGURE	The number *2* and the letter *Z* often look similar.
EMPHASIZED WORD	These *are* the right files.

38c Words not italicized

Italics are not used for a reference to a legal case by an unofficial name.

➤ All the major networks covered the O. J. Simpson trial.

But do italicize the shortened name of a well-known legal case.

➤ The Supreme Court decision in *Brown* forced racial integration of schools.

Italics are also not used for the names of trains, the models of vehicles, and the trade names of aircraft.

Orient Express   Ford Mustang   Boeing 787

EXERCISE 38.1

Identify words that require italics in the following sentences.

1. To celebrate an early book of poetry by James Joyce, Chamber Music, the Frye Art Museum exhibited paintings from its permanent collection to accompany Joyce's poems.

2. The website Frye Art Museum featured three of the paintings that were on display: The Birch Grove, Lady Curzon, and The Duel.

3. In an article published in Seattle Weekly, Brian Miller interviewed curator Scott Lawrimore.

4. Another exhibit at the Frye featured paintings, such as Sorrow and No. 21, commissioned to accompany music inspired by Joyce's poetry.

5. The songs can be found on an anthology album, also called Chamber Music.

6. Interactive is a key word for describing this exhibit, as there were also shelves of artifacts for people to examine.

Abbreviations and Numbers

An **abbreviation** is a shortened version of a word or phrase: *assn.* (association), *dept.* (department), *et al.* (*et alii*, or "and others"). An **acronym** is a special form of abbreviation formed by combining the initial letters and/or syllables of a series of words: *AIDS* (**a**cquired **i**mmune **d**eficiency **s**yndrome), *sonar* (**s**ound **na**vigation **r**anging).

39a Abbreviations of names or titles

If a person's name commonly appears with initials before the last name, follow each initial with a period and a space.

J. R. R. Tolkien   J. K. Rowling

When initials are used for an entire name, no spaces or periods are used.

MLK   LBJ

Certain abbreviations are used before and/or after a person's name.

Ms. Gretel Lopez   **Mrs.** Marcus

Kim Beck, **MD**   Samuel Levy **Jr.**

Dr. Redshaw   **Sen.** McCain

Prof. Elizabeth Chang   Lee Evans, **PhD**

Gen. David Petraeus   **Rev.** Talitha Arnold

Academic, government, military, and other titles are generally spelled out, especially when only a last name is used.

Professor Hood   President Lincoln   General Dunwoody

39b Addresses in correspondence

The names of states and words such as *Street*, *Road*, and *Company* are written out when they appear in formal writing and in letters, including in the address at the top of the page. However, they are abbreviated when used in the address on an envelope.

Derson Manufacturing Co.

200 Madison St.

Watertown, MN 55388

When addressing correspondence within the United States, use the two-letter state abbreviations established by the U.S. Postal Service.

39c Acceptable abbreviations in academic and professional writing

Some abbreviations have become so familiar that they are considered acceptable substitutes for full words (*math*, *exam*, *lab*). If you are unsure of whether an abbreviation is appropriate, spell out the word.

➤ The film ~~prof.~~ *professor* worked on a documentary about Walt Disney.

(1) Abbreviations for special purposes

Words such as *volume*, *chapter*, and *page* are abbreviated (*vol.*, *ch.*, and *p.*) in bibliographies and in citations of research sources, but they are written out within sentences.

(2) Abbreviations for time periods and zones

82 BC ("before Christ") or 82 BCE ("before the common era")

AD 95 (*anno Domini*) or 95 CE ("common era")

7:40 a.m. (*ante meridiem*) 10:00 p.m. (*post meridiem*)

4:52 EST (Eastern Standard Time)

(3) The abbreviation for the United States (U.S. or US) as an adjective

the U.S. Navy, the US economy

[COMPARE: They moved to the United States in 2015.]

The abbreviation *U.S.* or *US* should be used only as an adjective. When using *United States* as a noun, spell it out. The MLA recommends using the full form for an adjective as well but approves of the occasional use of *US*. The APA uses *U.S.* Either form is appropriate according to CMS.

(4) Some abbreviations for Latin expressions

Certain abbreviations for Latin expressions are common in academic writing.

cf. [compare]	et al. [and others]	i.e. [that is]
e.g. [for example]	etc. [and so forth]	vs. OR v. [versus]

39d   Acronyms

Introduce an acronym by placing it in parentheses after the group of words it stands for.

➤ The Federal Emergency Management Administration (FEMA) simulated a devastating earthquake in the Pacific Northwest.

MULTILINGUAL WRITERS
USING ARTICLES WITH ABBREVIATIONS, ACRONYMS, OR NUMBERS

When you use an abbreviation, an acronym, or a number, you sometimes need an indefinite article. Choose *a* or *an* based on the pronunciation of the initial sound of the abbreviation, acronym, or number: use *a* before a consonant sound and *an* before a vowel sound.

➤ **an IBM** computer [*IBM* begins with a vowel sound.]

➤ **a NASA** engineer [*NASA* begins with a consonant sound.]

➤ **a 1964** Mustang [*1964* begins with a consonant sound.]

39e Spelling out numbers

Depending on their uses, numbers are treated in different ways. MLA recommends spelling out numbers that are expressed in one or two words (*nine, ninety-one, nine hundred, nine million*). A numeral is used for any other number (*9½, 9.9, 999*), unless it begins a sentence. CMS advises spelling out whole numbers from zero through one hundred and any number followed by the word *hundred, thousand, hundred thousand,* or *million*.

➤ The register recorded 164 names.

APA advises spelling out only numbers below ten.
   Use words rather than numerals to begin a sentence.

➤ One hundred sixty-four names were recorded in the register.

When numbers or amounts refer to the same entities throughout a passage, use numerals when any of the numbers would be more than two words long if spelled out.

➤ Only 5 of the 134 delegates attended the final meeting. The remaining 129 delegates will be informed by e-mail.

39f   Common uses of numerals

Numerals are typically used for the following:

TIMES OF DAY	9:30 p.m.
DATES	September 11, 2001, or 11 September 2001, or 9/11
DECADES	the fifties or the 1950s
ADDRESSES	25 Arrow Drive, Apartment 1
IDENTIFICATION OF PROPER NOUNS	Edward III Highway 61
PARTS OF BOOKS AND PLAYS	chapter 1, page 15 act 2, scene 1 or Act II, Scene I
DECIMALS	a 2.5 average
PERCENTS	12 percent

When monetary amounts are mentioned frequently, they can be expressed with numerals and symbols: $20.00, 99¢, or $0.99.

EXERCISE 39.1

Edit the following sentences to correct the usage of abbreviations and numbers.

1. In 1817, construction on the Erie Canal was started in Rome, NY.

2. The original canal was 363 mi. long, running between Albany and Buffalo.

3. Pres. Thomas Jefferson refused to use fed. funds for the canal.

4. DeWitt Clinton, United States senator from NY, found support for the construction of the canal in the state legislature.

5. In 2000, the United States Cong. established the Erie Canalway National Heritage Corridor.

6. The Corridor is over 500 miles long and runs through 23 counties of upstate New York.

Answers to Even-Numbered Exercises

Exercise 12.1, page 111

2. CORRECT
4. Problematic–paraphrase is too close to original
6. Problematic–dropped quotation

Exercise 17.1, page 258

2. If (conjunction-subordinating) you (pronoun) are (verb), you (pronoun) should (verb-auxiliary) join (verb) the (article-definite) University Anime and Manga Club (noun-proper).
4. Memberships (noun-common) are (verb) free (adjective); however (conjunction-adverbial [also called conjunctive adverb]), donations (noun-common) are (verb) always (adverb) welcome (adjective).

Exercise 17.2, page 261

A slash separates the subject and predicate in each sentence. The complement is underlined and identified in square brackets.

2. He / showed slides of mountain lakes and heather meadows. [direct object]
4. Mountaineers and artists / consider the North Cascades the most dramatic mountains in the range. [direct object, object complement]
6. Many volcanoes / are in the Cascades. [no complement, "in the Cascades" is an adverbial prepositional phrase]
8. Many visitors to this area / hike the Pacific Crest Trail. [direct object]
10. The trail / begins in southern California, passes through Oregon and Washington, and ends in British Columbia. [no complement, "in southern California," "through Oregon and Washington," and "in British Columbia" are adverbial prepositional phrases]

422   **Answers**

Exercise 17.3, page 268

2. <u>The Charter of the United Nations</u> [noun phrase] <u>was written</u> [verb phrase] <u>in 1945</u> [prepositional phrase].
4. <u>The United Nations</u> [noun phrase] devotes most of its energies to <u>protecting human rights</u> [verbal phrase: gerund], <u>maintaining peace</u> [verbal phrase: gerund], and <u>encouraging social development</u> [verbal phrase: gerund].
6. <u>Its blue flag easily recognized everywhere</u> [absolute phrase], the United Nations now includes <u>193 member states</u> [noun phrase].

Exercise 17.4, page 271

Sentence 2.   1. if you make your living by swallowing swords [adverbial]

　　　　　　　　2. However: adverbial conjunction / if: subordinating conjunction

Sentence 4.   1. No dependent clauses

　　　　　　　　2. and: coordinating conjunction

Sentence 6.   1. No dependent clauses

　　　　　　　　2. No conjunctions

Exercise 18.1, page 275

Sentences 2, 3, 4, 6, 7, 9, 10, 12, and 13 are fragments.

Answers will vary. The following is one possible revision of the paragraph.

One of the most popular rides at any county fair or amusement park is the Ferris wheel. The original Ferris wheel, designed by George Washington Gale Ferris, Jr., for a national exposition in 1893, rose to a height of 264 feet and accommodated 2,140 passengers. Ferris's goal was to build something that would surpass in effect the Eiffel Tower, which was constructed just a few years earlier. Though Ferris's plans were not immediately accepted, once they were, and the wheel opened to the public, it became an immediate success, at times carrying thirty-eight thousand passengers a day. Since the nineteenth century, engineers have designed taller and taller Ferris wheels. The 541-foot Singapore Flyer holds the record, but the Beijing Great Wheel, currently under construction, will be over a hundred feet taller.

Exercise 19.1, page 280

Answers will vary. The following are possibilities.

2. He mentions, for example, research showing that measurements of happiness in the United States did not rise much over a period of fifty years: people responded to survey questions about their levels of happiness in much the same way as they did fifty years earlier.

4. Bok believes that people become accustomed to higher standards of living, not realizing how quickly they adapt, and so they do not become happier.

6. CORRECT

Exercise 20.1, page 285

2. ended   4. led   6. might have lost, had not fished

Exercise 20.2, page 289

Answers will vary depending on the tense chosen. All the sentences in the following paragraph are in the past tense.

I **had** already **been walking** for a half hour in the semi-darkness of Amsterdam's early-morning streets when I **came** to a red traffic signal. I **was** in a hurry to get to the train station and no cars **were** out yet, so I **crossed** over the cobblestones, passing a man waiting for the light to change. I never **looked** back when he **scolded** me for breaking the law. I **had** a train to catch. I **was** going to Widnau, in Switzerland, to see Aunt Marie. I **had** not **seen** her since I **was** in second grade.

Exercise 20.3, page 291

2. active   4. passive   6. passive

Exercise 20.4, page 293

2. Superstitious people think that if NASA had changed the number of the mission, the astronauts would have had a safer journey.

4. The crew used the lunar module as though it were a lifeboat.

6. If NASA ever planned a space mission on Friday the Thirteenth again, the public would object.

Exercise 20.5, page 299

2. include   4. is   6. know

Exercise 21.1, page 307

Answers will vary. The following are possibilities.

[1]When my brother and I were in middle school, we formed a band with our friends Jason and Andrew. [2]My grandmother had given Jake a guitar and me a drum kit for Christmas. [3]We practiced either alone or together for the rest of the winter. [4]Then, in the spring, we met up with Jason, whom we had known for years. [5]He and his cousin Andrew, whom we later called Android, were excited to join Jake and me. [6]Jason already had a guitar, and Andrew could sing. [7]After we played together one afternoon, we decided to call ourselves *The Crash*. [8]Jason and Andrew came over to our house to jam whenever their parents let them—which was most of the time. [9]Our parents did not mind our noise at all. [10]My dad said our playing reminded him of his own teenage garage band.

Exercise 21.2, page 307

2. They also recommended our hiring someone with extensive experience in statistical analysis.
4. CORRECT

Exercise 21.3, page 310

Answers will vary. The following are possibilities.
2. People should have the right to participate in a study only if they feel comfortable doing so.
4. Participants should be guaranteed that the information they provide will remain confidential.

Exercise 21.4, page 312

Answers will vary. The following are possibilities.
2. Because her father worked for the United Nations Education, Scientific and Cultural Organization (UNESCO), Baez lived in many different countries as a young girl.

4. Baez and her younger sister, Mimi Fariña, also a singer-songwriter, sometimes toured together.
6. In 2017, Baez was inducted into the Rock and Roll Hall of Fame in recognition of her influence on the development of rock in the 1960s.

Exercise 21.5, page 313

Answers will vary. The following are possibilities.
2. Daylight Savings Time was not adopted until 1918 as a fuel-saving measure during World War I.
4. Most people hate to reset clocks in the spring but enjoy the extra hour of sleep in November.

Exercise 21.6, page 315

Answers will vary. The following are possibilities.
2. For example, orangutans, African elephants, and Atlantic bottle-nose dolphins should roam freely rather than be held in captivity.
4. Like humans, animals such as these show emotions, self-awareness, and intention.
6. Clearly, they have the right to freedom.

Exercise 22.1, page 318

2. really
4. quietly

Exercise 22.2, page 320

2. less frequently
4. closest

Exercise 22.3, page 323

Answers will vary. The following are possibilities.
2. Hitchcock was identified with thrillers only after making his third movie, *The Lodger*.
4. Although his movies are known for suspense, sometimes moviego-ers also remember Hitchcock's droll sense of humor.
6. Originally a British citizen, Alfred Hitchcock was knighted by Queen Elizabeth II in 1980.

Exercise 22.4, page 324

Answers will vary. The following are possibilities.

2. In determining an appropriate challenge, climbers must consider safety precautions.
4. Although adding extra weight, a first-aid kit should be in every climber's pack.

Exercise 23.1, page 329

Answers will vary. The following are possibilities.

2. He convinced the audience that mass transit was affordable.
4. Hickey described what changes had been made to the farming operation.

Exercise 23.2, page 332

Answers will vary. The following are possibilities.

2. He drew a generic male face with metal teeth and long red ribbons of hair falling in front of it.
4. The evil visage of Darth Maul was so horrible that McCaig added elegant black feathers to balance the effect.

Exercise 24.1, page 336

Answers will vary. The following are possibilities.

The Lummis, a tribe in the Northwest, believe that grief is a burden that should not be carried alone. After the terrorist attack on the World Trade Center, Lummi carvers, wanting to help shoulder the burden of grief felt by others, crafted a healing totem pole for the citizens of New York, many of whom had family members who were killed in the terrorist attacks. The Lummis do not believe that it is the pole itself that heals but rather the prayers and songs said over it. For them, healing is not the responsibility of a single person; it is the responsibility of the community.

Exercise 24.2, page 338

Answers will vary. The following are possibilities.

2. Duct tape was originally called "duck tape" because, like ducks, it was water-proof and because it was made of cotton duck, a durable, tightly woven material.

4. Although many new colorful forms of duct tape are available, they are more expensive and less practical than standard silver.

Exercise 25.1, page 341

Answers will vary. The following are possibilities.

2. When she hired new employees for her department, she looked for applicants who were accomplished, hardworking, and articulate.
4. In her annual report, she wrote that her most important achievements were attracting new majors and increasing scholarship donations.
6. Whether planning for department meetings or conventions, Helen prepared her remarks in advance.

Exercise 26.1, page 345

Answers will vary. The following are possibilities.

2. Rudolph's Olympic achievement is impressive, but even more spectacular is her victory over a crippling disease.
4. Her determination was essential to her recovery, as were her siblings' willingness to help and her mother's vigilant care.

Exercise 27.1, page 349

Answers will vary. The following is a possibility.

2. With ideologies that could not be more different, both men see the Bible as the foundation from which the moral well-being of the United States should be reconstructed.

Exercise 27.2, page 350

Answers will vary. The following are possibilities.

2. After he pasted a map onto a piece of wood, he used a fine-bladed saw to cut around the borders of the countries.
4. Because the wooden pieces were cut by hand, the original puzzles were quite expensive.
6. After he recovered, built up his strength, and gained self-confidence, Lee's passion became mountain biking.
8. What kinds of activities can help survivors of traumatic brain injury toward recovery? Advocates believe that reviewing and practicing conversation and people skills are both essential to success.

Exercise 28.1, page 355

Answers will vary. The following are possibilities.

2. According to the weather reporter, this spring will be unseasonably cold and wet.
4. Professor Garcia mapped the evolutionary journey of the human species.

Exercise 29.1, page 360

Answers will vary. The following are possibilities.

2. Bottom line: She wanted to sell her car and the lowest figure she would accept was $12,000.
4. Mail it in: Because their contract for the project expires soon, the agency works with minimal effort.

Exercise 30.1, page 366

Answers will vary. The following are possibilities.

2. Originally, though, the magazine focused on rock and roll.
4. Its covers featured musical legends such the Beatles, Jimi Hendrix, Tina Turner, and Jim Morrison.
6. Since the late 1960s, *Rolling Stone* has become a newsstand mainstay around the world.

Exercise 31.1, page 369

Answers will vary. The following are possibilities.

2. In general, people notice goose bumps on their forearms, but some people also report having goose bumps on their legs.
4. The German and Italian languages also have words that refer to goose flesh, but French and Spanish translations refer to hens.
6. Not only humans experience piloerection, but other mammals do as well.

Exercise 31.2, page 370

2. However, while the comma may indicate pauses or grammatical boundaries (or sometimes both), the uses of the hashtag differ.
4. Once this metadata tag has been clicked, the viewer accesses posts that feature the tagged word.

6. CORRECT
8. Initially, scribes added a horizontal stroke through the top halves of each letter in the abbreviation. [A comma after a single introductory word may be omitted as long as no misreading occurs.]

Exercise 31.3, page 374

2. The largest cat on record, for example, was forty-eight inches long.
4. Most Maine Coons have exceptionally high intelligence for cats, which enables them to recognize language and even to open doors.
6. According to a legend, later proven to be false, Maine Coons are descendants from Turkish Angora cats owned by Marie Antoinette.

Exercise 31.4, page 376

2. On February 15, 1527, Cabeza de Vaca was appointed to an expedition headed for the mainland of North America.
4. Devastated by misfortune, the expedition dwindled rapidly.
6. His endurance now tested, Cabeza de Vaca lived as a trader and healer among Native Americans of the Rio Grande Basin, learning from them and eventually speaking on their behalf to the Spanish crown.

Exercise 32.1, page 378

2. The game is called soccer only in Canada and the United States; elsewhere it is known as football.
4. In amateur matches, players can be substituted frequently; however, in professional matches, the number of substitutions is limited.

Exercise 32.2, page 381

2. The process consists of six stages: recognizing a need or desire, finding information, evaluating options, deciding to purchase, purchasing, and assessing purchases.
4. The post-purchase assessment has one of two basic results: satisfaction or dissatisfaction with the product or service.

Exercise 33.1, page 385

2. an hour's drive
4. the eyewitness's report
6. Pat and Alan's new book
8. the neighbor's spying

Exercise 33.2, page 387

2. Hanson's book was published in the early 1920s.
4. More students enrolled during the academic year '13–'14.
6. They hired a rock 'n' roll band for their engagement party.
8. You'll have to include the ISBNs of the books you're going to purchase.

Exercise 34.1, page 391

2. In a speech delivered after being arrested for casting an illegal vote, Anthony asked this question: "Are women persons?"
4. Anthony suggests that not allowing women to vote is a violaton of "the supreme law of the land."
6. CORRECT

Exercise 35.1, page 400

2. Encouraging cultural diversity, fostering intercultural discussions, and promoting peace—these are just a few of UNESCO's goals.
4. According to a recent policy statement, the "Millennium Summit of Head of States [New York, September 2010] recognized the value of cultural diversity for the enrichment of humankind . . ." (UNESCO 4).

Exercise 36.1, page 405

2. desirable, readable, traceable, knowledgeable

Exercise 36.2, page 408

2. a forty-eight-inch television screen
4. a seventeenth-century painting
6. a food-borne virus

Exercise 37.1, page 412

[1]Swimmer **M**ichael **P**helps holds the record as the most decorated **O**lympian. [2]By the end of the 2016 **O**lympics in **R**io de **J**aneiro, **B**razil he had earned twenty-eight medals (**t**he previous record holder had eighteen). [3]In the 2008 **S**ummer **O**lympic **G**ames in **B**eijing, **C**hina, **P**helps finished first eight times. [4]Afterwards, with a bonus he was given by the sports company **S**peedo, **P**helps established a **f**oundation to promote healthy lifestyles and the sport of swimming, especially among children. [5]According to **P**helps, the swimming pool provided a place for him "**t**o have fun, stay healthy, set goals, work hard and gain confidence."

Exercise 38.1, page 415

2. The Frye Art Museum features three of the paintings that were on display: *The Birch Grove, Lady Curzon*, and *The Duel*.

4. Another exhibit at the Frye featured paintings, such as *Sorrow* and *No. 21*, commissioned to accompany music inspired by Joyce's poetry.

6. *Interactive* is a key word for describing this exhibit, as there were also shelves of artifacts for people to examine.

Exercise 39.1, page 420

2. The original canal was 363 miles long, running between Albany and Buffalo.

4. DeWitt Clinton, U.S. senator from New York, found support for the construction of the canal in the state legislature.

6. The Corridor is over five hundred miles long and runs through twenty-three counties of upstate New York.

Glossary of Usage

By learning about usage in this glossary, you will increase your ability to use words effectively.

Agreement on usage occurs slowly—often after a period of debate. An asterisk (*) before an entry indicates that a new usage has been reported by dictionary editors. This usage, however, might not yet be accepted by everyone.

a lot of   *A lot of* is conversational for *many, much,* or *a great deal of:* They do not have ~~a lot of~~ **much** time. *A lot* is sometimes misspelled as *alot.*

a while, awhile   *A while* means "a period of time." It is often used with the prepositions *after, for,* and *in:* We rested for **a while**. *Awhile* means "a short time." It is not preceded by a preposition: We rested **awhile**.

accept, except   The verb *accept* means "to receive": I **accept** your apology. The verb *except* means "to exclude": The policy was to have everyone wait in line, but mothers and small children were **excepted**. The preposition *except* means "other than": All **except** Joe will attend the conference.

advice, advise   *Advice* is a noun: They asked their attorney for **advice**. *Advise* is a verb: The attorney **advised** us to save all relevant documents.

affect, effect   *Affect* is a verb that means "to influence": The lobbyist's pleas did not **affect** the politician's decision. The noun *effect* means "a result": The **effect** of his decision on the staff's morale was positive and long lasting. When used as a verb, *effect* means "to produce" or "to cause": The activists believed that they could **effect** real political change.

all ready, already   *All ready* means "completely prepared": The rooms are **all ready** for the conference. *Already* means "by or before the time specified": She has **already** taken her final exams.

* **all right**   *All right* means "acceptable": The students asked whether it was **all right** to use dictionaries during the exam. *Alright* is not yet a generally accepted spelling of *all right*, although it is becoming more common in journalistic writing.

all together, altogether   *All together* means "as a group": The cast reviewed the script **all together**. *Altogether* means "wholly, thoroughly": That game is **altogether** too difficult.

allude, elude   *Allude* means "to refer to indirectly": The professor **alluded** to a medieval text. *Elude* means "to evade" or "to escape from": For the moment, his name **eludes** me.

allusion, illusion   An *allusion* is a casual or indirect reference: The **allusion** was to Shakespeare's *Twelfth Night*. An *illusion* is a false idea or an unreal image: His idea of college is an **illusion**.

alot   See **a lot of**.

already   See **all ready, already**.

alright   See **all right**.

altogether   See **all together, altogether**.

* **among, between**   To follow traditional usage, use *among* with three or more entities (a group): The snorkelers swam **among** the fish. Use *between* when referring to only two entities: The rivalry **between** the two teams is intense. Current dictionaries also note the possibility of using *between* to refer to more than two entities, especially when these entities are considered distinct: We have strengthened the lines of communication **between** the various departments.

amount of, number of   Use *amount of* before nouns that cannot be counted: The **amount of** rain that fell last year was insufficient. Use *number of* with nouns that can be counted: The **number of** students attending college has increased.

and/or   This combination denotes three options: one, the other, or both: a parent **and/or** a teacher. These options can also be presented separately with *or*: The student's application should be signed by a parent, a teacher, **or** both.

* **angry at, angry with**   Both *at* and *with* are commonly used after *angry*, although according to traditional guidelines, *with* should be used when a person is the cause of the anger: She was **angry with** me because I was late.

another, other, the other   *Another* is followed by a singular noun: **another** book. *Other* is followed by a plural noun: **other** books. *The other* is followed by either a singular or a plural noun: **the other book, the other books**.

anymore, any more   *Anymore* meaning "any longer" or "now" most frequently occurs in negative sentences: Sarah doesn't work here **anymore**. Its use in positive sentences is considered conversational; *now* is generally used instead: All he ever does ~~anymore~~ **now** is watch television. As two words, *any more* appears with *not* to mean "no more": We do not have **any more** time.

anyone, any one   *Anyone* means "any person at all": We did not know **anyone**. *Any one* refers to one of a group: **Any one** of the options is better than the current situation.

* **anyplace, everyplace, someplace**   These words are becoming increasingly common in academic writing. However, according to traditional usage rules, they should be replaced by *anywhere, everywhere,* and *somewhere*.

as   Conversational when used after such verbs as *know, say,* and *see*. Use *that, if,* or *whether* instead: I do not know ~~as~~ **whether** my application is complete. Also considered conversational is the use of *as* instead of *who, which,* or *that:.* Many of the performers ~~as~~ **who** have appeared on our program will be giving a concert this evening.

* **as, like**   According to traditional usage, *as* begins either a phrase or a clause; *like* begins only a phrase: My brother drives too fast, just ~~like~~ **as** my father did. Current dictionaries note the informal use of *like* to begin clauses after verbs such as *look* and *sound*.

assure, ensure, insure   *Assure* means "to state with confidence, alleviating any doubt": The flight attendant **assured** us that our flight would arrive on time. *Ensure* and *insure* are usually interchangeable to mean "make certain," but only *insure* means "to protect against loss": The editor **ensured** [OR **insured**] that the reporter's facts were accurate. Physicians must **insure** themselves against malpractice suits.

awhile   See *a while, awhile*.

bad   Unconventional as an adverb; use *badly* instead. The team played **badly**. However, the adjective *bad* is used after sensory verbs such as *feel, look,* and *smell*: I feel **bad** that I forgot to return your book yesterday.

being as, being that   Unconventional; use *because* instead.
~~Being as~~ Because the road was closed, traffic was diverted to
another route.

* **beside, besides**   According to traditional usage, these two words
have different meanings. *Beside* means "next to": The president
sat **beside** the prime minister. *Besides* means "in addition to"
or "other than": She has written many articles **besides** those on
political reform. Professional writers regularly use *beside* to convey this meaning, as long as there is no risk of ambiguity.

better, had better   *Better* is conversational. Use *had better* instead:
We ~~better~~ had better finish the report by five o'clock.

between   See **among, between**.

* **can, may**   *Can* refers to ability, and *may* refers to permission: You
can [are able to] drive seventy miles an hour, but you **may** not
[are not permitted to] exceed the speed limit. In contemporary
usage, *can* and *may* are used interchangeably to denote possibility
or permission, although *may* is used more frequently in formal
contexts.

capital, capitol   *Capital* means either "a governing city" or
"funds": The **capital** of Minnesota is St. Paul. An anonymous
donor provided the **capital** for the project. As a modifier, *capital*
means "chief" or "principal": This year's election is of **capital**
importance. It may also refer to the death penalty: **Capital** punishment is legal in some states. A *capitol* is a statehouse; the *Capitol* is the U.S. congressional building in Washington, DC.

cite, site, sight   *Cite* means "to mention": Be sure to **cite** your
sources. *Site* is a location: The president visited the **site** for the
new library. As a verb, *site* also means "to situate": The builder
sited the factory near the freeway. *Sight* means "to see": The
crew **sighted** land. *Sight* also refers to a view: What an incredible
sight!

climactic, climatic   *Climactic* refers to a climax, or high point:
The actors rehearsed the **climactic** scene. *Climatic* refers to the
climate: Many environmentalists are worried about the recent
climatic changes.

coarse, course   *Coarse* refers to roughness: The jacket was made of **coarse** linen. *Course* refers to a route: Our **course** to the island was indirect. *Course* may also refer to a plan of study: I want to take a **course** in nutrition.

* **compare to, compare with**   *Compare to* means "to regard as similar," and *compare with* means "to examine for similarities and/or differences": She **compared** her mind **to** a dusty attic. The student **compared** the first draft **with** the second. In current usage, this distinction is disappearing.

complement, complementary, compliment, complimentary   *Complement* means "to complete" or "to balance": Their personalities **complement** each other. They have **complementary** personalities. *Compliment* means "to express praise": The professor **complimented** the students on their first draft. Her remarks were complimentary. *Complimentary* may also mean "provided free of charge": We received **complimentary** tickets.

* **compose, comprise**   *Compose* means "to make up": That collection is **composed** of medieval manuscripts. *Comprise* means "to consist of": The anthology **comprises** many famous essays. Dictionary editors have noted the increasing use of *comprise* in the passive voice to mean "to be composed of."

conscience, conscious, consciousness   *Conscience* means "the sense of right and wrong": He examined his **conscience** before deciding whether to join the protest. *Conscious* means "awake": After an hour, the patient was fully **conscious**. After an hour, the patient regained **consciousness**. *Conscious* may also mean "aware": We were **conscious** of the possible consequences.

continual, continually, continuous, continuously   *Continual* means "constantly recurring": **Continual** interruptions kept us from completing the project. Telephone calls **continually** interrupted us. *Continuous* means "uninterrupted": The job applicant had a record of ten years' **continuous** employment. The job applicant worked **continuously** from 2000 to 2009.

could of   *Of* is often mistaken for the sound of the unstressed *have*: They **could ~~of~~ have** [OR might **have**, should **have**, would **have**] gone home.

couldn't care less   *Couldn't care less* expresses complete lack of concern: She **couldn't care less** about her reputation. *Could care less* is considered unconventional in academic writing.

council, counsel   A *council* is an advisory or decision-making group: The student **council** supported the new regulations. A *counsel* is a legal adviser: The defense **counsel** conferred with the judge. As a verb, *counsel* means "to give advice": She **counsels** people with eating disorders.

criteria, criterion   *Criteria* is a plural noun meaning "a set of standards for judgment": The teachers explained the **criteria** for the assignment. The singular form is *criterion*: Their judgment was based on only one **criterion**.

* **data**   *Data* is the plural form of *datum*, which means "piece of information" or "fact": When the **data are** complete, we will know the true cost. However, current dictionaries also note that *data* is frequently used as a mass entity (like the word *furniture*), appearing with a singular verb.

desert, dessert   *Desert* can mean "a barren land": Gila monsters live in the **deserts** of the Southwest. As a verb, *desert* means "to leave": I thought my friends had **deserted** me. *Dessert* refers to something sweet eaten at the end of a meal: They ordered apple pie for **dessert**.

device, devise   *Device* is a noun: She invented a **device** that measures extremely small quantities of liquid. *Devise* is a verb: We **devised** a plan for work distribution.

differ from, differ with   *Differ from* means "to be different": A bull snake **differs from** a rattlesnake in a number of ways. *Differ with* means "to disagree": Senator Brown has **differed with** Senator Owen on several issues.

* **different from, different than**   *Different from* is generally preferred for use with nouns, pronouns, and noun phrases: The school was **different from** most others. It may also be used with a noun clause: It was **different from** what we had expected. *Different* is also commonly used with adverbial clauses in which *than* is the conjunction: We are no **different than** they are.

discreet, discrete   *Discreet* means "showing good judgment or self-restraint": His friends complained openly, but his comments were quite **discreet**. *Discrete* means "distinct": The participants in the study came from three **discrete** groups.

disinterested, uninterested   *Disinterested* means "impartial": A **disinterested** observer will give a fair opinion. *Uninterested* means "lacking interest": She was **uninterested** in the outcome of the game.

distinct, distinctive   *Distinct* means "easily distinguishable or perceived": Each proposal has **distinct** advantages. *Distinctive* means "characteristic" or "serving to distinguish": We studied the **distinctive** features of hawks.

* **due to**   Traditionally, *due to* was not synonymous with *because of*: ~~Due to~~ Because of holiday traffic, we arrived an hour late. However, dictionary editors now consider this usage of *due to* acceptable.

effect   See **affect, effect**.

elicit, illicit   *Elicit* means "to draw forth": He is **eliciting** contributions for a new playground. *Illicit* means "unlawful": The newspaper reported their **illicit** mishandling of public funds.

elude   See **allude, elude**.

emigrate from, immigrate to   *Emigrate* means "to leave one's own country": My ancestors **emigrated from** Ireland. *Immigrate* means "to arrive in a different country to settle": The Ulster Scots **immigrated to** the southern United States.

ensure   See **assure, ensure, insure**.

especially, specially   *Especially* emphasizes a characteristic or quality: Some people are **especially** sensitive to the sun. *Especially* also means "particularly": Wildflowers are abundant in this area, **especially** during May. *Specially* means "for a particular purpose": The classroom was **specially** designed for music students.

etc.   Abbreviation of *et cetera*, meaning "and others of the same kind." Use only within parentheses: Be sure to bring appropriate camping gear (tent, sleeping bag, mess kit, **etc.**). Because *and* is part of the meaning of *etc.*, avoid using the combination *and etc.*

everyday, every day   *Everyday* means "routine" or "ordinary": These are **everyday** problems. *Every day* means "each day": I read the newspaper **every day**.

everyone, every one   *Everyone* means "all": **Everyone** should attend. *Every one* refers to each person or item in a group: **Every one** of you should attend.

everyplace   See **anyplace, everyplace, someplace**.

except   See **accept, except**.

explicit, implicit   *Explicit* means "expressed clearly and directly": Given his **explicit** directions, we knew how to proceed. *Implicit* means "implied or expressed indirectly": I mistakenly understood his silence to be his **implicit** approval of the project.

farther, further   Generally, *farther* refers to geographic distance: We will have to drive **farther** tomorrow. *Further* means "more": If you need **further** assistance, please let me know.

* **feel**   Traditionally, *feel* was not synonymous with "think" or "believe": I ~~feel~~ **think** that more should be done to protect local habitat. Dictionary editors now consider this use of *feel* to be a standard alternative.

fewer, less   *Fewer* occurs before nouns that can be counted: **fewer** technicians, **fewer** pencils. *Less* occurs before nouns that cannot be counted: **less** milk, **less** support. *Less than* may be used with measurements of time or distance: **less than** three months, **less than** twenty miles.

* **first, firstly; second, secondly**   Many instructors prefer the use of *first* and *second*. However, according to current dictionaries, *firstly* and *secondly* are also well-established forms.

former, latter   Used together, *former* refers to the first of two; *latter* to the second of two. John and Ian are both English. The **former** is from Manchester; the **latter** is from Birmingham.

further   See **farther, further**.

get   Considered conversational in many common expressions: The weather ~~got better~~ **improved** overnight. I did not know what he ~~was getting at~~ **meant**.

good, well   *Good* is an adjective, not an adverb: He pitched ~~good~~ **well** last night. *Good* in the sense of "in good health" may be used interchangeably with *well*: I feel **good** [OR **well**] this morning.

had better   See **better, had better**.

half   *A half a* or *a half an* is unconventional; use *half a/an* or *a half:* You should be able to complete the questionnaire in **a half ~~an~~** hour.

hanged, hung   *Hanged* means "put to death by hanging": The prisoner was **hanged** at dawn. For all other meanings, use *hung*: He **hung** the picture above his desk.

has got, have got   Conversational; omit *got*: I have ~~got~~ a meeting tomorrow.

he/she, his/her   Although used as a solution to the problem of sexist language, these combinations are not universally accepted. Consider using *he or she* and *his or her* or transforming the sentence with the plural *they* or *their*. See **28b**.

herself, himself, myself, yourself   Unconventional as subjects in a sentence. Joe and ~~myself~~ **I** will lead the discussion.

* **hopefully**   According to traditional usage, *hopefully* means "with hope," not "it is hoped": **Hopefully**, the negotiators discussed the proposed treaty. However, dictionary editors have started to accept the use of *hopefully* as a sentence modifier: **Hopefully**, the treaty will be ratified. If your instructor prefers you to follow traditional usage, use *I hope* in such a sentence: **I hope** the treaty will be ratified.

hung   See **hanged, hung**.

i.e.   Abbreviation of *id est*, meaning "that is." Use only within parentheses: All participants in the study ran the same distance (**i.e.**, six kilometers). Otherwise, replace *i.e.* with the English equivalent, *that is*: Assistance was offered to those who would have difficulty boarding, ~~i.e.,~~ **that is**, the elderly, the disabled, and parents with small children. Do not confuse *i.e.* with *e.g.*, meaning "for example."

illicit   See **elicit, illicit**.

illusion   See **allusion, illusion**.

immigrate   See **emigrate from, immigrate to**.

* **impact**   Though *impact* is commonly used as a verb in business writing, many instructors still use it as a noun only: The new tax ~~impacts~~ **affects** everyone.

implicit   See **explicit, implicit**.

imply, infer   *Imply* means "suggest without actually stating": Though he never mentioned the statistics, he **implied** that they were questionable. *Infer* means "draw a conclusion based on evidence": Given the tone of his voice, I **inferred** that he found the work substandard.

in regards to   See **regard, regarding, regards**.

inside of, outside of   Drop *of* when unnecessary: Security guards stood **outside** ~~of~~ the front door.

insure   See **assure, ensure, insure**.

irregardless   Unconventional; use *regardless* instead.

its, it's   *Its* is a possessive form: The committee forwarded **its** recommendation. *It's* is a contraction of *it is*: **It's** a beautiful day.

kind of a, sort of a   The word *a* is unnecessary: This **kind of** a book sells well. *Kind of* and *sort of* are not conventionally used to mean "somewhat": The report was ~~kind of~~ somewhat difficult to read.

later, latter   *Later* means "after a specific time" or "a time after now": The concert ended **later** than we had expected. *Latter* refers to the second of two items: Of the two versions described, I prefer the **latter**.

lay, lie   *Lay* (*laid, laying*) means "put" or "place": He **laid** the book aside. *Lie* (*lay, lain, lying*) means "rest" or "recline": I had just **lain** down when the alarm went off. *Lay* takes an object (to **lay** something), while *lie* does not. These verbs may be confused because the present tense of *lay* and the past tense of *lie* are spelled the same way.

lead, led   As a noun, *lead* means "a kind of metal": The paint had **lead** in it. As a *verb*, lead means "to conduct": A guide will **lead** a tour of the ruins. *Led* is the past tense of the verb *lead*: He **led** the country from 1949 to 1960.

less, less than   See **fewer, less**.

lie   See **lay, lie**.

like   See **as, like**.

literally   Conversational when used to emphasize the meaning of another word: I was ~~literally~~ nearly frozen after I finished shoveling the sidewalk. *Literally* is conventionally used to indicate that an expression is not being used figuratively: My friend **liter-ally** climbs the walls after work; his fellow rock climbers join him at the local gym.

lose, loose   *Lose* is a verb: She does not **lose** her patience often. *Loose* is chiefly used as an adjective: A few of the tiles are **loose**.

lots, lots of   Conversational for *many* or *much*: He has ~~lots of~~ **many** friends. We have ~~lots~~ **much** to do before the end of the quarter.

mankind   Considered sexist because it excludes women: All ~~mankind~~ **humanity** will benefit from this new discovery.

may   See **can**, **may**.

may of, might of   See **could of**.

maybe, may be   *Maybe* is an adverb: **Maybe** the negotiators will succeed this time. *May* and *be* are verbs: The rumor **may be** true.

* **media, medium**   According to traditional definitions, *media* is a plural word: The **media** have sometimes created the news in addition to reporting it. The singular form is *medium*: The newspaper is one **medium** that people seem to trust. The use of *media* as a collective noun taking a singular verb, although frequent, is still considered conversational.

most   Unconventional to mean "almost": We watch the news ~~most~~ **almost** every day.

myself   See **herself, himself, myself, yourself**.

nothing like, nowhere near   Unconventional; use *not nearly* instead: Her new book is ~~nowhere near~~ **not nearly** as mysterious as her previous novel.

number of   When the expression *a number of* is used, the reference is plural: **A number of** positions **are** open. When the *number of* is used, the reference is singular: **The number of** possibilities **is** limited. See also **amount of, number of.**

off of   Conversational; omit *of*. He walked **off ~~of~~** the field.

on account of   Conversational; use *because of* : The singer canceled her engagement ~~on account of~~ **because of** a sore throat.

* **on the other hand**   If you use *on the one hand* to introduce the first of two contrasting points, make sure that *on the other hand* introduces the second. However, *on the other hand* may be used

to introduce a contrasting point even if it is not preceded by *on the one hand.*

other   See **another, other, the other.**

passed, past   *Passed* is the past tense of the verb *pass*: Deb **passed** the other runners right before the finish line. *Past* means "beyond a time or location": We walked **past** the high school.

per   In ordinary contexts, use *a* or *an*: You should drink at least six glasses of water ~~per~~ a day.

percent, percentage   *Percent* (also spelled *per cent*) is used with a specific number: **Sixty percent** of the students attended the ceremony. *Percentage* refers to an unspecified portion: The **percentage** of students attending college has increased in recent years.

perspective, prospective   *Perspective* means "point of view": We discussed the issue from various **perspectives**. *Prospective* means "likely to become": **Prospective** journalists interviewed the editor.

phenomena, phenomenon   *Phenomena* is the plural form of *phenomenon*: Natural **phenomena** were given scientific explanations.

* **plus**   *Plus* joins nouns or noun phrases to make a sentence seem like an equation: Her endless curiosity **plus** her boundless energy makes her the perfect camp counselor. Note that a singular form of the verb is required (e.g., *makes*). In the past, *plus* was not used to join clauses: The candidate had three advanced degrees. ~~Plus~~ **In addition,** she had experience working abroad. The use of *plus* at the beginning of a clause is now considered acceptable by some dictionaries.

precede, proceed   To *precede* is to "go ahead of": A moment of silence **preceded** the applause. To *proceed* is to "go forward": After stopping for a short rest, we **proceeded** to our destination.

prejudice, prejudiced   *Prejudice* is a noun: They were unaware of their **prejudice**. *Prejudiced* is an adjective: She accused me of being **prejudiced**.

pretty   *Pretty* means "attractive," not "rather" or "fairly": We were ~~pretty~~ **fairly** tired after cooking all day.

principal, principle   As a noun, *principal* means "chief official": The **principal** greeted the students every day. It also means "capital": The loan's **principal** was still quite high. As an adjective, *principal* means "main": Tourism is the country's **principal** source of income. The noun *principle* refers to a rule, standard, or belief: She explained the three **principles** supporting the theory.

proceed   See **precede, proceed**.

prospective   See **perspective, prospective**.

quotation, quote   In academic writing, *quotation* refers to a repeated or copied sentence or passage: She began her speech with a ~~quote~~ quotation from *Othello*. *Quote* expresses an action: My coach **quotes** lines from television commercials.

raise, rise   *Raise* (*raised, raising*) means "to lift or cause to move upward, to bring up or increase": Retailers **raised** prices. *Rise* (*rose, risen, rising*) means "to get up" or "to ascend": The cost of living rose sharply. *Raise* takes an object (to **raise** something); rise does not.

real, really   *Really* rather than *real* is used to mean "very": He is from a ~~real~~ really small town. To ensure this word's effectiveness, use it sparingly.

* **reason why**   Traditionally, this combination was considered redundant: No one explained **the reason** ~~why~~ the negotiations failed. [OR No one explained ~~the reason~~ **why** the negotiations failed.] However, dictionary editors report its use by well-known writers.

regard, regarding, regards   Be sure to use the correct forms of these words: *in regard to, with regard to, as regards*, and *regarding* [NOT *in regards to, with regards to*, or *as regarding*].

* **relation, relationship**   According to traditional definitions, *relation* is used to link abstractions: We studied the **relation** between language and social change. *Relationship* is used to link people: The **relationship** between the two friends grew strong. However, dictionary editors now label as standard the use of *relationship* to connect abstractions.

respectfully, respectively   *Respectfully* means "showing respect": The children learned to treat one another **respectfully**. *Respectively* means "in the order designated": We discussed the issue with the chair, the dean, and the provost, **respectively**.

rise   See **raise, rise**.

should of   See **could of**.

sight   See **cite, site, sight**.

sit, set   *Sit* means "to be seated": Jonathan **sat** in the front row. *Set* means "to place something": The research assistant **set** the chemicals on the counter. *Set* takes an object (to **set** something); *sit* does not.

site   See **cite, site, sight**.

so   Instead of using *so* to mean "very," find a precise modifier: She was ~~so~~ **intensely** focused on her career.

someplace   See **anyplace, everyplace, someplace**.

sometime, sometimes, some time   *Sometime* means "at an unspecified time": They will meet **sometime** next month. *Sometimes* means "at times": **Sometimes** laws are unfair. *Some time* means "a span of time": They agreed to allow **some time** to pass before voting on the measure.

sort of a   See **kind of a, sort of a**.

specially   See **especially, specially**.

stationary, stationery   *Stationary* means "in a fixed position": Traffic was **stationary** for an hour. *Stationery* means "writing paper and envelopes": The director ordered new department **stationery**.

supposed to, used to   Be sure to include the frequently unsounded *d* at the end of the verb form: We are **supposed to** leave at 9:30 a.m. We **used to** leave earlier.

than, then   *Than* is used in comparisons: The tape recorder is smaller **than** the radio. *Then* refers to a time sequence: Go straight ahead for three blocks; **then** turn left.

their, there, they're   *Their* is the possessive form of *they*: They will give **their** presentation tomorrow. *There* refers to location: I lived **there** for six years. *There* is also used as an expletive (see **30a(3)**): **There** is no explanation for the phenomenon. *They're* is a contraction of *they are*: **They're** leaving in the morning.

theirself, theirselves   Unconventional; use *themselves*. The students finished the project by ~~theirselves~~ **themselves**.

then   See **than, then**.

to, too, two   *To* is an infinitive marker: She wanted **to** become an actress. *To* is also used as a preposition, usually indicating direction: They walked **to** the memorial. *Too* means either "also" or "excessively": I voted for her **too**. They are **too** busy this year. *Two* is a number: She studied abroad for **two** years.

toward, towards   Although both are acceptable, *toward* is preferred in American English.

try and   Conversational for *try to*: The staff will **try ~~and~~ to** finish the project by Friday.

uninterested   See **disinterested, uninterested**.

* **unique**   Traditionally, *unique* meant "one of a kind" and thus was not preceded by a qualifier such as *more, most, quite,* or *very*: Her prose style is **~~quite~~ unique**. However, *unique* is also widely used to mean "extraordinary."

use, utilize   In most contexts, *use* is preferred to *utilize*: We **~~utilized~~ used** a special dye in the experiment. However, *utilize* may suggest an effort to employ something for a purpose: We discussed how to **utilize** the resources we had been given.

used to   See **supposed to, used to**.

very   To ensure this word's effectiveness, use it sparingly. Whenever possible, choose a stronger word: She was **~~very satisfied~~ delighted** with her new digital camera.

ways   Conversational when referring to distance; use *way* instead: It's a long **~~ways~~ way** from home.

well   See **good, well**.

where … at, where … to   Conversational; omit *at* and *to*: **Where** is the library **~~at~~**? **Where** are you moving **~~to~~**?

with regards to   See **regard, regarding, regards**.

would of   See **could of**.

your, you're   *Your* is a possessive form: Let's meet in **your** office. *You're* is a contraction of *you are*: **You're** gaining strength.

yourself   See **herself, himself, myself, yourself**.

Glossary of Terms

This glossary provides brief definitions of frequently used terms. Consult the index for references to terms not listed here.

absolute phrase   A sentence-like structure containing a subject and its modifiers. Unlike a sentence, an absolute phrase has no verb marked for person, number, or tense: *The ceremony finally over*, the graduates tossed their mortarboards in the air. See **17d(6)**.

acronym   A word formed by combining the initial letters or syllables of a series of words and pronounced as a word rather than as a series of letters: *NATO* for North Atlantic Treaty Organization. See chapter **39**.

active voice   See **voice**.

adjectival clause   A dependent clause, also called a **relative clause**, that modifies a noun or a pronoun. See **17e**.

adjective   A word that modifies a noun or a pronoun. Adjectives typically end in suffixes such as *-able, -al, -ant, -ative, -ic, -ish, -less, -ous*, and *-y*. See **17a** and chapter **22**. **Coordinate adjectives** are two or more adjectives modifying the same noun and separated by a comma: a *brisk, cold* walk. See **31d**.

adverb   A word that modifies a verb, a verbal, an adjective, or another adverb. Adverbs commonly end in *-ly*. Some adverbs modify entire sentences: *Perhaps* the meeting could be postponed. See **17a** and chapter **22**.

adverbial clause   A dependent clause that modifies a verb, an adjective, or an adverb. See **17e(2)**.

adverbial conjunction   A word such as *however* or *thus* that joins one independent clause to another; also known as a **conjunctive adverb**. See **17a(7)**. COMPARE: **conjunction**.

agreement   Grammatical correspondence in number, person, or gender between pronouns and their antecedents and subjects and their verbs. See **20f** and **21c**.

antecedent   A word or group of words referred to by a pronoun. See **17a(3)**, **21a**, and **21c**.

appositive   A pronoun, noun, or noun phrase that identifies, describes, or explains an adjacent pronoun, noun, or noun phrase. See **17a** and **21b(4)**.

article   A word used to signal a noun. *The* is a definite article; *a* and *an* are indefinite articles. See **17a(4)**.

auxiliary verb, auxiliary   A verb that combines with a main verb. *Be*, *do*, and *have* are auxiliary verbs when they are used with main verbs. Also called **helping verbs**. **Modal auxiliaries** include *could*, *should*, and *may* and are used for such purposes as expressing doubt or obligation and making a request. See **17a**, **17d**, and **20a**.

Boolean operators   Words used to broaden or narrow database searches. These include *or*, *and*, *not*, and *near*. Also called logical operators. See **9b**.

case   The form of a noun or a pronoun that indicates its relationship to other words in a sentence. Nouns and pronouns can be subjects or subject complements (**subjective case**), objects (**objective case**), or markers of possession and other relations (**possessive case**). See **21b**.

claim   A statement that a writer wants readers to accept; also called a **proposition**. See **5b**, **6c**.

clause   A sequence of related words forming an independent unit (**independent clause** or **main clause**) or an embedded unit (**dependent clause** used as an adverb, adjective, or noun). A clause has both a subject and a predicate. See **17e**.

collective noun   A noun that refers to a group: *team*, *faculty*, *committee*. See **17a(2)**.

colloquial   A label for any word or phrase that is characteristic of informal speech. *Kid* is colloquial; *child* is used in formal contexts. See **28a(2)**.

common noun   A noun referring to any or all members of a class or group (*woman*, *city*, *holiday*) rather than to specific members

(*Susan, Reno, New Year's Day*). COMPARE: **proper noun**. See 17a(2).

complement A word or words used to complete the meaning of a verb. A **subject complement** is a word or phrase that follows a linking verb and categorizes or describes the subject. An **object complement** is a word or phrase that categorizes or describes a direct object when it follows such verbs as *make, paint, elect*, and *consider*. See 17c.

compound predicate A predicate that has two parts joined by a connecting word such as *and, or*, or *but*; each part contains a verb: Clara Barton *nursed the injured during the Civil War* and *later founded the American Red Cross*. See 17b.

compound subject Two subjects joined by a connecting word such as *and, or*, or *but: Students* and *faculty* are discussing the issue of grade inflation. See 17b.

compound word Two or more words functioning as a single word: *ice cream, double-check*. See chapter **36**.

conjunction A word used to connect other words, phrases, clauses, or sentences. **Coordinating conjunctions** (*and, but, or, nor, for, so*, and *yet*) connect and relate words and word groups of equal grammatical rank. See 17a(7). A **subordinating conjunction** such as *although, if*, or *when* begins a dependent clause and connects it to an independent clause. See 17a(7) and 17e(2). COMPARE: **adverbial conjunction**.

conjunctive adverb See **adverbial conjunction**.

coordinate adjective See **adjective**.

coordinating conjunction See **conjunction**.

coordination The use of grammatically equivalent constructions to link or balance ideas. See chapter **24**.

correlative conjunctions, correlatives Two-part connecting words such as *either . . . or* and *not only . . . but also*. See 17a(7).

count nouns Nouns naming things that can be counted (*word, student, remark*). See 17a(2). COMPARE: **noncount nouns**.

dangling modifier A word or phrase that does not clearly modify another word or word group. See 22e. COMPARE: **misplaced modifier**.

dangling participial phrase   A verbal phrase that does not clearly modify another word or word group. *Quickly calling 911, the wreck was frightening.* See **misplaced modifier**.

demonstrative pronouns   Four words (*this*, *that*, *these*, and *those*) that distinguish one individual, thing, event, or idea from another. Demonstratives may occur with or without nouns: *This law* will go into effect in two years. *This* will go into effect in two years. See **21a(6)**.

dependent clause   Also called *subordinate clause*. See **clause**.

determiner   A word that signals the approach of a noun. A determiner may be an article, a demonstrative, a possessive, or a quantifier: *a reason*, *this reason*, *his reason*, *three reasons*.

direct object   See **object**.

direct quotation   See **quotation**.

ellipsis points   Three spaced periods that indicate either a pause or the omission of material from a direct quotation. See **35g**.

elliptical construction (clause)   A construction, usually a clause, missing one or more words that are assumed to be understood. See **17e**, **21b(7)**, **30b**.

essential element   A word or word group that modifies another word or word group, providing information that is essential for identification. Essential elements are not set off by commas, parentheses, or dashes: The woman *who witnessed the accident* was called to testify. Also called a **restrictive element**. COMPARE: **nonessential element**. See **17e**, **21a(4)**, and chapter **31**.

ethos   One of the three classical appeals; the use of language to demonstrate the writer's trustworthy character, good intentions, and substantial knowledge of a subject. Also called an **ethical appeal**. See **6e**. See also **logos** and **pathos**.

expletive   A word signaling a structural change in a sentence, usually used so that new or important information is given at the end of the sentence: *There* were over four thousand runners in the marathon. See **30a**.

flat adverb   An adverb that shares the same form as a related adjective: Run *fast*.

genre   A literary category, such as drama or poetry, identified by its own conventions.

gerund A verbal that ends in *-ing* and functions as a noun: *Snowboarding* is a popular winter sport. See **17d(3)**.

gerund phrase A verbal phrase that employs the *-ing* form of a verb and functions as a noun: Some students prefer *studying in the library*. See **17d(3)**.

helping verb See **auxiliary verb**.

homophones Words that have the same sound and sometimes the same spelling but differ in meaning: *their*, *there*, and *they're* or *capital* meaning "funds" and *capital* meaning "the top of a pillar." See chapter **36**.

idiom An expression whose meaning often cannot be derived from its elements. *Burning the midnight oil* means "staying up late studying." See **29c**.

indefinite pronoun A pronoun such as *everyone* or *anything* that does not refer to a specific person, place, thing, or idea. See **21a(7)** and **21c**.

independent clause See **clause**.

indirect object See **object**.

indirect question A sentence that includes an embedded question, punctuated with a period instead of a question mark: My friends asked me *why I left the party early*. See chapter **35**.

indirect quotation See **quotation**.

infinitive A verbal that consists of the base form of the verb, usually preceded by the infinitive marker *to*. An infinitive is used chiefly as a noun, less frequently as an adjective or adverb: My father likes *to golf*. See **17d(3)**.

infinitive phrase A verbal phrase that contains the infinitive form of a verb: They volunteered *to work at the local hospital*. See **17d(3)**.

inflection A change in the form of a word that indicates a grammatical feature such as number, person, tense, or degree. For example, *-ed* added to a verb indicates the past tense, and *-er* indicates the comparative degree of an adjective or adverb.

intensifier See **qualifier**.

intensive pronoun See **reflexive pronoun**.

interjection   A word expressing a simple exclamation: *Hey! Oops!* When used at the beginnings of sentences, mild interjections are set off by commas. See **17a(8)**.

linking verb   A verb that relates a subject to a subject complement. Examples of linking verbs are *be, become, seem, appear, feel, look, taste, smell,* and *sound*. See **17a(1)** and **20a**.

logos   One of the three classical appeals; the use of language to show clear reasoning. Also called a **logical appeal**. See **6e**. See also **ethos** and **pathos**.

main clause   Also called **independent clause**. See **clause**.

misplaced modifier   A descriptive or qualifying word or phrase placed in a position that confuses the reader: I read about a wildfire that was out of control *in yesterday's paper*. [The modifier belongs after *read*.] See **22d**.

mixed construction   A confusing sentence that is the result of an unintentional shift from one grammatical pattern to another: When police appeared who were supposed to calm the crowds showed up, most people had already gone home. [The sentence should be recast with either *appeared* or *showed up*, not with both.] See **23c**.

mixed metaphor   A construction that includes parts of two or more unrelated metaphors: Her *fiery* personality *dampened* our hopes of a compromise. See chapter **23**.

modal auxiliary   See **auxiliary verb**.

modifier   A word or word group that describes, limits, or qualifies another. See chapter **22**.

mood   A set of verb forms or inflections used to indicate how a speaker or writer regards an assertion: as a fact or opinion (**indicative mood**); as a command or instruction (**imperative mood**); or as a wish, hypothesis, request, or condition contrary to fact (**subjunctive mood**). See **20e**.

nominalization   Formation of a noun by adding a suffix to a verb or an adjective: *require, requirement*; *sad, sadness*.

nominative case   Also called **subjective case**. See **case**.

noncount nouns   Nouns naming things that cannot be counted (*architecture, water*). See **17a(2)**. COMPARE: **count nouns**.

nonessential element   A word or word group that modifies another word or word group but does not provide information
essential for identification. Nonessential elements are set off by
commas, parentheses, or dashes: Carol Murphy, *president of the
university*, plans to meet with alumni representatives. Also called
a **nonrestrictive element**. See **17e** and chapter **31**. COMPARE:
essential element.

nonrestrictive element   See **nonessential element**.

noun   A word that names a person, place, thing, idea, animal,
quality, event, and so on: *Alanis, America, desk, justice, dog,
strength, departure*. See **17a(2)**. See also **collective noun,
common noun, count noun, noncount noun,** and **proper
noun**.

noun clause   A dependent clause used as a noun. See **17e**.

noun phrase   A noun and its modifiers. See **17d(1)**.

number   The property of a word that indicates whether it refers to
one (**singular**) or to more than one (**plural**). Number is reflected
in the word's form: *river/rivers, this/those, he sees/they see*. See **20b,
20f, 21b,** and **21c**.

object   A noun, pronoun, noun phrase, or noun clause that follows
a preposition or a transitive verb or verbal. A **direct object** names
the person or thing that receives the action of the verb: I sent
the *package*. An **indirect object** usually indicates to whom the
action was directed or for whom the action was performed: I sent
you the package. See **17c**. The **object of a preposition** follows a
preposition: I sent the package to *you*. See **17d(4)**.

object complement   See **complement**.

objective case   See **case**.

participial phrase   A verbal phrase that includes a participle and
serves as a modifier: The stagehand *carrying the trunk* fell over the
threshold. See **17d**. See also **participle** and **phrase**.

participle   A verb form that may function as part of a verb phrase
(had *determined*, was *thinking*) or as a modifier (a *determined*
effort; the couple, *thinking* about their past). A **present participle** is formed by adding *-ing* to the base form of a verb. A **past
participle** is usually formed by adding *-ed* to the base form of a

verb (*walked*, *passed*); however, many verbs have irregular past-participle forms (*written*, *bought*, *gone*). See **20a**.

particle A word such as *across*, *away*, *down*, *for*, *in*, *off*, *out*, *up*, *on*, or *with* that combines with a main verb to form a phrasal verb: *write down*, *look up*. See **20a**.

parts of speech The classes into which words may be grouped according to their forms and grammatical relationships. The traditional parts of speech are verbs, nouns, pronouns, adjectives, adverbs, prepositions, conjunctions, and interjections. See **17a**.

passive voice See **voice**.

past participle See **participle**.

pathos One of the three classical appeals; the use of language to stir the feelings of an audience. Also called an **emotional appeal** or a **pathetic appeal**. See **6e**. See also **ethos** and **logos**.

perfect progressive tense The form a verb takes to indicate that an action, condition, or event originating in the past is ongoing or incomplete (*he is talking*; *the brakes were failing*; *her film will be showing*). See **20b**.

perfect tense The form a verb takes to indicate actions performed or events completed before a particular time (*I have read that book already*; *The film had begun*; *By next term, I will have finished my internship*). See **20b**.

person The property of nouns, pronouns, and their corresponding verbs that distinguishes the speaker or writer (**first person**), the individuals addressed (**second person**), and the individuals or things referred to (**third person**). See **20b**, **21b**.

personal pronoun A pronoun that refers to a specific person, place, thing, and so on. Pronoun forms correspond to three cases: subjective, objective, and possessive. See **21a(1)**.

phrasal verb A grammatical unit consisting of a verb and a particle such as *after*, *in*, *up*, *off*, or *out*: *fill in*, *sort out*. See **20a**.

phrase A sequence of grammatically related words that functions as a unit in a sentence but lacks a subject, a predicate, or both: *in front of the stage*. See **17d**.

point of view The vantage point from which a topic is viewed; also, the stance a writer takes: objective or impartial (third person), directive (second person), or personal (first person). See **21e**.

possessive case See **case**.

predicate The part of a sentence that expresses what a subject is, does, or experiences. It consists of the main verb, its auxiliaries, and any complements and modifiers. The **simple predicate** consists of only the main verb and any accompanying auxiliaries. See **17b** and **17c**. COMPARE: **subject**.

preposition A word such as *at, in, by,* or *of* that relates a pronoun, noun, noun phrase, or noun clause to other words in the sentence. See **17a(6)**.

prepositional phrase A preposition with its object and any modifiers: *at* the nearby airport, *by* the sea. See **17d(4)**.

present participle See **participle**.

primary source A source that provides firsthand information. See **9a**. COMPARE: **secondary source**.

progressive tense The form a verb takes to indicate that an action or condition is in progress (*he is talking; the brakes were failing; her film will be showing*). See **20b**.

pronoun A word that takes the position of a noun, noun phrase, or noun clause and functions as that word or word group does: *it, that, he, them.* See **17a** and chapter **21**.

proper noun The name of a specific person, place, organization, and so on: *Dr. Pimomo, Fargo, National Education Association.* Proper nouns are capitalized. See **17a(2)**. COMPARE: **common noun**.

proposition See **claim**.

qualifier A word that intensifies or moderates the meaning of an adverb or adjective: *quite* slowly, *somewhat* reluctant. Words that intensify are sometimes called **intensifiers**. See **20a(5)**.

quotation A **direct quotation** (also called **direct discourse**) is the exact repetition of someone's spoken or written words. An **indirect quotation** is a report of someone's written or spoken words not stated in the exact words of the writer or speaker. See **11d** and chapter **34**.

reflexive pronoun A pronoun that ends in *-self* or *-selves* (*myself* or *themselves*) and refers to a preceding noun or pronoun in the sentence: *He* added a picture of *himself* to his web page. When used to provide emphasis, such a pronoun is called an **intensive pronoun**: The president *herself* awarded the scholarships. See **21a**.

refutation   A strategy for addressing opposing points of view by discussing those views and explaining why they are unsatisfactory. See **6d(2)** and **6f**.

relative clause   See **adjectival clause**.

relative pronoun   A word (*who*, *whom*, *that*, *which*, or *whose*) used to introduce an **adjectival clause**, also called a **relative clause**. An antecedent for the relative pronoun can be found in the main clause. See **17e**.

restrictive element   See **essential element**.

Rogerian argument   An approach to argumentation that is based on the work of psychologist Carl R. Rogers and that emphasizes the importance of withholding judgment of others' ideas until they are fully understood.

secondary source   A source that analyzes or interprets firsthand information. See **9a**. COMPARE: **primary source**.

signal phrase   A short phrase that identifies the source of a quotation: *according to Jones, Jones claims*. See **11c**.

simple tense   Present (*she talks*), past (*it failed*), or future (*I will dare*) forms of verbs. See **20b**.

split infinitive   The separation of the two parts of an infinitive form by at least one word: to *completely cover*. See **17d(3)**.

squinting modifier   A modifier that is unclear because it can refer to words either preceding it or following it: Proofreading *quickly* results in missed spelling errors. See **22d**.

subject   The pronoun, noun, or noun phrase that carries out the action or assumes the state described in the predicate of a sentence. Usually preceding the predicate, the subject includes the main noun or pronoun and all modifiers. A **simple subject** consists of only the main noun or pronoun. See **17b**. COMPARE: **predicate**.

subject complement   See **complement**.

subjective case   See **case**.

subordinating conjunction   See **conjunction**.

subordination   The connection of a grammatical structure to another, usually a dependent clause to an independent clause: *Even though customers were satisfied with the product*, the company wanted to improve it. See chapter **24**.

tense   The form of a verb that indicates time and sometimes completeness or duration of an action, an event, or a state of being. See chapter **20**.

thesis statement   The central point or main idea of an essay. See **2b**, **8d**.

tone   The writer's attitude toward the subject and the audience, usually conveyed through word choice and sentence structure.

topic   The specific, narrowed main idea of an essay. See **2b**.

topic sentence   A statement of the main idea of a paragraph. See **3a**.

Toulmin model   A system of argumentation developed by philosopher Stephen Toulmin in which a claim and supporting reasons or evidence depend on a shared assumption. See **5b**.

transitions   Words, phrases, sentences, or paragraphs that relate ideas by linking sentences, paragraphs, or larger segments of writing. See **3d(2)** and **19b(5)**.

verb   A word denoting action, occurrence, or existence (state of being). See **17a(1)** and chapter **20**.

verb phrase   A main verb and any auxiliaries. See **17a** and **20d**.

verbal phrase   A verb form functioning as a noun, an adjective, or an adverb. See **17a**. See also **gerund, infinitive**, and **participle**.

voice   A property of a verb that indicates the relationship between the verb and its subject. The **active voice** is used to show that the subject performs the action expressed by the verb; the **passive voice** is used to show that the subject receives the action. See **20d**.

warrant   According to the **Toulmin model**, the underlying assumption connecting a claim and data. See **5b.**

Index

Numbers and letters in **color** refer to chapters and sections in the handbook; other numbers refer to pages. Page numbers in *italics* indicate a glossary of usage term.

CITATION MAPS

Use these maps to help you quickly cite commonly used kinds of sources.

SPECIAL TOPICS FOR MULTILINGUAL WRITERS

REVISION SYMBOLS

ab	abbreviation **39a–c**		*main*	main idea **3a**
ac	acronym **39d**		*MLA*	MLA format **13**
adj	adjective **17a(4), 22a–b, 22d**		*mod*	modifier **22**
adv	adverb **17a(5), 22a–b**		*n*	number **33c, 39e–f**
agr	agreement **20f, 21c**		^	omission
APA	APA format **14**		¶	paragraph **3**
v̓	apostrophe **33**		//	parallelism **25**
arg	argument **6**		( )	parentheses **35e**
awk	awkward		.	period **34c(1), 35a**
cap	capital **37**		*pl*	plural **33a, c, 36c(5)**
CMS	CMS format **15**		*pro*	pronoun **21, 24a(2)**
coh	coherence **4a, 22d–e**		?	question mark **34c(3), 35b**
:	colon **32b, 34c(2)**		" "	quotation marks **34**
,	comma **31, 34c(1)**		*red*	redundant **30a(1)**
con	conciseness **30**		*ref*	reference **21d**
coor	coordination **24b–c**		*rep*	repetition **25b, 26c**
cred	source credibility **10**		;	semicolon **32a, 34c(2)**
cs	comma splice **19**		*sg*	singular **20f, 21c, 33a**
CSE	CSE format **16**		/	slash **35h**
—	dash **34c(3), 35d**		*sp*	spelling **36a–d**
✔	delete		*sub*	subordination **24a, 24c**
dev	development **3**		[ ]	square brackets **35f**
. . .	ellipsis points **35g**		*t*	tense **20b**
evid	evidence **6d**		*thesis*	thesis statement **2b**
!	exclamation point **34c(3), 35c**		*trans*	transition **3d(4)**
frag	fragment **18**		∽	transpose
fs	fused sentence **19**		*u*	unity **4a, 23**
hy	hyphenation **36e**		*usg*	usage **Glossary of Usage**
inc	incomplete **18, 23f–h**		*var*	variety **27**
irreg	irregular verb **20a**		*v*	verb **20**
ital	italics **38**		*wc*	word choice **23e–g, 28a–b**
log	logic **6d–e**		*w*	wordiness **30a**
lc	lowercase **37**		*ww*	wrong word **29a–c**

Contents